Teaching Success Guide for the Advanced Placement Classroom

Advanced Placement Classroom

Julius Caesar

Emily,

Enjoy the book!

Advanced Placement Classroom

Julius Caesar

Timothy J. Duggan, Ed.D.

PRUFROCK PRESS INC.
WACO, TEXAS

Library of Congress Cataloging-in-Publication Data

Duggan, Timothy J.
 Julius Caesar / by Timothy J. Duggan.
   p. cm. -- (Teaching success guide for the advanced placement classroom)
 At head of title: Advanced placement classroom
 Includes bibliographical references.
 ISBN 978-1-59363-834-4 (pbk.)
 1. Shakespeare, William, 1564-1616. Julius Caesar. 2. Shakespeare, William, 1564-1616--Study and teaching (Higher)
 3. Caesar, Julius--In literature. I. Title. II. Title: Advanced placement classroom. III. Series.

 PR2808.D84 2012
 822.3'3--dc23

                    2011030633

Edited by Lacy Compton

ISBN-13: 978-1-59363-834-4

At the time of this book's publication, all facts and figures cited are the most current available. All telephone numbers, addresses, and website URLs are accurate and active. All publications, organizations, websites, and other resources exist as described in the book, and all have been verified. The author and Prufrock Press Inc. make no warranty or guarantee concerning the information and materials given out by organizations or content found at websites, and we are not responsible for any changes that occur after this book's publication. If you find an error, please contact Prufrock Press Inc.

•AP and Advanced Placement Program are registered trademarks of the College Entrance Examination Board, which was not involved in the production of, and does not endorse, this book.

Prufrock Press Inc.
P.O. Box 8813
Waco, TX 76714-8813
Phone: (800) 998-2208
Fax: (800) 240-0333
http://www.prufrock.com

For Heidi, Eamon, and Liesel, the triumvirate of my Rome.

Contents

Acknowledgments xi

Chapter **1**

"I wish your enterprise today may thrive": Introduction 1

Chapter **2**

"I shall be glad to learn": Teaching Shakespeare 9

Chapter **3**

"Are we all ready?": Teaching *Julius Caesar* 37

Chapter **4**

"Into what dangers would you lead me?":
Entering the Text of *Julius Caesar* 55

Chapter **5**

"A vision fair and fortunate": Reading *Julius Caesar* 75

Chapter **6**

"Friends, Romans, countrymen, lend me your ears":
Talking About *Julius Caesar* 139

Chapter **7**

"Speak, hands, for me!": Performing *Julius Caesar* 173

Chapter **8**

"What meanst thou by that?":
Understanding and Writing About *Julius Caesar* 203

Chapter **9**

"Is there no voice more worthy than my own?":
Additional Resources 237

References 241
About the Author 247

Acknowledgments

I would like to thank those who introduced me to William Shakespeare's works and held me accountable for more than a cursory reading, especially Homer Swander and Steven Hilliard. I thank the family of the Nebraska Shakespeare Festival for putting me in a position to extend my teaching and acting skills in the 1990s. Thanks to Lisa Hazlett at the University of South Dakota for teaching me the value of editing and for the great Shakespeare bobblehead adventure.

A huge thanks to Marilyn Halperin and Barbara Gaines of the Chicago Shakespeare Theater for making me a part of their team, and to the participants in the workshops I have taught there. Many of the strategies described in this book were developed specifically for CST's Bard Core professional development course and related sessions. Thanks to my colleagues at Northeastern Illinois University, especially my department chair, Katy Smith, for respecting my need to complete this work. Thanks to the Illinois Association of Teachers of English, especially Deborah Will, for their encouragement and support for my workshops. Thanks, also, to Penny Hirsch at Northwestern University. Thanks to Michael LoMonico for first giving me the opportunity to share my workshop approach with a wider audience through *Shakespeare* magazine.

Thanks to Lacy Compton, my fearless editor, whose competence and supportive demeanor made this process enjoyable. Thanks to Joel McIntosh and the other fine folks at Prufrock Press for continuing our relationship.

Thanks to my friends for keeping me active as an artist and for sharing their talents. Finally, thanks to my children, Eamon and Liesel Duggan, and to my wife, Heidi Nickisch Duggan.

"I wish your enterprise today may thrive": Introduction

Welcome to *Advanced Placement Classroom:* Julius Caesar. What this book presents is a guide to teaching Shakespeare's famous Roman tragedy, with theory, practical activities, and resources included. This book does not simply offer a unit plan with sequential lesson plans followed by a summative assessment. Instead, it presents a large menu of options from which you, as the teacher, may choose the explanations, activities, and assignments that will help you fulfill your own vision of a great educational experience for your students.

I have always loved *Julius Caesar*, and I am not entirely sure why. It may be that this was the first Shakespeare play I ever taught, back at Sonora Union High School in 1984. After struggling through a 9-week grammar unit with my sophomores, we embarked on a journey that allowed me to take what Dr. Homer Swander of the University of California at Santa Barbara had taught me and put it into practice. The students read, performed scenes, and not only survived the experience, but also thrived. I have taught the text of *Julius Caesar* on several occasions, and have never grown tired of it, even in the preparation of this book. The memorable speeches, the competition between the leading characters, and the descent from civilized discourse to mob violence speak powerful warnings about what motivates us as citizens, requiring us to continually reexamine how we govern ourselves.

That being said, many Shakespeare lovers, people who know his work well and advocate for it, do not like this particular work. Cohen (2006) imagined (somewhat humorously) that Shakespeare wrote the play out of a revulsion for the idea that his works would become popular commodities in succeeding centuries, and that he wanted to destroy his own reputation by creating a work that school-aged children would dread reading. Certainly, the play contains no great lovers, as do *Romeo and Juliet* and *Antony and Cleopatra*. It contains no transcendent leading character, as do *Hamlet* and *Macbeth*, and no memorable villain, as do *Othello* and *King Lear*. Although we may feel that the play keeps us at a distance from the main characters, particularly Caesar himself, we do get to know several major characters whose personalities are governed by different humors and whose historical significance is unquestioned. Julius Caesar was by far the most famous historical protagonist in Shakespeare's canon, and it is important to note that Shakespeare not only pays homage to his source, Plutarch's *Lives of the Noble Greeks and Romans* (1898; in the Thomas North translation), but also adapts the historical narrative to fit his own theatrical (and perhaps political) needs.

In American schools, *Julius Caesar* traditionally was taught during the same year (typically, 10th grade) as high school composition and speech. The pairing made sense, as the work contains many rhetorical speeches, and writing instruction was based around rhetorical modes of writing, including argument and persuasion. Theoretically, then, *Julius Caesar* would provide models for persuasive discourse applicable to writing instruction for high school students, and teachers today can continue to exploit these opportunities for instruction in different forms of persuasion.

I have been reading, viewing, and enjoying Shakespeare for nearly 30 years, but Shakespeare's works still pose difficulties for me when I sit to read them, and I often make use of the explanatory notes in whatever edition I happen to be using, even if I sometimes dispute them when they don't make sense to me. As this book will demonstrate, reading the text as a script with clues for performance will help unlock meaning, as will exercising the many skills of analytical reading and writing at the core of language arts standards. Reading Shakespeare is difficult, but rigor and challenge are what schools should be about, and Shakespeare rewards our work with hard-earned understanding. Let me give a short example of the approach presented in this book.

Here is an excerpt from Act 3, scene 1 of *Julius Caesar*. In this scene, Caesar has gathered with his senate, and he is surprised to find that several of them, including Brutus and Cassius, are kneeling before him (and perhaps surrounding him), pleading for Caesar to overturn a decision he had previously made to banish the brother of one of the senators, Metellus Cimber. Caesar has come to the capitol on this particular day against the advice of his wife, Calphurnia, who had horrible dreams of Caesar's death. Furthermore, the night before had been filled with strange storms and sights. Here is the speech Caesar makes in response to the men's request:

> *Caesar:* I could be well moved, if I were as you.
> If I could pray to move, prayers would move me.
> But I am constant as the Northern Star,

Of whose true fixed and resting quality
There is no fellow in the firmament.
The skies are painted with unnumbered sparks;
They are all fire, and every one doth shine.
But there's but one in all doth hold his place.
So in the world: 'tis furnished well with men,
And men are flesh and blood, and apprehensive.
Yet in the number I do know but one
That unassailable holds on his rank,
Unshaked of motion; and that I am he
Let me a little show it, even in this:
That I was constant Cimber should be banished
And constant do remain to keep him so. (3.1.64–79)

I'd like for us to consider that inside this speech is not a man, but a range of possible men called Caesar. Our job as readers/teachers/students/directors/performers is to find in these words the "man" Caesar that makes sense to us. For example, imagine a Caesar who speaks this speech in a commanding voice. He is physically imposing and he takes his time, staring down the senators, establishing eye contact with each, building his iteration to a commanding climax. This is Caesar.

Now imagine the same words delivered by a soft-spoken, somewhat doughy middle-aged man, who pauses occasionally to look nervously over his shoulder, perhaps not even convinced by his own words. This, too, is Caesar, if we choose him to be so. One set of words, two very different Caesars, and thus, two different plays. When referring to the words in *Julius Caesar*, I will try to use the word *script* as opposed to *play*, as a play is something people pay to attend in the theatre. The point is that we decide what play resides within the script, based on the vision of the story we wish to present. Teaching students that Shakespeare allows us to create the play anew with each reading allows them to become coauthors and directors. It is not just the words of the script that allow us to build differing interpretations, but the context of the play itself. We can take Caesar out of Ancient Rome and set him in the context of a large contemporary corporation. We can place him in a school setting, as a sort of dictatorial principal. Shakespeare's works, by virtue of their genre, create marvelous opportunities for constructivist teaching and learning. Such opportunities are what this book is about.

My hope is that you will find useful and challenging activities here to guide and enhance your students' experience reading, performing scenes, and writing in response to the text. Ultimately, when students have arrived at their own initial interpretations, they will venture into the world of *Julius Caesar* criticism, and this book should help you in your efforts to make that journey sensible for them as well.

As the teacher, creating a unit of study covering *Julius Caesar* is a little like mounting a production of the play. You have a number of decisions to make prior to starting, you hope things will go as planned, and you hope the outcome will be a phenomenal success. I believe you, the teacher, can create your own units with whatever tools you see fit to use, because you know your students, your curriculum standards, and the other pressures on your work life that allow or disallow certain options. As director of your students' experience with *Julius Caesar*, you will be able to determine how the material here fits with your goals for instruction.

John Dewey (1938) said that the best type of experience for a learner is that which leads the learner to seek a further, similar experience. Our job in teaching Shakespeare and in teaching *Julius Caesar* is to make an introduction and to guide the experience our students have with the text in such a way that will foster their desire to have another experience with Shakespeare. Shakespeare has much to teach us.

How to Use This Book

There are many, many discussion topics and classroom ideas in this book. Activities that involve students in work outside the classroom often include a Student Activity Sheet (SAS) at the end of the chapter, which you can modify as you please or give to your students as a set of instructions. Those activities that are teacher directed and can be done in the classroom are explained in the chapters themselves, with no handouts. In descriptions of activities throughout the book, I specify what students may produce as a result of the activity, but it will be up to you to assess student progress based on your own expectations. At the end of Chapter 3 is a suggested unit timeline.

Use this teaching guide as best suits your own background, needs, and preferences. Chapter 2 considers different challenges that Shakespeare's work poses, and Chapter 3 takes a general look at *Julius Caesar*. Chapters 4–8 lead us through the student experience with the text, including prereading activities and a scene-by-scene reading guide, followed by ideas for discussion, performance, and writing. Most of the activities in the book reflect back on the script of *Julius Caesar*, assuming that you and your students will reexamine the text often following your initial reading. In a 3–6 week unit on *Julius Caesar*, you won't have time for everything here, but you should have a good variety of approaches that challenge your students and build understanding on a number of levels.

Source citations in this book follow APA format, and act/scene/line indications for passages pulled from the scripts follow contemporary formatting, with numerals separated by points, such as 3.2.20 for Act 3, scene 2, line 20. Line indications are taken from the Folger Shakespeare Library editions of the script (Shakespeare, 1623/1992b) edited by Barbara Mowat and Paul Werstine.

I believe in student involvement, and Shakespeare demands it, through the relationship between a script, which is what we have in our hands, and a play, which is a theatrical experience. If this book makes nothing else clear, it should make the point that Shakespeare wrote scripts for actors. Although reading Shakespeare without thinking about performance can be pleasurable, reading the text as a set of instructions for actors will open up possibilities for you and your students that will bring the work to life. This book is written with the goal of getting you and your students to spend much of your time with *Julius Caesar* up on your feet, speaking the lines and moving around. Certainly no approach to teaching anything is hegemonic, and you will find many alternative activities in this book that don't involve performance. My general method for teaching involves students in individual contemplation, group exploration, and whole-group sharing. I believe that as teachers we need to distribute our students' attention between the text, each other, technology (media), and ourselves. We should bring something to the mix when we teach Shakespeare, which includes not only what we know of the work, but our spirit to become learners with our students. The kinds of thinking students do should alternate between receiving information, processing information, and expressing knowledge gained through speech, writing, or performance.

A Note on Standards

The activities in this book address virtually every standard put forth by the National Council of Teachers of English and the International Reading Association (1996), which are listed below.

NCTE/IRA Standards
1. Students read a wide range of print and nonprint texts to build an understanding of texts, of themselves, and of the cultures of the United States and the world; to acquire new information; to respond to the needs and demands of society and the workplace; and for personal fulfillment. Among these texts are fiction and nonfiction, classic and contemporary works.
2. Students read a wide range of literature from many periods in many genres to build an understanding of the many dimensions (e.g., philosophical, ethical, aesthetic) of human experience.
3. Students apply a wide range of strategies to comprehend, interpret, evaluate, and appreciate texts. They draw on their prior experience, their interactions with other readers and writers, their knowledge of word meaning

and of other texts, their word identification strategies, and their understanding of textual features (e.g., sound-letter correspondence, sentence structure, context, graphics).

4. Students adjust their use of spoken, written, and visual language (e.g., conventions, style, vocabulary) to communicate effectively with a variety of audiences and for different purposes.

5. Students employ a wide range of strategies as they write and use different writing process elements appropriately to communicate with different audiences for a variety of purposes.

6. Students apply knowledge of language structure, language conventions (e.g., spelling and punctuation), media techniques, figurative language, and genre to create, critique, and discuss print and nonprint texts.

7. Students conduct research on issues and interests by generating ideas and questions, and by posing problems. They gather, evaluate, and synthesize data from a variety of sources (e.g., print and nonprint texts, artifacts, people) to communicate their discoveries in ways that suit their purpose and audience.

8. Students use a variety of technological and information resources (e.g., libraries, databases, computer networks, video) to gather and synthesize information and to create and communicate knowledge.

9. Students develop an understanding of and respect for diversity in language use, patterns, and dialects across cultures, ethnic groups, geographic regions, and social roles.

10. Students whose first language is not English make use of their first language to develop competency in the English language arts and to develop understanding of content across the curriculum.

11. Students participate as knowledgeable, reflective, creative, and critical members of a variety of literacy communities.

12. Students use spoken, written, and visual language to accomplish their own purposes (e.g., for learning, enjoyment, persuasion, and the exchange of information).

A new movement toward a national set of standards has gained much momentum through the establishment of Common Core Standards. In my state of Illinois, the Common Core Standards will become operational in 2014. The standards are well articulated and focused to a great extent on higher level thinking and deep comprehension, the kinds of understanding that work with Shakespeare's texts is designed to engender in students. Throughout this book are suggestions and activities related to the Reading Literature, Writing, Speaking and Listening, and Language strands at both the 9–10 and 11–12 grade levels. The heavy emphasis on integrated language arts in the Common Core Standards fits well with the approach adopted here in Chapters 4–7, and the high demand for evidentiary reasoning, the ability to cite specific textual elements in written analysis of literature, fits well with the writing suggested in Chapter 8. Student activity sheets provided here identify specific Common Core Standards that the various activities address.

Before we jump into a focused study of *Julius Caesar*, the next chapter presents an overview of characteristics of Shakespeare's works that make them both challenging and fun. Enjoy.

CHAPTER 2

"I shall be glad to learn": Teaching Shakespeare

Shakespeare stands at the center of the language arts literature curriculum in high schools for a number of reasons, and we are smart to revisit the reasons why we teach Shakespeare at any level. Especially now, with a multitude of new literacy forms and means of communications, with stories told through electronic books, films, television shows, and online networks, the dusty scripts of a playwright from Elizabethan England can appear a bit distant from the world of 21st-century adolescents. That being said, we must consider the permanence of Shakespeare's works throughout the past 400 years as testament that his many themes have been questioned before for relevance and passed the test. Shakespeare continues to be performed in theaters and festivals around the world, and Shakespeare still inspires more literary criticism than any other author.

On the other hand, saying that we should teach Shakespeare just because our predecessors have taught Shakespeare is not going to convince a skeptical student, nor should it. The work must stand on its own and endure the scrutiny of fresh, young eyes in order to survive. We cannot and will not be able to "make" our students love Shakespeare or see its value just because we love it or see its value. What we can do is give Shakespeare a good chance by teaching his work well, and then let the chips fall where they may.

These are strange times in the teaching of English language arts generally, including Advanced Placement English Literature and other English classes. In a climate of test preparation and concern over standardized assessments, many teachers and schools opt for fewer literary works covered, with skills-focused instruction replacing deep, critical discussions of challenging literature. At the same time, the proliferation of high-quality young adult literature has provided teenagers with nearly endless opportunities to engage in critical reading of texts set in today's world with current issues and fast-paced action. Some of these works even tip their hats to Shakespeare. So we have the situation of less time in the curriculum devoted to literature and more literature from which to choose to fill that time.

If you are skeptical about teaching Shakespeare or have had a negative experience in school with Shakespeare's works, your biggest challenge when faced with the requirement to teach his work will be to get over your own fear or dread (or plain dislike) in order to help your students approach Shakespeare with open minds. As someone who has always loved teaching Shakespeare more than any other work, I've learned to make my case to doubters as clearly as possible. In examining the value of Shakespeare in our curriculum, then, the following arguments may prove convincing—if not to your students, at least to yourself.

Reason One: Shakespeare's Stories

It is almost a cliché to say that Shakespeare's stories are universal. I am not exactly sure saying so will convince skeptical students who have not experienced a great deal in life, but if you just take the main conflicts of the stories and present them, they are compelling in their own right. For example, a boy from one family falls in love with a girl from a rival family, and they must keep their love secret to avoid all-out war between the families (*Romeo and Juliet*). Although it is the rare student who will be in a situation of serious and public family feuds, several will relate to falling for someone their parents don't approve of. Complicate the story by adding a mercurial friend on one side who likes to stir things up and a jealous cousin on the other side who likes to fight, then put those strong personalities together and see what happens. There's your story.

Students like good stories. What about the young man who is supposed to be with his father, the king, learning to become a worthy heir to the throne, but instead is hanging out with the wrong crowd and being "corrupted" by an older man in a tavern (*King Henry IV, Part 1*)? When rebellion erupts and the young man must prove his worth, will he be ready? There's your story. The stories of Shakespeare resonate because the conflicts are real and they reveal humans struggling with their insecurities and their weaknesses. Shakespeare often found his stories or adapted stories his audience knew and loved. *Julius Caesar* is an adaptation of a popular book in Shakespeare's day, Thomas North's translation of Plutarch's *Parallel Lives of the Greeks and Romans*. Actually, North made a translation of a French translation of Plutarch by James Amyot, and the resultant title is *The Lives of the Noble Grecians and Romans, compared together by that grave learned Philosopher and Historiographer, Plutarch of Chaeronea: Translated out of*

Greek into French by James Amyot, Abbot of Bellozane, Bishop of Auxerre, one of the King's privy council, and great Amner of France, and out of French into English, by Thomas North (Spencer, 1968, p. 9). Shakespeare's audience, at least a good number of them, would have attended Shakespeare's play aware that he was doing an adaptation of North for the theatre, and they would have been pleased to find many exact quotes lifted from Plutarch and set in the dialogue of the play. In this sense, Shakespeare was doing nothing different from what contemporary moviemakers do in adapting popular literature for the screen. And like those movie directors, the changes Shakespeare made to his source reveal the kind of story he wished to tell (Thomas, 1992).

In our classrooms, we have the freedom to tell Shakespeare's stories to spark student interest. With younger students (middle school and younger), telling them the story before they encounter the script will help them address the script itself. I have told stories of Shakespeare to children of all ages, and they are more engaged, immediately, with the conflicts in the stories than they are with any other elements, although character is what they eventually hold on to the longest. For example, I have told the following introduction many times:

> An old king wants to retire, but still go on being called king. He has three daughters, and he intends to divide the kingdom equally among them. But the king is vain, and before he divides the kingdom, he sets up a little contest with his daughters by making them tell him how much they love him. He starts with his oldest daughter, and she says, "Oh, my father, my love is dearer than eyesight, space, and liberty, beyond what can be valued, rich, or rare. I love you more than child ever loved a parent." She lays on the flattery, and her father is pleased. "Very good," he says, and making a motion toward a map of the kingdom, continues, "You get this third, with rivers wide and forests, and pleasant farm land." Then he turns to his second daughter and commands her to tell how much she loves him. "Oh," she says, "I am just like my sister, and I love you just as she does, only I find she comes too short in proclaiming her love, for I am only happy in my love for you."
>
> "Very good," the old king chuckles, "you can have this third of the kingdom," he points to the map on the floor, "no less than what was given to your sister."
>
> Then he turns to his third daughter, who is his favorite. He has been saving the nicest third of his kingdom for her, and it is time for her to claim it by telling how much she loves him. And she truly does love him, unlike her lying sisters, but she stands with her head down when he speaks to her. "Now, my youngest, what can you say to draw a third more opulent than your sisters?"

"Nothing, my lord."

"Nothing will come of nothing, speak again." The king looks irritated.

"Nothing, my lord. I cannot heave my heart into my mouth like my sisters."

The king grows angry at once, and says, "Mend thy tongue lest you mar your fortunes!" But the daughter stands silently, unwilling to lavish him with sweet testament of her love. He gives her one more chance and says, "So young and so untender?"

She replies, "So young, my lord, and true."

"Fine," he shouts. "Thy truth shall be thy dowry. I hereby disown you!" And he gives the other two sisters her third of the kingdom, casting his youngest daughter away.

By this point in the storytelling, kids are already fastened to the story. How could the father king be so vain? Why doesn't the youngest daughter speak up and receive her land? What are the other two false daughters going to do? What will happen to the youngest daughter? If kids decide to actually read the script of *King Lear*, they will have a struggle ahead, but knowing what they know of the story, and discovering the subplot of Gloucester and his sons, they will advance with an open mind and a desire to know what will happen.

Romeo and Juliet, Henry IV, Part I, Julius Caesar, and *King Lear* are just four of the many stories that Shakespeare tells through his medium of the stage. *Hamlet, Macbeth, Othello,* and the comedies, such as *A Midsummer Night's Dream, Twelfth Night, As You Like It,* and *Measure for Measure,* all have compelling stories to tell, and in some cases, such as *Hamlet, Romeo and Juliet,* and *Macbeth,* the stories have become the archetypes of many stories told since. It is not a coincidence, for example, that Disney's *The Lion King* roughly follows the plot of *Hamlet*—it is a great plot to follow, full of complications, intrigue, and a heightened sense of drama as the story progresses. Nor is it a coincidence that so many film remakes of Shakespeare's works have been produced, even when they only loosely follow the originals. Examples include *O* for *Othello, 10 Things I Hate About You* for *Taming of the Shrew, Scotland, PA,* for *Macbeth,* and *She's the Man* for *Twelfth Night.*

Reason Two: Script Reading and Reading Ability

It is not just the stories of Shakespeare that make his work worth teaching. Remember that Shakespeare wrote scripts, not plays. Scripts not only tell stories, but also are sets of instructions for directors and actors, from which they may develop plays, which are theatrical experiences including text, sound, action, and visual effects, such as lighting. Reading the text of *Julius Caesar* as a set of instructions requires us to understand that the script contains clues or signals for actors. Signals can be stage directions in dialogue, such as when Egeus, in *A Midsummer Night's Dream* (Shakespeare, 1600/1993a) tells Demetrius to "Stand forth" (1.1.25) or when Julius Caesar says, "Then fall Caesar" (3.1.85). Other signals, however, are not so obvious and can only be teased out through the physical act of creating a stage space and filling it with actors. Line length, rhythm, poetry, imagery, punctuation, sequence of speakers, implied action—all of these can be signals for actors to follow. Students read the scripts of Shakespeare looking for clues that tell them how to perform and then transform those clues into their own interpretations of scenes from the plays. Implied in this approach is the notion that the dramatic process unveils the literary treasures in the play that are undiscoverable through quiet, independent reading. In other words, until we have students make the choices that actors and directors have to make, much of the literary text will remain frozen on the page.

The scripts themselves, which offer the opportunity to learn a dynamic way of reading, are the basis of Shakespeare's place in the curriculum. If we teach students how to read Shakespeare as though they are looking at a blueprint for action (or a possible range of actions) on a stage, as a story that has within it a complex set of stage directions for actors and directors, they may come to see what good theatre directors know: Within the confines of a single set of words are many different plays. We will thus start our students on a journey of critical reading that engages all of the senses and that will affect everything they read from that point onward. My contention is that learning to read Shakespeare as a script to be performed will increase your students' engagement with any words in any text they encounter in any academic subject or in their recreational reading. There is no turning back once one learns to find signals in printed words that translate to action. This book will address that technique often, so that you can teach your students the process.

Reason Three: Language and Poetry

Most defenses of Shakespeare in the curriculum mention the language and the poetry of Shakespeare as reasons to teach his works. In Shakespeare, we certainly have a poet/playwright who had the greatest command of the English language ever shown, and whose power of sheer imagery, both literal and metaphorical, can take the breath away. The facts that Romeo and Juliet speak sonnets to one another when they first meet, that Richard III opens his play with unforgettable lines, that Shakespeare inhabits no fewer than 66 pages in Bartlett's *Familiar Quotations* (1980) all demonstrate this illustriousness in language. Nearly everyone who has studied Shakespeare with any seriousness has favorite passages they can cite at will. What is it about the power of the words themselves that compels us to remember them? The words often take on lives of their own outside the context of their plays, transferring themselves into our own realities. I can still remember a passage from *Othello* (Shakespeare, 1623/1993b) that I copied and taped to my wall in college: "The robbed that smiles steals something from the thief, / He robs himself that spends a bootless grief" (1.3.238–240). Often we quote Shakespeare in our common sayings, not even knowing that we are. I recently overheard a group of high school students talking about a friend who had done something embarrassing, and a girl among them said, "Oh, he's a piece of work" (Shakespeare, *Hamlet*, 1603–1605/1992a, 2.2.327).

ACTIVITY (SAS #1): THAT SOUNDS FAMILIAR!

Have students browse the Internet for lists of common phrases taken from Shakespeare, then share their findings with each other. I suggest Michael LoMonico's *The Shakespeare Book of Lists* (http://www.lomonico.com/bookch4.html) as a starting point. See SAS #1 (p. 32) for a handout to facilitate the activity.

ACTIVITY: THE WALL OF NOTABLE QUOTES.

As a follow-up to the activity above, create a background on a bulletin board or a wall of your classroom for students to mount "notable quotes" from Shakespeare and specifically from *Julius Caesar*. Ask each student to contribute at least one line he or she finds interesting or memorable. Build the wall of notable quotes as you work through *Julius Caesar* and afterward. Students can add as many quotes as they like, and any student can add a comment on any quote.

Shakespeare often takes the most basic of human expressions and transforms them into stunning imagery, and he even gives unlikely characters some sense of poetry in their speech. Instead of saying, for instance, "It's not dark yet," a murderer in *Macbeth* (Shakespeare, 1623/1992c) says, "The west yet glimmers with some streaks of day" (3.3.7) And the most well-known passages from Shakespeare are well-known precisely because they crystallize in some way what we commonly recognize as truth into an exact and profound expression of clear thinking: "To be or not to be—that is the question" (Shakespeare, 1603–1605/1992a, *Hamlet*, 3.1.64).

Furthermore, studying the language of Shakespeare extends our students' verbal agility and range of expression. Active engagement with Shakespeare also increases their vocabulary and can inspire them to engage in creative expression of their own. You will want to give your students opportunities to write poems, sonnets, blank verse, soliloquies, dramatic dialogue, and other creative forms during their study of Shakespeare.

Reason Four: Cultural Heritage

Another compelling reason to study Shakespeare is in the service of sharing and extending our cultural heritage. Shakespeare no longer belongs solely to 16th- and 17th-century England. I remember an episode of *Star Trek: The Next Generation* in which Patrick Stewart recites a passage from Shakespeare, and his Klingon companion says, "You should hear it in the original Klingon." Shakespeare belongs to us all, and although we can learn much about Elizabethan England by starting with Shakespeare (Greenblatt, 2004; Shapiro, 2005) and studying Elizabethan England can help us interpret some passages of Shakespeare, neither approach is necessary for the work to have value for us. Nor will the historical perspectives impute value to a 21st-century teen if the work has no significance to the here and now. To be an educated person in our society and be ignorant of Shakespeare is to be culturally handicapped (Bloom, 1994; Hirsch, 1987). Even if one rejects Shakespeare as outdated and politically incorrect, as some have done, to not know Shakespeare, at least the greatest works that are part of our cultural conscience, is to stand at a disadvantage in literate society.

Certainly, Shakespeare is often misinterpreted in the cultural consciousness. "Romeo, Romeo, wherefore art thou Romeo" is still often misunderstood in quotations ("wherefore" meaning "why" and not "where"), and as Metzger (2004) pointed out when referring to Hirsch's misuse of Brutus's "There is a tide in the affairs of men" (4.3.249), quotes taken out of context can end up representing something very different from what they represent in Shakespeare. But having the language of Shakespeare, the character archetypes, the symbolic stories, the personalities of the memorable characters, and yes, the quotations available to us is part of why we continue our fascination with his work.

Reason Five:
Rigor and Challenge in the Curriculum

Another reason to teach Shakespeare is that Shakespeare is challenging. I would submit that this is an important reason for teaching Shakespeare in any class, but most certainly in Advanced Placement classes. In order to extend our literacy skills and broaden our scope of possibility for learning, we must encounter literature that is at the appropriate level of challenge for our students. Vygotsky (1978) knew that children must engage in material at their zone of proximal development. If we employ a variety of teaching techniques for Shakespeare, his works provide us with material that can meet many different levels of student development. Students who bump (gently) against the walls of their ignorance push those walls backward, broadening their knowledge and making the next bump easier to take. As students challenge themselves and as you challenge them to read, discuss, debate, and perform Shakespeare, they and you both extend literacy and build confidence that can be used in the next reading task.

Two conflicting, yet equally damaging, beliefs often get in the way of success in teaching Shakespeare:

1. Shakespeare is not difficult.
2. Students can't understand Shakespeare.

The first statement falls into the category of lies that teachers tell students when they think students are not going to put in effort. Along these same lines are "This is going to be fun" and "Shakespeare is going to be your favorite writer." You can't know whether your students are going to like Shakespeare before they encounter it. Some will and some won't, but you telling them what experience they are going to have is likely to turn them away from the experience because, if nothing else, kids want to have their own experiences and make up their own minds about those experiences. The second statement, implying that Shakespeare is beyond the students' comprehension, dooms all teaching from the outset because the teacher will be working under the pall of self-imposed futility, waiting to get "through" Shakespeare or, worse yet, explaining every passage so that students get the teacher's interpretation of the meaning rather than their own. Students have the capacity to understand Shakespeare, as understanding is always a continuum rather than a doorway. Understanding of Shakespeare is always in progress and incomplete. Small victories in comprehension of difficult passages can build confidence in readers of all ability levels.

Finally, and perhaps most importantly, remember that Shakespeare will teach our students more than we will teach Shakespeare. Dewey's (1938) point that the best kind of educational experience is one that leads the learner to seek another, similar experience should linger in the backs of our minds when we teach Shakespeare. Our job is to make the introduction and guide the relationship, providing what opportunities and experiences we can with the texts so that our students will have experiences that they will want to repeat, either with us or on their own.

Reason Six: Shakespeare Study Translates Well to College-Level Work

Partially for the reasons outlined above and partly for the sheer fact that Shakespeare surfaces on AP exams, AP classes are natural places to examine Shakespeare because students are motivated to do well, or they wouldn't be pursuing the rigor of the AP curriculum. Free-response and multiple-choice questions on the exams often are matched with passages or works from Shakespeare.

Just as Shakespeare is ubiquitous in high school language arts curriculum, his work is also common in university studies of English. Most introductory courses in college literature include selections from Shakespeare. Even if a student does not take any college coursework directly related to Shakespeare, the skills of analysis gained by deep consideration of nearly any Shakespeare text transfer to the kinds of analysis vital to performing well in college-level writing and reading. The ability to take apart sentences and lines, unpack the syntax, and clearly identify pronoun antecedents without being intimidated or frustrated by archaic and unusual vocabulary will help students in any college course. Shakespeare provides a great playing field for the teaching of critical thinking. Consider the situations in Shakespeare: Should Hamlet pursue his revenge? Why doesn't Brutus listen to Cassius's advice after joining the conspiracy? How is the Friar who marries Romeo and Juliet responsible for their fates? Are we to laugh at Malvolio or pity him? Consideration of these questions and others that routinely arise in the plays allows for challenging discussion and both informal and formal writing opportunities. Even individual passages from Shakespeare can provide material for analysis. Consider this example:

Macbeth: If it were done when 'tis done, then 'twere well
It were done quickly: if the assassination
Could trammel up the consequence, and catch
With his surcease success: that but this blow
Might be the be-all and the end-all—here,
But here, upon this bank and shoal of time,
We'd jump the life to come. But in these cases
We still have judgment here; that we but teach
Bloody instructions, which, being taught, return
To plague the inventor: this even-handed justice
Commends the ingredients of our poisoned chalice
To our own lips. He's here in double trust;
First, as I am his kinsman and his subject,
Strong both against the deed; then, as his host,
Who should against his murderer shut the door,
Not bear the knife myself. Besides, this Duncan
Hath borne his faculties so meek, hath been
So clear in his great office, that his virtues
Will plead like angels, trumpet-tongued, against
The deep damnation of his taking-off;
And pity, like a naked new-born babe,
Striding the blast, or heaven's cherubim, horsed
Upon the sightless couriers of the air,
Shall blow the horrid deed in every eye,

That tears shall drown the wind. I have no spur
To prick the sides of my intent, but only
Vaulting ambition, which o'erleaps itself
And falls on the other. (1.7.1–28)

In this soliloquy from *Macbeth* (Shakespeare, 1623/1992), the title character produces a series of arguments against committing a murder he will soon commit anyway. He progresses from thinking about how the deed will come back to haunt him ("justice / commends the ingredients of our poison'd chalice / to our own lips"), to thinking about the king as his kin and as his guest, both good reasons not to kill him. Macbeth then calls up the image of heavenly sanction against the deed by imagining "angels," "new-born babes," and "heavenly cherubim" that will "blow the horrid deed in every eye." Students could write an analysis of Macbeth's reasons against committing the murder, then compare them to the reasons Macbeth's wife gives later in the same scene to refute that analysis. By comparing the reasons, they can decide why Macbeth found her argument more persuasive than his own.

Even single exchanges of dialogue in Shakespeare can provide material for discussion and writing (see Chapters 6 and 8). For example, in *Julius Caesar*, Caesar meets a soothsayer who tells him to beware. Caesar calls the man before him, thinking to intimidate him, and they have the following exchange.

Caesar: What say'st thou to me now? Speak once again.
Soothsayer: Beware the ides of March.
Caesar: He is a dreamer. Let us leave him. Pass. (1.2.26–28)

Much can be discussed regarding this close exchange, and performance options can illuminate discussion and writing. Is Caesar visibly shaken by the soothsayer's words? Does he really believe the soothsayer's words are those of a "dreamer"? Why does Caesar's last line contain three sentences? Why did Caesar haul the soothsayer in front of him in the first place? What does this exchange reveal about Caesar? These are the kinds of analytical investigations that Shakespeare's scripts invite. College-level literature courses demand that students dig beneath the texts to fashion a defensible interpretation. One never runs out of possible topics to explore in Shakespeare.

Helping Students Understand Shakespeare: Addressing Their Concerns

The best way to help students understand Shakespeare and to address their concerns is not to lie to them about Shakespeare. As mentioned above, don't kid them that it's going to be easy, and always hold out the possibility that they can understand it, then provide the tools to allow them to grapple successfully with it (see Sizer & Sizer, 1999). Most important to remember in this is not to do the grappling for them, because the struggle is what, more than any other process, will draw them into Shakespeare, or any other literature, for that matter (Blau, 2003).

This book will provide you with specific advice for working through *Julius Caesar* with your students, and although many of the activities and topics are only applicable to *Julius Caesar,* the general process is similar to what I would advocate using with any Shakespeare script, and any challenging literature, for that matter. That process attempts to maximize the interaction between the reader and the text, directed by the reader, using the tools available to the reader, courtesy of the teacher, the reader's past experience, and whatever other sources the reader pursues. These tools are complemented by the reader's own motivation. Let's take a look at typical concerns students have when reading Shakespeare, and discuss how we might address those concerns.

Relevance

The first concern that students often mention when faced with a unit on Shakespeare is its apparent lack of relevance to their lives, but this concern is more likely to be an issue in the early stages of their experience with Shakespeare. Once students are engaged in meaningful study of the texts, they forget that they thought it irrelevant. That being said, I would caution you against preparing an elaborate verbal or written defense of Shakespeare's relevance in order to combat apathy or real complaining as you start into *Julius Caesar* with your students.

A better approach to this concern is to say to the student who calls into question Shakespeare's relevance or the relevance of *Julius Caesar,* "I appreciate that sentiment, and I want us to address it, but I'm going to ask you a favor. Let's postpone that discussion until we've worked through the unit, and I promise we'll return to it." After a rigorous encounter with Shakespeare that challenges them to read, discuss, perform, and write critically, the conversation at the end can be powerful, and even those who argue against Shakespeare's relevance will do so with knowledge of the experience behind them.

Difficulty

Another problem that students often encounter with Shakespeare is how relentlessly difficult the opening scenes can be. Because so much exposition is loaded into the first act of any script, and because we are not only learning to listen to the characters, but also trying to fill in the details of the world around them, we must be willing to spend more time scaffolding student work in the early stages than in the later stages, even though most of the exciting action happens from Act 2 onward. If students understand that the first few parts will be more difficult and that establishing the world of the play is part of their job, they will exercise more patience and see their role as detectives, rather than expecting you to provide the information for them. Chapter 4 in this book offers specific activities for orienting students and preparing them to enter the text of *Julius Caesar*, and Chapter 5 will continue with close reading strategies for the entire script.

Language

Another concern many express, usually in tandem with the difficulty of the early scenes in a script, is that Shakespeare's language isn't like ours. True, but we can also make the opposite statement: Shakespeare' language *is* like ours. If you have your students approach the text initially as though it is a foreign language, and then have them pick out the words, lines, and sentences that they understand, they may be surprised at their ability. Sometimes perceived difficulty is a matter of perspective.

ACTIVITY (SAS #2): SHAKESPEARE AS A FOREIGN LANGUAGE.

Give students a segment of *Julius Caesar* from the first act, maybe even the opening scene, and ask them to treat it as though it is a different language from ours, similar to German, French, or even Middle English. Ask them to pick out the words and phrases they understand, and those that they don't, and make lists. Then ask them to evaluate their ability to understand, on a basic level, how Shakespeare's characters speak. You may need to adapt the activity for English language learners, but they, too, will find the activity helpful.

One problem students often encounter in understanding Shakespeare's language is simply that they aren't given sufficient time to wrestle with it, so they lose patience. Slow down when first reading the script. Give your students the time they need to check explanatory notes and consult their dictionaries. The time will be well spent.

For younger students, the exotic nature of Shakespeare's language is one of the qualities that most attracts them to his work. The fact that the characters, many of whom are kings, queens, princes, and other nobles, sound different from the students and use strange words, even pronouns like "thou" and "thee" and verb variations such as "doth" and "dost," attracts some young readers. The one caveat to this point is that the students need to hear themselves speak those words.

Young readers are young actors, and it is cool for them to encounter the language of Shakespeare's characters if they get to speak the exotic words and, by extension, inhabit the exotic characters. High school students, while generally more reticent, often react the same way once they realize that they don't need to be perfect in their pronunciations and representations.

For example, kids have no problem with the fact that Flavius, in the opening scene of *Julius Caesar*, uses words like "hence," "idle creatures," and "naughty knave," when they come to realize that he sees himself as better than the common people. Have students read this passage using the punctuation provided, and they will understand that Flavius and Marullus are angry, even if they don't yet know why. Kids may ask why Marullus and Flavius are angry with the tradesmen, which gives you an opening to begin discussing the scene.

Flavius:	Hence! Home, you idle creatures, get you home!
	Is this a holiday? What, know you not,
	Being mechanical, you ought not walk
	Upon a laboring day without the sign
	Of your profession?—Speak, what trade art thou?
Carpenter:	Why, sir, a carpenter.
Marullus:	Where is thy leather apron and thy rule?
	What dost thou with thy best apparel on?—
	You, sir, what trade are you?
Cobbler:	Truly, sir, in respect of a fine workman, I am but, as you would say, a cobbler.
Marullus:	But what trade art thou? Answer me directly.
Cobbler:	A trade, sir, that I hope I may use, with a safe conscience, which is indeed, sir, a mender of bad soles.
Flavius:	What trade, thou knave, thou naughty knave, what trade? (1.1.1–17)

You may need to explain to students that the word *cobbler* meant not only a repairer of shoes, but also a *bungler*, as the Folger Shakespeare Library edition puts it, someone who does poor quality work. Thus, we understand the frustration of the two tribunes that leads to their scolding, but we very soon learn that they are mainly upset that the commoners are celebrating the victory of Caesar. Students have no trouble reading aloud, with emotion, the indignation of Marullus once he learns why the workmen are on the streets.

Marullus:	Wherefore rejoice? What conquest bring he home?
	What tributaries follow him to Rome
	To grace in captive bonds his chariot wheels?
	You blocks, you stones, you worse than senseless things!

O you hard hearts, you cruel men of Rome,
Knew you not Pompey? (1.1.36–42)

Young people, more so than the rest of us, like to experiment with language; therefore, letting them hear themselves speak the words of Shakespeare is a good way to encourage them to take chances. We must always be sensitive to the fact that we are asking students to confront the limits of their abilities as literate adults at a time when there is considerable social capital connected with knowing things and appearing knowledgeable. This is especially true in AP classes, and as Tracy Cross (2001) pointed out, gifted students may shy away from challenging material that puts them in a position of appearing to not know something. A climate of acceptable error must pervade any class wishing to have an authentic and meaningful experience with Shakespeare. I mentioned earlier that we all own Shakespeare, which also implies that we can be wrong about Shakespeare and not lose our confidence. Here are a few details related to Shakespeare's language and style that may prove helpful to you and your students.

Shakespearean Style and Language

Nearly every printed edition of Shakespeare's works includes an essay on Shakespeare's language, and invariably they point to the rhythm, the vocabulary, the syntax, and the puns included. I here offer a perspective on the language and the difficulties it poses without trying to recreate the explanations students will have the opportunity to read in their own texts. If at all possible, students should have a copy of the script that is portable enough for them to carry in one hand. The versions set in large (and heavy!) literature anthologies do not work well for in-class scene work. The Folger Library Series of *Julius Caesar* contains a nice essay on Shakespeare's language by editors Barbara Mowat and Paul Werstine, and I recommend it. Other editions, such as the Signet, contain similar aids.

Many of the initial difficulties students have with reading Shakespeare can be traced to two essential problems, the first being the students' inability to fill in the action narrative that they typically would see in a novel or short story, related to the need mentioned above for them to conceptualize the works as scripts for performance. The second problem, also mentioned above, is the linguistic style and language Shakespeare uses. The first difficulty, not knowing how to read the texts as scripts, simply takes training, for which this book will provide materials and methods. The second problem, style and language differences, stems from the different time periods in which we live, and the fact that Shakespeare's characters are often speaking in the highly stylized language of poetry. We must realize that students also have difficulty reading contemporary poetry because of its density of language, even without the differences in time period. Shakespeare poses the dual problems of poetry and archaism, as well as the difficulty of sometimes very complicated meaning. Even in plain language, difficult concepts are difficult concepts. What follows are a few tips for addressing style and language difficulties, intended to augment rather than replace the introductory language essays provided by printed versions of the scripts.

Vocabulary

Shakespeare lived more than 400 years ago. Our language has changed in the past 20 years, let alone the past 400, and we can address those changes with our students as a way of helping them to accept the differences in Shakespeare's language and our own, but also as a way of thinking about the similarities between our language and his.

The Words to Know Activity (SAS #3) will get students started reading text with notes, but will also allow them to see that the differences in Shakespeare's language and our own are not insurmountable. Students can choose new words or expressions that they encounter and construct a "Word Wall" in the classroom. See Dakin (2009) for extensive and engaging vocabulary study related to Shakespeare, including what she calls "heartspeak," or tone vocabulary.

Rhythm

Rhythm in the speeches is very important, and Shakespeare made use of a wide variety of poetic meters and prose rhythms to signify changes in action, the importance of characters, and a variety of other stage concerns. The major poetic meter Shakespeare uses, by far, is iambic pentameter, a five-beat line that follows an unstressed-stressed pattern repeated five times. If we were to write it out as beats, it would sound like this:

Puh-PUMP, Puh-PUMP, Puh-PUMP, Puh-PUMP, Puh-PUMP

There are so many examples of this pattern in Shakespeare and in other literature that you should have no problem teaching your students to listen for it. *Julius Caesar*, a play of speeches, is written almost entirely in iambic pentameter. I like to make up sentences in iambic pentameter and have students repeat after me, not knowing that they are speaking in iambic pentameter, then slip effortlessly into Shakespeare's language:

i HAVEn't HAD a THING to EAT all DAY.
i WISH that I could GO to BURger KING.

ACTIVITY (SAS #3): WORDS TO KNOW.

Have students generate a list of words that we commonly use today that didn't exist or that didn't have the same meaning for their parents' generation. Many of the words will be words that already existed but that either changed meanings or changed parts of speech. Examples they will readily be able to come up with include "texting," "facebook," or "multitasking." Have students reflect on what forces are changing language in our lives.

Then have students look at one scene from *Julius Caesar* and pick out all of the words they find that are not in use today. Have them seek definitions for those words either in the notes accompanying the text or in a dictionary. For example, in Act 3, scene 1 of *Julius Caesar*, we see Mark Antony over the body of the newly slain Julius Caesar, having just confronted the men who killed Caesar. Those men, Brutus, Cassius, and the rest, leave Antony alone on stage, and he delivers this speech to Caesar's body:

Antony: O pardon me, thou bleeding piece of earth,
That I am meek and gentle with these butchers.
Thou art the ruins of the noblest man
That ever livèd in the tide of times.
Woe to the hand that shed this costly blood!
Over thy wounds now do I prophesy
 (Which like dumb mouths do ope their ruby lips
to beg the voice and utterance of my tongue)
A curse shall light upon the limbs of men;
Domestic fury and fierce civil strife
Shall cumber all the parts of Italy;
Blood and destruction shall be so in use
And dreadful objects so familiar
That mothers will but smile when they behold
Their infants quartered with the hands of war,
All pity choked with custom of fell deeds;
And Caesar's spirit ranging for revenge,
With Ate by his side come hot from hell,
Shall in these confines with a monarch's voice
Cry "Havoc!" and let slip the dogs of war,
That this foul deed shall smell above the earth
With carrion men groaning for burial. (3.1.280–301)

Students will list words such as these: ope, cumber, quartered, fell, ranging, Ate, havoc, carrion. In the Folger edition of the text, all but two of the words listed above are defined in the marginal notes, as are several other words and passages, such as "mute" for "dumb" and "customary" for "in use." Those that aren't included, "ope" and "carrion," fall into two categories. "Carrion" may be looked up easily, and some students in the class will know the word, so you could just ask the group. The word "ope" gives an example of a common practice in Shakespeare that trips up students: a simple omission of a letter to show speech pattern; "ope" is just "open" as a verb without the "n", which effectively makes it fit the rhythm of iambic pentameter. Sometimes Shakespeare removes a letter from inside a word (e.g., "ta'en" for "taken") to make a two-syllable word into a one-syllable word and to reflect dialect in his characters. These changes to conventional words are clues to actors speaking the lines.

and MAYbe GET a WHOPper AND some FRIES
These SCHOOLhouse LUNCHes JUST don't FILL me UP.
But SOFT what LIGHT through YONder WINdow BREAKS?
It IS the EAST and JULiet IS the SUN.
Shall I comPARE thee TO a SUMmer's DAY?
Thou ART more LOVEly AND more TEMperATE.
You BLOCKS! you STONES! You WORSE than SENSEless THINGS!

Students can and do get the hang of speaking and hearing iambic pentameter. Going back to Antony's speech in the activity above, we see that he is speaking in iambic pentameter, and we can also see that the rhythm, while dominant, is not entirely consistent, as Shakespeare uses variations on the iambic pentameter to attract our attention and to avoid his characters falling into sing-song speech. Actors make use of those variations in rhythm as clues for performance. Maybe they will lend special emphasis to a line that inverts the rhythm. Here are some lines from Julius Caesar that, while essentially following rhythm, contain notable variance from the pattern.

Brutus:	Look how he makes to Caesar. Mark him.
Cassius:	Casca, be sudden, for we fear prevention.—
	Brutus, what shall be done? If this be known,
	Cassius or Caesar never shall turn back,
	For I will slay myself.
Brutus:	Cassius, be constant.
	Popilius Lena speaks not of our purposes,
	For look, he smiles, and Caesar doth not change. (3.1.20–27)

Often, as in this case, characters will finish each other's lines to complete the iambic pentameter, and editors indicate this practice by placing words of the second speaker further to the right on the page, such as in Brutus's response to Cassius.

Also of note are instances where characters speak in prose as opposed to poetic meter. Students can examine those instances in the script to determine why Shakespeare chose to shift into prose. A good example in *Julius Caesar* is Brutus's funeral oration.

Students in advanced English classes should know not only iambic rhythm, but other metrical feet as well: trochees, anapests, and dactyls. They should know dimeter, trimeter, tetrameter, and other rhythmic features, such as spondee and caesura. Shakespeare gives us plenty of opportunities to make such literary terms operational for our students.

Figurative Language

Another challenge that Shakespeare's style presents us with, which varies from character to character, is the use of figurative language, such as metaphor and its family members, simile and personification. If you look at Mark Antony's speech reproduced above, you will see that he uses a wide range of metaphors, direct and implied, in just the first several lines. He calls Caesar's body a "bleeding piece of earth" and then "the ruins of the noblest man that ever livèd in the tide of times," thus comparing Caesar to a building, or perhaps a ship (given the further "tide of times" metaphor). He employs the metaphorical device of synecdoche in "woe to the hand that shed this costly blood," with "costly" providing yet another metaphor. He then constructs a simile for Caesar's wounds, which "like dumb mouths do ope their ruby lips." Granted, not everyone in Shakespeare or in *Julius Caesar* speaks with as much figurative language as Antony, and he will prove his rhetorical mastery in his funeral oration, but any character in any Shakespeare play is liable to create a metaphorical image at any time. Students who are put on alert for such images will find that they can understand metaphors and construct their own.

Sometimes the metaphors or personification will be short and clear, and other times, the figures of speech will take twists and turns. Although not all imagery in Shakespeare is figurative, he creates worlds where people aren't always content to just speak plainly. They provide details that color the world, both for the actor who needs to bring that world to light, and for the reader who wishes to understand the speeches. Ironically, what is sometimes most difficult in reading Shakespeare, the figurative language, is part of what makes it most memorable. For example, "Friends, Romans, countrymen, lend me your ears" is more memorable than, "Hey, listen up!"

Syntax

Another aspect of Shakespeare's style and language that poses difficulty is the syntax. Tracing the sentence construction in Shakespeare can not only help students to understand Shakespeare, but Shakespeare's creative use of sentence structure can help students understand the possibilities presented by different grammatical forms. Grammar is best taught in context anyway, and close analysis of Shakespeare's sentences can broaden one's grasp of the possibilities. One need never look far in Shakespeare for examples of inverted syntax. Often he does so in service of the verse. Look at the following:

> *Antony:* Over thy wounds now do I prophesy
> (Which like dumb mouths do ope their ruby lips
> to beg the voice and utterance of my tongue)
> A curse shall light upon the limbs of men; (3.1.285–288)

In this sentence, Antony inverts the subject/auxiliary verb/main verb form ("I do prophesy" or just "I prophesy") to auxiliary verb/subject/main verb ("do I prophesy"), which students may mistakenly read as a question even in the absence of a question mark. He then inserts a long parenthetical adjective clause describing metaphorical "wounds" before completing the sentence with a noun clause. But you will note that beyond the opening trochee "over," the verse is strictly iambic. Students can be taught to read Shakespeare always on the lookout for such instances of inverted sentence construction, and for the insertion of lengthy phrases and clauses of description.

Along with picking out examples of sentences that use variations on typical sentence construction, students can analyze their own writing and construct examples of sentences that use unusual forms. For example, one of us may write a sentence like, "The players were tired by the end of the game." But the same sentence could be written, "Tired were the players by the end of the game." Or "By the end of the game, tired the players were."

Listening to the Language and Variations in Meaning: Operative Words

In a Folger Shakespeare workshop I attended in 2010, the leader of the workshop, Michael LoMonico, presented a single line of dialogue and asked his participants to say the line aloud. I've changed the line slightly, but it went something like this:

He didn't say that he had beat his dog.

You will notice that the line is written in iambic pentameter. What LoMonico then did was project the line several different times and have us repeat it aloud, emphasizing the boldfaced word. Try it yourself:

He didn't say that he had beat his dog.

He **didn't** say that he had beat his dog.
He didn't **say** that he had beat his dog.
He didn't say that **he** had beat his dog.
He didn't say that he **had** beat his dog.
He didn't say that he had **beat** his dog.
He didn't say that he had beat **his** dog.
He didn't say that he had beat his **dog.**

As we discovered in the workshop, and as I'm sure you discovered in reading these lines, emphasizing different words changes the meaning of the statement. The boldface words become what theatre people would call the "operatives," or the key words for an actor to emphasize to communicate meaning to an audience so that they may construct a similar meaning. Typically there would be more than one operative in a given line, but only through hearing different emphases can we identify ranges of possible meaning in the lines. In looking at Shakespeare's scripts, we will naturally pick out different words as operatives, but it may be useful to try other alternatives to test how they affect our reading. Try this passage from Julius Caesar, during the argument between Brutus and Cassius:

> *Brutus:* You say you are a better soldier.
> Let it appear so, make your vaunting true,
> And it shall please me well. For mine own part,
> I shall be glad to learn of noble men. (4.3.56–59)

Which words do you see as operatives? Try reading the passage aloud and emphasizing different words to see what is communicated, then imagine the response of the other character.

Pronoun and Verb Forms

One other aspect of Shakespeare's language to consider here is the more mundane use of pronouns and archaic forms of verbs that students have problems with at first but which they can master in a short time if they have the will and the guidance to do so. I am speaking of "thou" and "thee" and "doth" and "dost" and "whilst" and "shouldst" and other such forms. The short explanation for the second person pronoun is that "thou" is the subject form and "thee" is the object form of you, and while Shakespeare uses "you" also, he often uses thee and thou, which in his day represented a more familiar form (although these words sound formal to us). The variant forms of verbs such as "dost" and "whilst" are easy to master, and students will not need explanation after they have been reading Shakespeare for a little while.

ACTIVITY (SAS #4): SYNTAX.

Have students write for 10 minutes, recalling a story from their lives that was dramatic in some way. Have them tell in detail what happened. When they have finished their free-write, ask them to review the sentences they've written and determine the sentence structure. You will find that they typically employ a subject/verb/object construction, with the occasional adverb clause thrown in at the beginning. Then have them take a few of the most important sentences that describe action and reverse the order so that the main information comes last. Have students also reverse the order of noun and verb if it works for them. An example might be sentences like the following:

I parked my truck in the parking lot, and I walked inside. I was looking for my brother.

A student can turn it into:

In the parking lot parked I my truck and, looking for my brother, inside walked.

Then have students increase the drama with the addition of thoughts such as:

Full of trepidation, yet driven blindly onward, in the parking lot parked I my truck and without hesitation, my brother seeking with great anxiety, inside the cavernous and dark entrance walked I.

Although the sentences they arrive at may seem silly, they will get the hang of it with practice, and will enjoy creating a sense of drama when they read their revised versions. Students' writing patterns tend to be fairly consistent and without a great deal of variety, so this exercise can do more than simply help them to understand Shakespeare. Such play with language will teach them to think of language as something malleable that they can control and perhaps translate to their own storytelling. But they will also begin to see how Shakespeare uses language to create a sense of tension. Have them compare times when the characters use this inverted syntax with times when they speak plainly.

What will be more of a challenge, however, related to the variations of sentence structure and the complicated metaphors Shakespeare uses, is the ability to match pronoun forms with their proper antecedents. Shakespeare's sonnets provide short and digestible samples to use in teaching this skill, and your students can then apply that skill to some of the longer speeches in Shakespeare that use complicated pronoun/antecedent relationships. Let's look at Sonnet 116 (Shakespeare, 1593–1609/1969) as an example:

Let me not to the marriage of true minds
Admit impediments; love is not love
Which alters when it alteration finds,
Or bends with the remover to remove.
O, no, it is an ever-fixéd mark
That looks on tempests and is never shaken;
It is the star to every wand'ring bark,
Whose worth's unknown, although his height be taken.
Love's not Time's fool, though rosy lips and cheeks
Within his bending sickle's compass come;
Love alters not with his brief hours and weeks,
But bears it out even to the edge of doom:
If this be error and upon me proved,
I never writ, nor no man ever loved.

In lines 7–8, the pronoun "It" (referring to Love), is "the star" (the North Star) to every wandering "bark" (ship) "whose worth's unknown, although his height be taken." The pronoun "his" refers to "star," which, again, is a metaphor for "love." Two lines later, however, "his" refers to "Time," which is portrayed as a false lover and a carrier of a "bending sickle." Notice how "Love" is the antecedent for the pronoun "it" through the first octave of the poem, but another noun has become the antecedent for "it" in line 12: "But bears it out even to the edge of doom." What is the antecedent for "it" in line 12? "Time," perhaps. And finally, the pronoun "this" reflects on the speaker's assertion regarding love, which forms the text of the poem. Students can very quickly get mired in pronoun-antecedent relationships, making them a good tool for examination when passages are murky.

A Note on Language in *Julius Caesar*

One of the particular qualities of *Julius Caesar* is the directness of language as compared to Shakespeare's other scripts. Shakespeare could count on his audience to know the story he was telling, as well as something about Roman oratory. The style of the language in *Julius Caesar* has been called lucid and vigorous (Humphreys, 1984) and flexible and strong (McMurtry, 1998). Both Humphreys and McMurtry make note of the style in language serving the play's enormous concern with rhetoric, and for Spevack (2003), the style is influenced by the story's conflation of the public and the private spheres. In any case, your students will have less trouble navigating the language and speech structures in *Julius Caesar* than they would have with *Hamlet*, *Romeo and Juliet*, or most of the other Shakespeare scripts. They will find, however, that the simple language masks deep meaning.

Chapter Materials

Name: ______________________________ Date: ______________________

Student Activity Sheet #1: That Sounds Familiar!

Applicable Portion of Play: Prereading

Objective: Students will be able to recognize common sayings and words that originated with Shakespeare, and choose those that are least familiar to them to investigate further.

Common Core Standard(s): 11-12.L.4, 11-12.L.4.c

Directions: Alone or in pairs, open an Internet browser and type in the search phrase "common phrases from Shakespeare." You will see several sites open, including the following:

- http://www.worsleyschool.net/socialarts/shakespeare/sayings.html
- http://www.lomonico.com/bookch4.html

Investigate these sites and pick 10 phrases that are very familiar to you, 10 phrases that are moderately familiar to you, and 10 phrases that are not familiar to you at all. Compare your lists with those of your classmates, and then gather as a class to discuss the meanings of the unfamiliar lines. Then, write sentences or dialogue using the lines in a way that makes sense to you.

Very Familiar	Moderately Familiar	Not Familiar

Student Activity Sheet #2:
Shakespeare as a Foreign Language

Applicable Portion of Play: Prereading

Objectives: 1. Students will demonstrate an understanding of the similarities between Shakespeare's English and contemporary English.
2   Students will assess their knowledge of Shakespeare's English.

Common Core Standard(s): 11-12.L.4, 11-12.L.4.a, 11-12.L.4.d

Directions: Examine the opening scene of *Julius Caesar* as though it is a foreign language. Use a blank piece of paper or two columns on a computer screen. Divide the page into two columns, and label one "Known" and the other "Unknown."

Pick out the words and phrases that you know and list them on one side of a blank page. Then pick out the words and phrases you don't know or understand. Pair up with a classmate and share your lists. When everyone has compared their lists, the class will discuss the difficulty of the language and the passage.

Again, read the passage out loud and listen to it, then return to your lists and see if any words or phrases make more sense to you. Discuss.

Reflection: Based upon the size of your two lists, how confident are you that you know the language? Would you be able to function and communicate in a society that spoke this way? What is most difficult about it?

_____

_____

_____

_____

_____

_____

_____

_____

_____

_____

_____

_____

_____

Student Activity Sheet #3:
Words to Know

Applicable Portion of Play: Prereading and Act III, scene 1.

Objectives:
1. Students will identify words they use that did not exist until recently.
2. Students will be able to identify unfamiliar words in one passage of *Julius Caesar*, then define them by using explanatory notes and a dictionary.

Common Core Standard(s): 11-12.L.4, 11-12.L.4.a, 11-12.L.4.c, 11-12.L.5, 11-12.R.L.4

Directions: In groups of four, generate a list of words that we commonly use today that didn't exist or that didn't have the same meaning for your parents' generation. Some of the words will be words that already existed but that either changed meanings or changed parts of speech. How many can you come up with? Share words with the other groups to compile a list for the entire class.

Next, read the following passage from *Julius Caesar*, Act 3, scene 1:

> *Antony:* O pardon me, thou bleeding piece of earth,
> That I am meek and gentle with these butchers.
> Thou art the ruins of the noblest man
> That ever livèd in the tide of times.
> Woe to the hand that shed this costly blood!
> Over thy wounds now do I prophesy
> (Which like dumb mouths do ope their ruby lips
> to beg the voice and utterance of my tongue)
> A curse shall light upon the limbs of men;
> Domestic fury and fierce civil strife
> Shall cumber all the parts of Italy;
> Blood and destruction shall be so in use
> And dreadful objects so familiar
> That mothers will but smile when they behold
> Their infants quartered with the hands of war,
> All pity choked with custom of fell deeds;
> And Caesar's spirit ranging for revenge,
> With Ate by his side come hot from hell,
> Shall in these confines with a monarch's voice
> Cry "Havoc!" and let slip the dogs of war,
> That this foul deed shall smell above the earth
> With carrion men groaning for burial. (3.1.280–301)

Reread the passage and pick out any words or phrases that we no longer use, or that you are unfamiliar with. List them, then look at the explanatory notes in your script to see how many of those words or phrases are explained. Note the explanations next to your list. Any words from your list that are not defined in the notes will need to be looked up in a dictionary. Share notes with your classmates.

Finally, reread the passage to register your new understanding.

Reflection: How long was your list? How many of the difficult words were explained in the notes? How difficult was the process of checking the notes?

_____

_____

_____

_____

_____

_____

_____

_____

_____

_____

_____

_____

_____

_____

Student Activity Sheet #4:
Sentences Reordered

Applicable Portion of Play: All

Objectives: 1.   Students will understand how Shakespeare manipulates sentence structure for dramatic effect.
2.   Students will be able to manipulate sentences in their own writing for dramatic effect.

Common Core Standard(s): 11-12.L.3.a, 11-12.W.2.c

Directions: First, find a few sentences in *Julius Caesar* that use an unusual sentence order. Write one sentence on a separate piece of paper and identify the subject noun, the verb or verbs, and any other elements. Discuss the sentences you picked with a partner or in a small group.

Next, write for 10 minutes recalling a story from your life that was dramatic in some way. Tell in detail what happened. When you have finished your free-write, review the sentences you have written and determine the sentence structure. Pick three or four of the most important or interesting sentences in the story and reverse the structure of the sentence, so what is near the end comes first.

An example might be a sentence like the following:

I parked my truck in the parking lot, and I walked inside, looking for my brother.

You can turn it into:

In the parking lot parked I my truck and, looking for my brother, inside walked I.

Next, increase the drama with the addition of thoughts and details such as:

Full of trepidation, yet driven blindly onward, in the parking lot parked I my truck and without hesitation, my brother seeking with great anxiety, inside the cavernous and dark entrance walked I.

Incorporate your revised sentences into your story for dramatic effect.

Reflection: How did playing with your own sentences affect your ability to read sentences you find in *Julius Caesar*? What is gained or lost when we write in unusual sentence order?

_____

_____

_____

_____

_____

CHAPTER 3

"Are we all ready?": Teaching *Julius Caesar*

Teaching *Julius Caesar* will present many of the same challenges that all Shakespeare texts present, such as the elements discussed in the previous chapter. The script of *Julius Caesar* is more accessible than many of Shakespeare's texts because the plot is uncomplicated, the language is less convoluted than the language in *Romeo and Juliet* or *Hamlet,* and the story of Caesar's assassination is well known. The biggest challenge in teaching *Julius Caesar* may present itself by virtue of what the play lacks rather than what it contains. The Romanness, or "romanitas," as Humphreys (1984) referred to it, an essence built on personal virtue and public spirit, in some way prevents us from getting close to the characters, even if they reveal their weaknesses and demonstrate human frailty and vice. This is a political play, a play of public speeches, a play of competing men. This chapter discusses particular aspects of *Julius Caesar* that distinguish it from the rest of Shakespeare's work, including character sketches, plot summary, and suggestions for building a unit of study.

Much has been written over the years in connection with *Julius Caesar,* and students may be overwhelmed if you bury them in critical material before they start reading. This is not to say that critical prose should be avoided, but I would recommend letting students first encounter the text of *Julius Caesar* with a fairly naïve stance as readers, unencumbered by predigested interpretations of others. Looking at published criticism can add to rereadings, discussions, and ultimately to performing scenes and writing in response to the play, but frontloading students with piles of information, even extensive background information, can lessen interest and convince them that they are no match for the task of studying *Julius Caesar.* Instead, students can build background and broaden interpretive context through their interactions with the text, particularly through rereading. That is not to say, however, that students can't adopt certain critical stances when studying the script through various inquiry questions; such stances will be addressed in Chapter 8.

Concerns Particular to the Play

Julius Caesar presents a world that is foreign to your students, layered through another world that is equally foreign. Students are two millennia away from the time of the Roman republic and four centuries removed from Elizabethan England. We may look for hints of Shakespeare's world in the play set in Ancient Rome (Shapiro, 2005), and we may learn a number of things about Rome through Shakespeare's manifestation of it in *Julius Caesar*. But Shakespeare was writing a stage adaptation of a book that was popular in his time. He was interested in presenting famous figures as human beings interacting with one another in times of crisis. Also, he was presenting Rome in a way that his audience would understand and perhaps accept, which may differ from how we see Rome today. Ultimately, Shakespeare was shaping his audience's perception of Rome and, by extension, he has helped to shape our perception as well.

One of the chief concerns particular to this play is the ambiguity of audience sympathy. Shakespeare presents us with a script that can be interpreted in Caesar's favor, making Mark Antony a righteous avenger and Brutus and Cassius the traitors that Dante perceived them to be. The script can just as easily present Caesar as deluded and dangerous, Mark Antony as contriving, and Brutus and Cassius as righteous defenders of Roman republicanism. A good director can present all of the characters in the fullness of their good and bad qualities. But for high school students, having a clear "good guy" and "bad guy" helps orient them, and they sometimes resist the challenge of interpreting characters as a mix of sympathetic and antisympathetic characteristics. A good teacher, with the right tools, can move students past their insistence on black-and-white interpretations.

Another problem that *Julius Caesar* presents for students is the tone of speech characteristic of the play. In nearly every scene, iambic pentameter dominates, and characters use the high style of oratory in public and in private. Every scene in the first four acts contains an argument of some type. Some scholars, such as Barbara Baines (2005), note that the play itself is about language and its uses. Particularly in the first two acts, when students typically are making up their minds about how well they like the script and the story, the text is filled with rhetorical speeches on Rome, honor, and nobility, not necessarily the three top conversational topics of contemporary teens.

A third concern presented by this play is the dominance of men, or put another way, the lack of female characters and female energy. Other than the wives of Caesar and Brutus, both of whom appear in only two scenes, the play presents a festival of testosterone. You may need to do some investigation of different critical perspectives to help your female students take an interest in the script (see Gillespie, 2010). Some critics have found the gender politics of *Julius Caesar* compelling (Cohen, 2006; Kahn, 1992; Knight, 1931; Paster, 2002). Cohen, who viewed the play unfavorably and questioned its place in the school curriculum, saw the gender approach, wherein the men steal from their "wholesome" beds and the life-giving love of their wives, as a driving force in the violence and tragedy that follow.

Related to the concern above is the lack of the kind of love interest present in Shakespeare's comedies and the other tragedy students will most likely be familiar with, *Romeo and Juliet*. We have no character who pours out his heart to the audience, as Hamlet and Macbeth (to an extent) do, although Brutus does soliloquize. The style and the relationships in this play can come across as stiff and abstract. The powerful tent scene between Brutus and Cassius is the exception to this tone, as Cassius reveals deep personal hurt to Brutus.

On the other hand, there is plenty of blood in *Julius Caesar*, and while it is not nearly as violent as Shakespeare's first Roman play, *Titus Andronicus*, we do see a gang stabbing, a mob killing, and several suicides. What will appeal to some students will repel others.

Given the concerns presented here, I would suggest approaching *Julius Caesar* with an open mind, telling your students that you are going to experience the world from both inside and out, taking on the roles of the characters and thus penetrating their personalities, applying a variety of reading, discussion, performance, and writing tools to examine the world Shakespeare suggests to us. Through such investigations, we can develop our sense of what the script suggests that a production of the play might be about. Our students' construction of meaning in the text will make it a part of the permanent architecture of their literary worlds.

What Is This Play About?

Every time I read a critical essay on *Julius Caesar*, a critical introduction to one of the various editions of the play, or an account of a different production, I am led to reconsider my position on the text. Although this may say more about my own intellectual fickleness than about *Julius Caesar*, my point is that the play provides rich ground for interpretation. Two compilations of critical essays that have appeared in the past 10 years (Wilson, 2002c; Zander, 2005b) are rich with alternative readings based on close consideration of language, parallel cultural history, or application of critical lenses. At the same time, new theatre productions continue to push the envelope of our conception of the play.

On its face, the play is about the plot to assassinate Julius Caesar, the major players in the conspiracy, and the aftermath of the assassination (including violence in the streets of Rome and civil war) leading to the suicides of the main conspirators. It can also be seen as a play about "emulation," or a struggle among male competitors to establish dominance over their peers (Kahn, 2005; Rebhorn, 2002). The play may also be seen as a commentary on social class and structure (Hawkes, 2005; Rebhorn, 2002). As such, the class society of Rome has been compared to the class society of Shakespeare's day, and can be compared to our own. Northrop Frye (1968) saw the play as representing order and the restoration of it following upheaval. For many, the play is about language and rhetoric, and how language operates in private and political contexts (Baines, 2005; Barker, 2005).

The play is about what it means to be Roman (Humphreys, 1984), male relationships (Kahn, 1992; Knight, 1931), violence (Hawkes, 2005; Parker, 2005), time and its signification (Candido, 2005; McMurtry, 1998; Spevack, 2003), and constancy (Spevack, 2003). The play presents us with a common citizenry that is changeable and potentially violent, led by men who are in turns vain, honorable, jealous, conniving, kind, and self-destructive. Some critics have seen the play as presenting a commentary on acting and the role of theatrical ritual in society (Holmes, 2001; Wilson, 2002b). Related to the play's preoccupation with language and rhetoric is its concern with interpretation, and several writers have commented on the lines of Cicero in Act 1, scene 3, "But men may construe things after their fashion / Clean from the purpose of the things themselves" (34–35), seeing these lines as emblematic of the central theme in the text (Baines, 2005; Holderness & Nevitt, 2005).

Critics argue over nearly every scene presented in the script, including the intense, seemingly brutal mob killing of an innocent poet (Act 3, scene 3) that either signifies a ritual of killing art (Taylor, 2002), a parody of violence (Holmes, 2001) or, as I see it, a commentary on the potentiality of anarchy in any society. The play is also about the historic and larger-than-life figures of its main characters, and as mentioned before, in presenting an adaptation of Plutarch's series of biographies translated into English, Shakespeare put language into the mouths of these figures in an attempt to bring them to life for the patrons of his theatre. As a study of the intersection between individual personalities and political crisis, *Julius Caesar* presents greatness even as it questions greatness, juxtaposes personal affection and loyalty against civic responsibility, and examines the necessity of building personal connection as a means of survival.

Ultimately, what the play is about depends upon what you and your students decide to make it about. By taking the approach of interpreters through shared reading, discussion, performance, and writing, you and your students will mine the words Shakespeare has left us in order to create, out of the script, a world that is not only Ancient Rome in the names and events it depicts, but our own world in the reality your interpretation represents.

The character descriptions below and the plot summary that follows them will inevitably reflect my own biases, although I try to portray the characters in terms of potentialities rather than fixed realities. As Mary Ellen Dakin (2009) pointed out, dominant readings of characters can and should be challenged in the process of reading and doing Shakespeare in the classroom. If we focus on the process of converting script to performance (Rocklin, 2005), then new possibilities will present themselves related to character, plot, and ultimately the play itself.

Characters

Julius Caesar

Given that he was the most famous man in the world during his time, and given that the Elizabethan public was very interested in ancient Rome, Caesar's many exploits as a military leader and conqueror would have been familiar to most educated Elizabethans, and his lore would have been familiar even to the uneducated. Shakespeare only makes occasional reference to Caesar's long and storied military career in the script of the play that bears his name, focusing instead on the man's physical characteristics and his personal interactions with those closest to him. Caesar only appears in three scenes in the play and is assassinated shortly into Act 3. Following his death, Caesar's spirit appears to Brutus twice, once on stage at the conclusion of Act 4. Directors sometimes choose to bring the actor playing Caesar on stage for the spirit role, and sometimes they pursue other visions. If we are to see Caesar as the protagonist of this play, his influence on the events following his death requires acknowledgment, and there is evidence in the script for such emphasis. Both Brutus and Cassius address Caesar's memory in their dying words. Some productions have even featured an oversized bust of the man in the background (see Spevack, 2003, p. 60).

While alive, Caesar is presented in contrasts. When we first meet Caesar in public procession, he orders Mark Antony to touch Calphurnia (Caesar's wife) in the Lupercal chase in order to help her conceive a child. Caesar's apparent superstition is inconsistent, however, as he ignores later omens from his wife and his augurers who would not have him go to the capitol for fear of danger. He is powerful, yet weak. He is commanding in public and affable in his residence, inviting the very men who will shortly kill him to "taste some wine . . . like friends" (2.2.134-135). He often refers to himself in the third person, and claims that he is more "terrible" than danger itself, yet he is deaf in one ear, has frequent epileptic seizures, and fears Cassius's "lean and hungry look" (1.2.204). One of the challenges of any director producing this play is to present Caesar in his complexity. He can be presented as an arrogant and distant dictator who deserves his fate, or a glorious and benevolent leader who is ruthlessly murdered. Caesar separates himself from others, claiming to be "constant as the Northern Star, / of whose true fixed and resting quality / There is no fellow in the firmament" (3.1.66–68), and yet he leaves himself vulnerable to death by stabbing. When Antony reads Caesar's will, we learn that Caesar was a great public benefactor. One of the primary characteristics of Shakespeare's script is its potential ambiguity in sympathy toward characters. How Caesar is presented to the audience, then, often depends on how a director decides to present the other major characters.

Marcus Brutus

Typically considered the protagonist in the play or the "tragic hero" (McMurtry, 1998; Spevack, 2003), Brutus is often referred to as the most "honorable" of the conspirators against Caesar. He is a Roman Praetor, or civic administrator. He is a friend of Julius Caesar, and also a reputed lover of his country. He is seduced by Cassius into the conspiracy against Caesar, although he had already been troubled by Caesar's growing power. One argument for presenting Brutus as the protagonist is the garden soliloquy at the beginning of Act 2, scene 1, wherein Brutus contemplates the idea of assassinating Caesar. He rationalizes the killing not based on what Caesar is, but on what he may become. Tradition has sometimes claimed that Brutus was Julius Caesar's illegitimate son (Bloom, 1998). No other character is given as much direct intimacy with the audience. Having joined the conspiracy, Brutus takes command of the plans and makes a series of tactical blunders against the advice of Cassius, eventually leading to his defeat and suicide. He is married to Portia and shows affection for her and for his servant boy, Lucius. He and Cassius have a complicated and troubled relationship, which climaxes in their famous argument scene in Act 4, scene 3. They part, however, as friends, and often refer to each other using the word "love."

Brutus is associated with the Stoic philosophy, which prevents him from showing great emotion, most notably demonstrated when he learns of his wife's violent death by her own hand. The dominant reading of him is of a "naive idealist" (Dakin, 2009), but other readings are possible. He is eulogized positively by his enemies and loved by his inferiors. Once again, how Brutus is presented, either as a righteous would-be savior of the republic, a treacherous traitor, or a shortsighted idealist, is in the hands of a director.

Caius Cassius

Cassius is a senator and the lead organizer of the conspiracy against Julius

Caesar. He dominates Act 1, scenes 2 and 3 in his quest to recruit Brutus and others to assassinate Caesar, and he participates in the assassination, even if he barely suppresses a panic attack prior to the deed. Although he is generally dismissed as "not a serious candidate for the play's leading character" (McMurtry, 1998, p. 42), I find him the most compelling character in the play, and even McMurtry admitted that actors are eager to play Cassius. He presents a combination of intelligence, passion, bitterness, and self-destruction that make him the most consistently human of the main characters. As an Epicurean, he puts little stock in superstition. He is personally disgusted by Caesar's rise to power, and he is not beneath lying to get Brutus to join him in the plot. Perhaps Cassius's tragic flaw is his singleness of purpose to seduce Brutus, and he learns, to his great downfall, that Brutus is better as a symbol of the conspiracy than as the actual leader of it. Cassius advises the conspirators to take an oath and is rejected by Brutus. He advises that Antony die, too, and is rejected. He warns Brutus not to let Antony speak in Caesar's funeral and is overruled, and he advises that the armies of Brutus and Cassius not attack Antony and Octavius at Philippi, only to be overruled again. Cassius's inability to dissuade Brutus from making tactical errors in a sense costs him his life.

Cassius historically was Brutus's brother-in-law, but in the play, the feminine influence is suppressed, as symbolized by Portia's death and the absence of reference to Cassius's wife. A homosexual reading of the script would find ample evidence to indicate a bond between Brutus and Cassius that goes beyond friendship, and their famous squabble in Brutus's military tent in Act 4, scene 3 reads like a bitter marriage brawl. Cassius speaks his mind from early on, and his growing frustration with Brutus's bad decisions culminates in a pathetic plea to Messala to bear witness that he is going to battle against his better judgment. He threatens to kill himself if Caesar is crowned king, and nearly kills himself when he thinks the plot is discovered. Eventually, when he misreads the events on the battlefield, he succumbs to the Roman "honor" of suicide. A director wishing to give a sympathetic reading to Caesar can easily vilify Cassius. One of many arguments against such vilification is the fact that his officer, Titinius, kills himself when he sees Cassius dead, and that Brutus calls him "the last of the Romans."

Mark Antony

Although some see Mark Antony as a candidate for the leading role in the play, I disagree. He has a major role, the role of Caesar's avenger, and his oration in Caesar's funeral is the most famous argument in the play, and perhaps in all of literature. The 1953 (Houseman & Mankiewicz) movie starring Marlon Brando as Mark Antony made him into a rival protagonist to James Mason's Brutus. In the script, Antony is a minor character through the first half of the play, then dominates the last half of Act 3. He appears again in Act 4, scene 1, the "proscription scene," and then disappears until Act 5, when he appears once to parley with Brutus and Cassius and twice on the battlefield.

His personality is complicated. He is described early on as a sort of party animal, even by Caesar, which sets him in contrast with Cassius in Caesar's eyes. He gains great audience sympathy through his genuine reaction to Caesar's death and his brilliant rhetorical piece that sways the Roman citizens to mutiny. But he also "prophesies" great destruction that goes far beyond bringing Caesar's killers to justice, and he, Octavius, and Lepidus organize a reign of terror that leaves 70–100 senators dead. Shakespeare paints brilliant contrasts by presenting the Antony of the funeral speech, followed shortly by the Antony of the proscription scene, marking down names of those who will die. We must also remember that Antony in this play is prelude to Antony, the titular hero of *Antony and Cleopatra*, one of Shakespeare's greatest later tragedies.

The Other Conspirators: Casca, Decius, Cinna, Metellus Cimber, Ligarius, and Trebonius

Casca. First appears as Caesar's crowd silencer, then becomes the man who strikes the opening blow against Caesar with his knife. His line, "Speak, hands, for me!" (3.1.84) is one of the most quoted lines from the script. He is a sharp-tongued conspirator who shows a clear disdain for the common people in his description of Mark Antony offering Caesar a crown in Act 1, scene 2. In the following scene (1.3), he appears completely unwound by the storm until Cassius wins him to the conspiracy.

Decius. Flatters Caesar to bring him to the Capitol by reinterpreting Calphurnia's dream. Palmer (1968) saw him as representative of the public servant who is "accustomed to dealing with persons in high office" (p. 18) and for whom insider status and the ability to manipulate his superiors is his greatest quality.

Cinna. Appears in the storm scene already a part of the conspiracy. Perhaps best distinguished as the man whose name resulted in the death of an innocent poet of the same name.

Metellus Cimber. Is concerned for the public perception of the assassination in Act 2, scene 1. Begs for his brother's enfranchisement as a ploy to allow the conspirators to surround Caesar in order to kill him.

Ligarius. Either sick or pretending sickness before joining the conspiracy. Not listed as being on stage in the assassination scene, but a director may choose to include him.

Trebonius. Draws Mark Antony out of the way at the assassination.

None of these co-conspirators appears after the assassination scene, and the last we see them is when Mark Antony individually shakes their bloody hands. We assume that some or all of them are killed by the triumvirate's proscription, though historically, according to McMurtry (1998), Casca is reputed to have fought with Cassius's army against Antony and Octavius. In Shakespeare's company and today, the actors playing these characters most likely would "double" as the soldiers who are introduced in Acts 4 and 5.

The Women: Portia and Calphurnia

Portia. Wife to Brutus, who argues with her husband about his strange behavior and convinces him to share knowledge of the conspiracy against Caesar. She is the daughter of Cato, which makes her the sister of an unfortunate young soldier who dies on stage in Act 5. She herself dies a horrible death, swallowing coals. She is based on the historical woman whose argument with her husband and violent death are described in Plutarch. She appeals to Brutus's sense of duty to her as his wife and stabs herself in the thigh to prove her "constancy." She can be portrayed as logical and sane or irrational and unhinged, depending upon what we think of her self-mutilation and her speech. She calls the conspiracy what it is before she even knows the details, and some have implied that the fact of Brutus having "ungently . . . stole from [her] bed" (2.1.257–258) is the cause of all the trouble in this play (Cohen, 2006). When she appears for the second time in Act 2, scene 4, she is clearly nervous for Brutus, indicating that she knows of the conspiracy.

Calphurnia. Wife to Caesar, who in the opening scene is portrayed by her own husband as having a "sterile curse," but her husband's curse is his inability to listen to her warnings. Calphurnia's argument with Caesar in Act 2, scene 2 does not have the same result as Portia's argument with her husband, but whereas Portia just wants information, Calphurnia is trying to save her husband's life. She has had bad dreams the night before, and though she claims she "never stood on ceremonies" (2.2.13), she is frightened. She persuades Caesar at last to listen to her, but is easily overturned by Decius's flattery of Caesar. She seconds the indication in the script that feminine energy is eliminated before blood is shed. If Caesar had stayed home with his wife, he would have lived for another day.

Roman Public: Plebeians, Including the Carpenter and the Cobbler

No source that I have consulted lists the plebeians as a major character, but I see them as central to the theme of public opinion that runs throughout the text. They appear in the opening scene, where the tribunes castigate them for their fickleness, which foreshadows their further treatment. Casca ridicules them in his description of their reactions to Caesar, and they are swayed into almost polar opposite views of Caesar's assassination merely by listening to speeches. They are first moved to accept Caesar's death by the oration of Brutus, but then are whipped into a frenzy of revenge by Mark Antony. They may be portrayed on stage as intelligent consumers of logic or idiotic and dangerous fools, unfit to govern themselves. Their role crescendos in the horrifying mob murder of the innocent poet with the unfortunate name of Cinna. Shakespeare strays from his source (Plutarch) in portraying the death of Cinna the poet by having the crowd acknowledge that they hear him claim to be a different person from the conspirator. Yet they kill him anyway (unless, as Holmes [2001], argued, they don't really kill him but only rough him up). Shakespeare thus comments on the quality of mob mentality. Some have questioned Shakespeare's presentation of a fickle mob, and the killing of the poet can be read as a humorous take on Shakespeare's own profession as poet.

Minor Characters

Octavius Caesar. The nephew of Julius Caesar, and historically adopted by Caesar, Octavius will be a major character as an antagonist in *Antony and Cleopatra*. Octavius is referred to as being young, and he establishes a contrarian relationship with Mark Antony, even as they work together to defeat Brutus and Cassius.

Marullus and Flavius. Two tribunes who scold the plebeians in the opening scene of the play. Tribunes, historically, were from among the plebeian class, and they represented their interests in the government. These tribunes seem to lack respect for those they represent, and we learn later that they are "put to silence" for removing decorations from Caesar's images.

Soothsayer and Artemidorus. Both of these men attempt to warn Caesar, one enigmatically, the other very specifically. Both appear in Plutarch also. The presence of the soothsayer is especially intriguing because it sets up for us the theme of superstition in the play. The role of Artemidorus serves to show just how close Caesar is to discovering the plot while there is still time to stop it.

Cinna the Poet. This character is on stage for less than a minute, yet like so many minor characters in Shakespeare, he burns himself into our memory and serves to reflect on the major characters. Cinna has the bad fortune of sharing the same name as one of the conspirators, and he finds himself in the wrong place at the wrong time with an angry mob.

Lucius. Serving boy of Brutus and Portia. Lucius is one of the only characters to appear in the early acts and again in the later ones. As Brutus's personal servant, he runs errands and, through his interactions with his master, humanizes Brutus as a tender and caring man.

Lepidus. Triumvir with Antony and Octavius. Lepidus appears briefly in one scene and is trivialized by Mark Antony. His presence serves to open the first debate between Antony and Octavius.

Servants to Antony and Octavius. Both of these servants see the body of Caesar. Both of them give speeches and interact directly with the major characters. Antony's servant recites a message from Antony to Caesar's assassins. Octavius's servant, in his emotional reaction to seeing Caesar's body, brings Antony to tears.

Other Patricians

Cicero. Famous Roman senator. Not a part of the conspiracy, but suffers the consequences of it, being put to death by the triumvirate. He is not a friend to Caesar. Cicero meets Casca during the storm scene, but betrays no alliances.

Publius. A senator who prevents Artemidorus from getting his warning to Caesar. Brutus's dialogue with Publius indicates that he is old and not involved with the conspiracy.

Popilius Lena. A senator whose offhanded comment to Cassius nearly aborts the conspiracy.

Soldiers of Brutus and Cassius

Lucilius, Titinius, and Messala. Officers in the armies of Brutus and Cassius. Lucilius and Messala are taken by Mark Antony. Titinius kills himself over the body of Cassius, using Cassius's sword.

Varro and Claudius. These two men sleep in Brutus's tent, but don't see the appearance of the ghost.

Young Cato. Similar to Young Siward in *Macbeth*, this young soldier goes freshly to field and is quickly killed, reminding us that war = death. Historically, the brother of Portia.

Strato, Volumnius, Dardanus, and Clitus. Soldiers to Brutus who appear in his final scene. Each is asked to kill Brutus, and all but Strato refuse. Strato holds Brutus's sword while he runs on it.

Miscellaneous Characters

Second poet. Attempts to stop an argument between Brutus and Cassius after it has already run its course. He is kicked out of the tent, and neither Brutus nor Cassius acknowledges the accuracy of the poet's concern for them.

Pindarus. Cassius's slave who stabs Cassius at his request, then runs away.

Messengers and soldiers. Depending upon production budgets and director wishes, many extras can be cast in the armies or the citizenry of Rome.

Basic Plot

Julius Caesar can be seen as following the traditional arc of Shakespearean drama, with exposition in the first scenes, rising action developed through Act 2, a climax in Act 3, and the falling action and denouement taking place in the final two acts. What separates the plot of this play from others is the division between the first three acts, all taking place in various public and private spaces in Rome, and the final two acts that take place, primarily, in the field of war. Also significant is the almost complete turnover in casting, with only a handful of principal characters continuing on in the final acts. Following the death of Caesar, we no longer see any of the conspirators, save Brutus and Cassius, and we no longer see Portia and Calphurnia, nor any of the minor characters except the serving boy, Lucius. A new cast of soldiers takes the place of the citizenry, and Shakespeare's effect is to turn the Roman public, before our eyes, into a killing force in the final scene of Act 3. Another feature of note in *Julius Caesar*, and one reason why the play moves quickly, is the lack of subplots. The beginning of a subplot, the conflict between Antony and Octavius, is not developed, perhaps anticipating its full development in the later work, *Antony and Cleopatra*. Below is a short plot summary. For other summaries, consult McMurtry (1998) or the Folger edition of the script, which includes scene summaries in the marginal notes. For a detailed, scene-by-scene reading analysis, see Chapter 5.

Act 1

The script opens on a public street during the pagan feast of Lupercal, with commoners celebrating the return of Caesar to Rome. They are scolded and told to return to work by two tribunes, Marullus and Flavius, who note the changeability of the people's hearts, who before had supported Pompey, Caesar's rival. Caesar parades through the streets and commands Antony to "touch" Caesar's wife, Calphurnia, to help her bear a child. Thus, superstition is established as a theme. A soothsayer warns Caesar to "beware the Ides of March." When Caesar and the crowd go off-stage to see the running of the Lupercal race, Brutus and Cassius stay behind. Cassius sounds Brutus out on his feelings toward Caesar, and finds that Brutus does not want Caesar to be crowned king. Cassius then explains his personal distaste for Caesar's power, and encourages Brutus to see himself as having the same stature as Caesar. When Caesar and the rest return from the race, Caesar tells Antony to watch out for men with a "lean and hungry look" (1.2.204), mentioning Cassius specifically. Casca tells Brutus and Cassius that Caesar was offered a crown by Antony, and that he refused it three times, pleasing the common people. Casca also describes Caesar's epileptic fit after he refused the crown. Brutus promises to think about what Cassius has said regarding Caesar's power. In the final scene, a great thunderstorm is raging, and Casca is nervous about what it may mean. He talks to Cicero, who tries to calm him down, and then he sees Cassius, who uses the storm to recruit Casca to the conspiracy against Caesar. Cinna informs Cassius that others wait for him at his house, and Cassius tells Cinna to throw messages in Brutus's window that will flatter him into joining them.

Act 2

In the middle of the night, Brutus wrestles with his conflicting thoughts about Caesar, resolving to kill him not because of what he is, but because of what he may become. Brutus is visited by the other conspirators, who hide their faces. Once Brutus officially joins the cause, the conspirators talk about strategy. Brutus over-rules Cassius on whether or not to take an oath, whether or not to include Cicero in the conspiracy, and whether or not to kill Mark Antony along with Caesar. Following the men's departure, Portia questions Brutus on his behavior and purposes. She wounds herself in the thigh, prompting Brutus to promise to tell her what is happening. Another man, Caius Ligarius, enters and throws off his sickness, pledging to follow Brutus. In the next scene, at Caesar's house, Calphurnia argues with Caesar regarding her dreams and the strange weather, warning him not to leave home for fear of death. Caesar commands that his priests do sacrifice, and they return with an unfavorable omen. When Calphurnia tells him his wisdom is "consumed in confidence" and kneels, he decides to stay home. Decius enters, reinterprets Calphurnia's dream, and convinces Caesar to go to the capitol. In scene 3, Artemidorus is shown with his letter revealing the conspiracy, and he vows to give it to Caesar. In the final scene, Portia appears in great agitation, wondering if Brutus is successful in his mission. The soothsayer passes by, on his way to warn Caesar, and the act ends in anticipation of the murder scene.

Act 3

Caesar comes to the capitol. He sees the soothsayer, who warns him again of the Ides of March. Artemidorus tries unsuccessfully to get Caesar to read his petition revealing the conspiracy. Popilius Lena wishes Cassius success, at which point Cassius fears that their purpose is discovered and vows to kill himself. Brutus calms him, and they proceed to surround Caesar with the other conspirators. When Metellus Cimber starts to plea for his brother's return from banishment, Caesar expounds on his greatness and his constancy that exceeds all others. Casca stabs him, followed by the other conspirators and finally Brutus. Caesar says to Brutus, "*Et tu Brute?* Then fall Caesar" (3.1.85) and dies at the base of the statue of Pompey. In the immediate aftermath of the assassination, Antony's servant announces Antony's desire to meet with the conspirators. Antony confronts them and convinces Brutus to let him speak at Caesar's funeral, against the advice of Cassius. Mark Antony is left alone with the body and prophesies bloody war. A servant announces the arrival of Caesar's nephew, Octavius, to Rome.

The next scene takes place in the public forum, where Brutus gives his reasons for killing Caesar, and the crowd supports him. He leaves to allow Mark Antony his opportunity to speak, having set conditions that Mark Antony not blame the conspirators but only speak well of Caesar. Mark Antony uses the conditions to his advantage, ironically referring to Brutus and the others as "honorable men" while giving extensive evidence that their claims about Caesar's "ambition" were false. After he shows the citizens Caesar's bloody cloak, then his body, and then his will naming the citizens as heirs, they run off to burn the houses of the conspirators. Antony prepares to meet Octavius, and in the final scene, the rampaging citizens kill an innocent poet who has the same name as the conspirator Cinna.

Act 4

The three new rulers of Rome, Octavius, Antony, and Lepidus, meet to decide who among their possible rivals will die. Antony asks Lepidus to get Caesar's will so they can figure out how to take away some of the money that has been promised to the public. Antony claims to Octavius that Lepidus is unworthy to rule with them, but Octavius doesn't indicate that he agrees. In the next two scenes, Brutus and Cassius meet in Brutus's military camp at Sardis, and they argue both outside and inside Brutus's tent. Cassius pours out his frustration with Brutus, and Brutus accuses Cassius of corruption. Their words indicate the threat of violence against each other, but Brutus gains the upper hand, reminding Cassius of the reasons why Caesar was killed. Cassius offers his naked breast for Brutus to kill him, and complains that Brutus loved Caesar more than he loves Cassius. The two men calm down, and Brutus tells Cassius that Portia has killed herself. Titinius and Messala come in with news of the killing of senators in Rome, and Messala informs Brutus (again) of Portia's death. They discuss military strategy, and Brutus overrules Cassius's argument to stay at Sardis, deciding instead to march to Phillipi to meet the forces of Antony and Octavius. After the other men exit, Brutus calls to Lucius to play music, and invites two soldiers to sleep in his tent. He is visited by the ghost of Caesar, who calls himself "Thy evil spirit, Brutus" and tells Brutus that he will see him at Philippi. None of the others present in Brutus's tent see the ghost.

Act 5

The leaders of the opposing armies meet on the field to parley, hurling insults at each other and confirming the necessity of battle over diplomacy. Cassius tells

Messala that he is questioning his philosophy of Epicureanism, having seen a bad omen on the way to Philippi. He also mentions that it is his birthday, and asks Messala to bear witness that he goes to battle against his will. Brutus and Cassius say farewell to each other, musing on the possibility that they may not meet again. The next few scenes shift from one part of the battlefield to another. Brutus gives Messala an order to attack Octavius, then Cassius is shown with Titinius, who claims that "Brutus gave the word too early" (5.3.5). Cassius receives an inaccurate report of the battle from his slave, Pindarus. Believing he is defeated, Cassius asks Pindarus to kill him, which he does. When Titinius returns with good news but finds Cassius dead, he kills himself with Cassius's sword. Brutus arrives and finds Cassius dead, calling him "last of the Romans" (5.3.111). Antony is shown taking Lucilius prisoner, who was posing as Brutus. Brutus gathers a group of soldiers around him and asks them, one by one, to kill him. At last, the stoic Brutus gives in to emotion and cries. One of his men, Strato, holds Brutus's sword while he runs on it. Antony and Octavius enter in victory and are led to Brutus's body. Antony calls Brutus "the noblest Roman of them all" (5.5.74) and Octavius orders that Brutus's body lie in his tent, as an honorable soldier.

Julius Caesar in the Shakespeare Canon

The techniques used by Shakespeare scholars to determine date of composition vary from examination of the script itself and whatever format of the script survives, to other evidence such as contemporary references to the play, implied references in other dramatic works, and actual records, such as the stationer's registry of published writing. The first full script of *Julius Caesar* is the one found in the Folio of 1623, the collected works of Shakespeare compiled by John Heminge and Henry Condell 7 years after Shakespeare's death. Evidence exists, however, in the journal of a German tourist named Thomas Platter, to believe that the play was staged in 1599. Several other pieces of evidence indicate that the play was first produced that year, and may have been the first play staged at the Globe Theatre. See Spevack (2003), Humphreys (1984), Thomas (1992), or McMurtry (1998) for full discussions of the sources establishing date of composition. James Shapiro (2005), in his *A Year in the Life of William Shakespeare: 1599*, presents extensive evidence to support the claims of the others, and recreates a compositional process for Shakespeare, drawing parallels between the characters and themes in *Julius Caesar* and contemporary events in England such as the Irish rebellion, the ambition of the Earl of Essex, and even the confusion over calendar dates and newly formed holidays.

Placing *Julius Caesar* in 1599 puts it after the English history plays, in fact immediately after the triumphant *Henry V*, and also after many of Shakespeare's comedies. It appears before what are considered the "great" tragedies, *Hamlet,*

Othello, Macbeth, and *King Lear,* and well before the last two Roman plays, *Antony and Cleopatra* (a kind of sequel to *Julius Caesar*) and *Coriolanus.* Therefore, we may assume that this was not a novice play for Shakespeare. He was approaching the height of his creative powers and had moved past the elaborate language of the sonnets and the great romances of *Romeo and Juliet* and *A Midsummer Night's Dream.* Horst Zander (2005a) called *Julius Caesar* a "turning point" in Shakespeare's writing, leading him away from the chronicles and whimsical comedies toward the deeply introspective tragedies that we typically identify as his greatest work. According to Shapiro, Shakespeare may have been drafting *Hamlet* even as he was working on *Julius Caesar.*

Bloom (1998) found the play to be flawed, though he mentioned that it anticipates the great work to come, specifically *Hamlet.* If we think of *Julius Caesar* as an opener for the new theatre on the south side of the Thames, we can imagine Shakespeare choosing a subject that was popular with Renaissance theatregoers. As Shapiro (2005) explained, Shakespeare's audience would also be interested in a play on political assassination, as attempts on the life of Queen Elizabeth were frequently rumored. The play gives us a text that is well structured (though some have found fault with the final two acts); that uses language as rhetoric to a high degree, in keeping with the Elizabethan notion of Roman republicanism providing a model of civic discourse; and that develops characters fully. What it does not give us is the penetrating identification with individual heroes that Shakespeare was able to achieve with the greater tragedies. According to Greenblatt (2004), however, in one speech by Brutus, Shakespeare evidenced a watershed in his development as a playwright. Brutus's soliloquy in Act 2, scene 1 (lines 10–36) demonstrates, for the first time, "the unmistakable marks of actual thinking" (p. 301) that characterize the great soliloquys in *Hamlet,* which Shakespeare may have been working on as he finished *Julius Caesar.* (See Chapter 7 for a choral reading activity using Brutus's speech).

Possible Unit Structure

How many weeks you spend studying *Julius Caesar* with your students will, of course, depend upon your curricular requirements and the context of your class. In an AP class or a regular survey class, you may be mixing literature study with test preparation, explicit writing instruction, grammar review, media study, or any number of other activities. In most cases, however, I suggest that you give this play what amounts to your undivided attention for a span of 4–6 weeks in order to allow your students an experience that has some depth. Anything less than that would require rushing, and anything more than that would risk deterioration in student interest, where the sheer volume of interpretive discourse wears down the students. You want your students to have an experience with the play. This doesn't mean it will be their last, and you certainly don't want them to emerge from their study of *Julius Caesar* wanting it to be their last encounter with the play or the playwright. In other words, you don't have to feel the pressure to exhaust all interpretive options for every single line of the script. You can leave something for next time.

If students were to experience this play in the theater for the first time without reading it, the experience would last between 2 and 3 hours, with no rereading or stopping to analyze. Stretching a 3-hour theatrical experience into an 8- or 10-week instructional unit does a disservice to your mission, your students, and Shakespeare. Even if the script is read, analyzed, and written about in tandem with other activities, such as partner contemporary texts and other elements of language arts instruction, the experience will get too diffuse to maintain student engagement, so 4 weeks, perhaps 6 if you include student performances, is sufficient. With students who have been reading Shakespeare and for whom the conventions of his works are known, you may be able to do the play justice in 3 weeks.

And how will you want to spend those weeks? I suggest that you spend only a day or two with preliminary or prereading activities, such as the movie trailer exercise in Chapter 4, perhaps a summary of the biography of Julius Caesar in *Plutarch's Lives of the Noble Greeks and Romans*, and some cursory background on reading Shakespeare (see Chapter 2). You will want to spend more time on Acts 1, 2, and 3 than on 4 and 5, as the students are getting oriented, learning the characters, the conflicts, and the subtle elements of the text, such as imagery and tone. Act 3, being the pivotal act and containing both the assassination and the funeral orations, should provide a good week's worth of attention. As you shift more of the interpretive burden to students in the later parts of the script, you may pick up the pace and move into some of the dynamic discussion, performance, and writing opportunities described in Chapters 6–8. Below is a model calendar for treatment of the play in class with related chapters from this book that will be helpful. This calendar allows for full consideration of the performance activities outlined in Chapter 7.

- **Week One:** Sources, prereading activities, Shakespeare orientation (Chs. 2–4).

- **Week Two:** Begin reading, Acts 1 and 2 in class with activities (Ch. 5).

- **Week Three:** Continue reading, with discussion and increased independent reading and discussion (Chs. 5–6).

- **Week Four:** Complete first reading and begin considering interpretive activities (Chs. 7–8).

- **Week Five:** Student groups do scene work and interpretive work (Chs. 7–8).

- **Week Six (if necessary):** Performance of scenes, final writing assessments and reflections.

"Into what dangers would you lead me?": Entering the Text of *Julius Caesar*

*T*his chapter will present several prereading and introduction strategies to prepare you and your students to begin the task of reading *Julius Caesar* as performers. Although traditional prereading activities, such as studying Shakespeare's life and works or looking at Elizabethan England, can be productive, the activities presented here are quick, active, student centered, and challenging. The entire span of activities here (Movie Trailers, Problem Situations, Cast Party/Post-Party Chat, and When in Rome . . .) can be done within a couple of days, or with extensions, may become integral to the entire unit. The chapter also will also provide literature circle ideas for parallel supplemental reading related to the text of *Julius Caesar*.

Movie Trailers

Students will be familiar with the concept of the movie trailer, as they've seen them many times in the theater and at the front of DVDs or online rentals. This activity creates a "live" movie trailer in the classroom through what amounts to a quick, reader's-theater-style reading mixing music, selected lines from the script, and quick, dramatic narration. There are enough speaking parts for most members of an average-size class, and other students can be involved in doing the sound effects.

On the next page is a script for the *Julius Caesar* Movie Trailer. Although I include a suggested soundtrack, you may want to use different music. Encourage students to read "over the top" in their volume and their emotions, as the trailer is designed to create interest in the play (movie). Also, have students read quickly, to give the sense of fast-paced action. There are 13 individual speaking parts (14

Note: All italicized passages are read by the narrator, typically the teacher.

Opening: cue music, Beethoven's "Coriolan Overture" (or other of teacher's choosing)

Speaker		Sound effect
*Narrator:	*Ancient Rome...*	Crowd noise
*Flavius:	Home, you idle creatures, get you home!	
	A crowd of people celebrates...	
*Cobbler:	We make holiday to see Caesar!	Cheering
	But not everyone is happy...	
*Marullus:	You blocks, you stones, you worse than senseless things!	
	A man on the verge of dominance...	
**Plebeians:	Hail, Caesar!	More cheering
	But a threat looms...	
*Soothsayer:	(in spooky voice) CAESAR!	Abrupt silence
*Caesar:	Who calls so loud?	
Soothsayer:	Beware the Ides of March!	Gasps
	A conspiracy forms in the Roman senate...	
*Cassius:	Tell me, good Brutus, can you see your face?	
*Brutus:	Into what dangers would you lead me, Cassius?	
	Amidst one man's rise...	
Plebeians:	Caesar!	Crowd cheers
	Others aim to bring him down...	
Brutus:	I do fear the people choose Caesar for their king!	
Cassius:	Then must I think you would not have it so.	
	Warning signs abound...	
Caesar:	Yond Cassius has a lean and hungry look.	
	But warnings are not heeded...	
*Antony:	Fear him not.	
	In a time of confusion...	
*Casca:	It was Greek to me!	
	And strange eruptions in nature...	
Casca:	All the sway of Earth shakes like a thing unfirm! Ahhh!	Thunder
	A friend becomes a rival...	
Brutus:	It must be by his death.	
	And women fear for their husbands...	
*Portia:	Y' have ungently, Brutus, stolen from my bed!	

*Calphurnia:	Caesar, you shall not stir out of your house today!	More thunder
	But their warnings are for naught . . .	
*Decius:	This dream is all amiss interpreted!	
Caesar:	Caesar shall forth!	
	Suddenly surrounded by those he thought he could trust . . .	
*Metellus:	Most high, most mighty, and most puissant Caesar!	
	Witness as a dictator stands his ground . . .	
Caesar:	I spurn thee like a cur out of my way!	Ugh!
	And as the threat closes in . . .	
Brutus:	I kiss thy hand, Caesar.	
Caesar:	What, Brutus!	
Cassius:	Pardon, Caesar, Caesar, pardon!	
	He resists . . .	
Caesar:	I am constant as the Northern Star!	
	Until violence erupts!	
Casca:	Speak, hands, for me!	Arrrr!
		Stabbing sounds
Caesar:	Et tu, Brute? Then fall Caesar (dying sound)	
	See Rome in turmoil . . .	
Cinna:	Liberty! Freedom! Tyranny is dead!	Frightened screams
Brutus:	People and senators, be not affrighted.	
	A questioning public . . .	
Plebeians:	We will be satisfied! Let us be satisfied!	
	And a friend, sworn to vengeance . . .	
Antony:	Cry "Havoc!" and let slip the dogs of war!	
	See the power of persuasion . . .	
Antony:	Friends, Romans, Countrymen, lend me your ears.	
	A turning of the tide . . .	
Antony:	If you have tears, prepare to shed them now!	
Plebeians:	We'll burn the house of Brutus!	Shouts
	And the shedding of innocent blood . . .	
Plebeians:	Tear him to pieces!	More shouts
	How will it end? Will Caesar be revenged, or will conspiracy succeed?	
	This is William Shakespeare's Julius Caesar! *In theatres soon!*	
		End music

if you include the narrator), plus the role of the plebeians, which can be anywhere from 2–10 people, depending on your class size, and the role of "sound effects," which, again, can vary in the number of students. The sound effects should be done without the benefit of tools or technology for this reading. The flexibility of the two plural roles allows you to cast everyone, whether you have 15 students or 30 in your class. I have indicated with an asterisk each time a new speaker is introduced to help you in assigning roles. The plebeians and sound effects people have multiple asterisks to indicate plural roles. I strongly suggest that you take on the role of the narrator, so that you can control the pace of the trailer.

The benefits of the movie trailer activity are many. First, the trailer provides a fun way to preview the story, without the teacher having to lecture. Second, it provides a nonthreatening way to involve the entire class in performance before entering the script for further study. They will immediately associate the text with performance. Third, the activity is quick, as it can be cast quickly, set up in 10 minutes or so (depending upon student willingness to volunteer), and will take less time than that to perform. Finally, the trailer allows the opportunity for students to suggest how they might take the activity and develop it after they have read the script. A small group of students may decide to produce an actual movie trailer with this script or another of their own making, including a video with graphics and sound. As a differentiation strategy, producing a filmed movie trailer will allow students with a talent for and an interest in video technology to interpret the story in their own unique way.

Problem Situations

Another great way to help students enter the text of *Julius Caesar* is to have them face the "problem situations" the characters will face. The activity will not only start them down the road to seeing similarities between these high-ranking, ancient personages and themselves, but the students will be able to anticipate the situations and will look for them to come up in the reading. The suggested situations are not exhaustive, so you may construct your own problem situations or revise my descriptions to suit your needs. The problem situations activity is a small-group activity, and it should take no more than 10 minutes for students to work in groups to address the scenarios they are given. Following the group time, have each group report on what its situation was and how students decided to address it. You may want to project the situations on a screen, so that all students have a visual of the situations other groups were given. The activity box contains eight situations, enough to split an average-sized class into groups of 3–4 students.

Following the problem situations activity, allow students to write in their journals what questions the activity has raised for them, and allow them to ask

ACTIVITY (SAS #5): PROBLEM SITUATIONS.

Instruct students working in groups of 3–4 to read the problem situation they have been assigned. Have them spend 5–7 minutes discussing the situation and brainstorming possible responses on the sheet provided. When time is called, have each group report its ideas.

Situation 1: You want to do something that may be risky, and you have a friend whom you want to recruit to join in that activity. Knowing that there are risks, but also knowing that the friend may already want to join you, how will you persuade the friend to do so?

Situation 2: You have been warned by several sources that something bad may happen to you if you go to a certain place to meet a group of people. You want to go, and you don't want to give the impression that you are afraid. Although you are confident that you will be fine, you are not entirely sure. What do you do? What are your options?

Situation 3: Someone you love has a secret that he or she isn't telling you. You observe that the person has changed, and appears to be troubled, and you are worried that the secret is damaging the person's health. What do you do? What are your options?

Situation 4: You are worried for someone you love, say a spouse or other family member, and you see warning signs that disaster is coming for that person. But he or she will not listen to the warnings. What are your options? What would you do?

Situation 5: You receive anonymous notes telling you that you are a great person and that you should challenge someone who is in a position of authority. You have thought about challenging that person before, but weren't sure if you should. What would you do? What are your options?

Situation 6: You are working on a project with someone, and that person is the leader of the project, but you see that he or she is making what you believe to be wrong decisions. You know that the person has the support of others, but you are sure the decisions are wrong. What are your options? How do you proceed?

Situation 7: You are in a place where a group of people mistakes you for someone else and wants to hurt you because it thinks you are that other person. What are your options? What would you do?

Situation 8: You are in an argument with a friend and it turns very negative. You are angry with that person and that person is angry with you. In the course of the argument, the person tells you that he or she has just lost a loved one to death. What are your options? How should you respond?

questions of you regarding the script of *Julius Caesar*. During the class reading of the script (see Chapter 5), you may want to return to the problem situations as they arise and let the groups comment on how the characters' actions mirrored or differed from their own ideas.

Julius Caesar Cast Party and Post-Party Chat

The *Julius Caesar* cast party activity takes the common necessity of introducing the characters, or dramatis personae, and makes it into a student-centered, fun, and beneficial psychomotor activity. Immediately, students will make the connection between the concept of a "cast" and the reality that they are reading the script of a play, rather than a short story or novel. They will begin to make sense of who the characters are and, more importantly, what their relationships are. The activity requires some prep work prior to class, but can be executed in the same class period as the Movie Trailer or the Problem Situations, and it can be extended throughout the reading process. Here's how it works.

ACTIVITY (SAS #6): *JULIUS CAESAR* CAST PARTY AND POST-PARTY POSTING.

You may introduce this activity by having a short conversation with your class about parties or other gatherings where they meet new people. Ask them how they remember the names and information about people they have just met, especially those they want to remember. Tell them that they are going to simulate such a party, and the overall goal is to remember as much as possible about as many people as possible.

Here are step-by-step instructions for the activity:

1. Print the names of all of the cast members from *Julius Caesar* on stick-on nametags.
2. Make a set for each class you have that is reading the script.
3. Copy the character descriptions provided on pp. 71–73.
4. Attach the descriptions to the matching nametags with a paper clip.
5. Distribute one description and nametag to each student. Note: There are more than 40 character descriptions available. Because you will most likely have more cards than students, you can eliminate some of the minor characters and/or reduce the number of plebeians.
6. Have the students read the information given on the index card for the character they have been assigned and attach their nametags to their chests.

---

7. Direct the students to stand up and mingle around the room with the goal of (a) meeting as many other cast members as they can and (b) finding the other characters with whom they are connected.
8. Allow the mingling to go on for around 10 minutes, until everyone has had the opportunity to meet everyone else.
9. Ask students to group up with characters who are connected to them in some way.
10. Discuss what they have learned about the characters while they are still standing in party groups.

Following the party and discussion, it is important to have students write what they remember about the characters they have met, using either a list (a graphic organizer may help) or their journals. Students should not be expected to remember what they learned about every character, just as they would not remember everyone they met at an actual party. But chances are that someone else will remember those other characters, and that's where the online "post-party posting board" comes in handy. Using any school-approved, safe, online social networking venue or discussion board (e.g., Facebook, Google groups, Ning, Blackboard), students may continue "in character" or as themselves to share their impressions of the cast party and the characters they met who were memorable by posting comments to the board and responding to each other's posts. For example:

Messala: I met my fellow cast members at the party. I especially remember Titinius, with whom I will work, and my leaders, Brutus and Cassius. I'm not sure yet what my connection is to Mark Antony and Octavius, because they are supposed to be the enemy.

Antony: I'm wondering that, too, but we'll find out. I know that I will revenge Caesar's death, and that Octavius and I will rule with Lepidus. I also met Calphurnia, who is the wife of Caesar, and Portia, who is the wife of Brutus. Not sure whether I'm connected to them, but it was nice to find out about them.

Through the cast party and post-party postings, students will increase their collective memory of character relationships and self-monitor by correcting each other when memories are inaccurate. Once the activity is completed, you may either abandon the character discussion board or continue it through the reading process, allowing students to post their reflections on the reading and how it influences their thoughts on the characters. Another follow-up option is to have students generate character webs for each character and a cast web on the classroom wall that shows relationships between characters. Figure 1 includes an example of a character web for the Soothsayer.

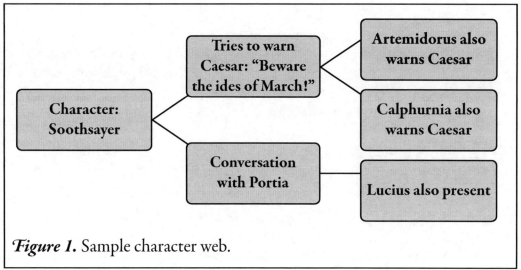

Figure 1. Sample character web.

When in Rome . . .
(A Student-Driven Investigation of Setting)

Teachers often wonder how much frontloading is necessary regarding the time period and setting of Shakespeare's plays (and of Shakespeare's own life and times). There is no right answer to this question because too many variants exist in the time you may have available in the curriculum, the background and interests of your students, and your own previous knowledge (see Chapter 3 for discussion). *Julius Caesar* is a play that invites attention to the setting because Ancient Rome is such a famous and larger-than-life civilization in our cultural imagination. My concern with taking too much time to frontload information on setting or any other typical background information (such as published critical interpretations) prior to diving into the script is that students may get bogged down, the class may get sidetracked, and enthusiasm for the reading to come may dissipate rather than build.

This activity, "When in Rome . . . ," requires students to do some background work on their own, sharing responsibility with the teacher to build knowledge of Rome while studying Shakespeare's script. The activity is especially viable if you are reading *Julius Caesar* as part of a broader unit on Rome, and it will help students to build skills in source research, verification, collaboration, and sharing. Here's how it works.

ACTIVITY (SAS #7): WHEN IN ROME . . . .

Project the following famous statement, attributable to St. Ambrose through a quote in a letter from St. Augustine: *When in Rome, do as the Romans do.* Ask the students what the quote means and how it is used today. Then ask them what they know about Roman customs. In other words, ask them, "What DID the Romans do in Rome?" Post a large blank posterboard on the wall of your classroom (or open an online posting board if you have the technology) with the phrase, "When in Rome . . . ." Underneath the phrase, students can then post information on Roman political or social structure, customs, statistics, or facts that they find through their own investigations. Have them include identification of the sources where they find the information. On the righthand side of the posterboard, place a space or a box for "corroborations" or confirmations by other students using other sources. Decorate your wall around the posterboard with pictures of Ancient Rome, illustrations by students, and the Wall of Notable Quotes (see Chapter 2).

Challenge your students to "fact check" the information provided by their classmates, and require everyone from the class to contribute something. What you will end up with is a pile of information, provided by your students, corroborated by your students (and you, if you choose to participate, which you should), and taken from sources that your class can then evaluate for their quality and their authenticity. A couple of examples may look like Figure 2.

When in Rome . . .

Information	Source	Corroborated?
You may find graffiti on the walls	http://www.roman-empire.net	Yes http://www.explore-italian-culture.com/ancient-roman-daily-life.html
Wear purple if you are in power	http://www.explore-italian-culture.com/ancient-roman-daily-life.html	Yes http://www.vroma.org/~bmcmanus/clothing.html

Figure 2. Example of "When in Rome . . ." activity.

Remind your students that Ancient Rome was a civilization that lasted hundreds of years. The death of Julius Caesar, in a sense, marked the end of the Roman republic and started the chain of events that would lead to Octavius Caesar becoming the first Roman emperor. Therefore, ask students to provide the time frame for the customs or facts on Rome that they share, if possible. The "When in Rome . . ." activity can continue through the unit, and students can use what they learn to discuss ideas for how they "see" staging *Julius Caesar* as a play, and what details to include. They may also compare what they discover about Roman customs with the behavior of the characters in Shakespeare's script.

Parallel Reading and Literature Circles

If you wish to augment your students' experience with *Julius Caesar,* and you have the time, you may want to engage them in supplementary reading. Similar to the "When in Rome . . . " activity above, parallel reading and literature circles can be a great way to differentiate instruction based on student interests and ability levels. Collectively, the class can read more material in literature circles than if everyone were to read everything together as a class, so literature circles can also provide an opportunity for students to teach each other. As Mary Ellen Dakin (2009) pointed out in her book *Reading Shakespeare With Young Adults*, the roles of students in literature circles can help them to participate in a meaningful way as productive individuals in a group. "Reading in companies," as Dakin calls it, can be done with the script of *Julius Caesar* itself, but I suggest using the literature circles for parallel reading that will augment students' experience with the play. For young students, young adult novels with themes related to *Julius Caesar* may work. For AP classes, however, more challenging fare will be necessary even if students aren't required to read them in their entirety. Here are my top candidates for parallel reading texts:

- *Plutarch's Lives of the Noble Greeks and Romans*, Thomas North, Translator: Excerpts from: "Julius Caesar," "Marcus Brutus," and "Mark Antony." This was Shakespeare's main source. Many versions are available (see Reference list at the back of this book).

- *Antony and Cleopatra*, William Shakespeare: For a group of students who are familiar with Shakespeare and want to see how things turn out for Antony and Octavius after the deaths of Brutus and Cassius, this will be a good choice. Many editions are available.

- *A Year in the Life of William Shakespeare: 1599*, James Shapiro (2005): This book discusses an exciting time in Elizabethan England and examines several factors related to the writing and performance of *Julius Caesar*, as well as other great Shakespeare plays.

- *Caesar: Politician and Statesman*, Mattias Gelzer (1968): This is the standard among biographies of Julius Caesar. There are also newer biographies out, if you so choose. This book is 368 pages, so excerpts may be good enough. Your history buffs will do well with this book.

This chapter has presented a number of activities to prepare your students to enter the text of *Julius Caesar*. The next chapter will provide a scene-by-scene reading guide with journal/discussion prompts, activities, and interpretive notes.

Chapter Materials

Student Activity Sheet #5:
Problem Situations

Applicable Portion of Play: Prereading, All

Objectives: 1.   Students will project themselves into situations similar to those faced by characters in *Julius Caesar*.
2.   Students will connect their own thinking in response to the problem situations with the decisions made by characters in *Julius Caesar*.

Common Core Standard(s): 11-12.SL.1.c, 11-12.R.L.1

Directions: Choose one of the situations below (or allow your teacher to assign groups) and work in a group of 3–4 students to generate a list of responses. Following discussion of the different situations, write responses to the situations you were not assigned.

Situation 1: You want to do something that may be risky, and you have a friend whom you want to recruit to join in that activity. Knowing that there are risks, but also knowing that the friend may want to join you, how will you persuade the friend to do so?

_____

_____

_____

_____

_____

_____

Situation 2: You have been warned by several sources that something bad may happen to you if you go to a certain place to meet a group of people. You want to go, and you don't want to give the impression that you are afraid. Although you are confident that you will be fine, you are not entirely sure. What do you do? What are your options?

_____

_____

_____

_____

_____

_____

Situation 3: Someone you love has a secret that he or she isn't telling you. You observe that the person has changed and appears to be troubled, and you are worried that the secret is damaging the person's health. What do you do? What are your options?

_____

_____

_____

_____

_____

_____

Situation 4: You are worried for someone you love, say a spouse or other family member, and you see warning signs that disaster is coming for that person. But he or she will not listen to the warnings. What are your options? What do you do?

_____

_____

_____

_____

_____

_____

Situation 5: You receive anonymous notes telling you that you are a great person and that you should challenge someone who is in a position of authority. You have thought about challenging that person before, but weren't sure if you should. What should you do? What are your options?

_____

_____

_____

_____

_____

_____

Situation 6: You are working on a project with someone, and that person is the leader of the project, but you see that he or she is making what you believe to be wrong decisions. You know that the person has the support of others, but you are sure the decisions are wrong. What are your options? How do you proceed?

_____

_____

_____

_____

_____

Situation 7: You are in a place where a group of people mistakes you for someone else and wants to hurt you because it thinks you are that other person. What are your options? What do you do?

_____

_____

_____

_____

_____

Situation 8: You are in an argument with a friend and it turns very negative. You are angry with that person and that person is angry with you. In the course of the argument, the person tells you that he or she has just lost a loved one to death. What are your options? How do you respond?

_____

_____

_____

_____

_____

Reflection (after reading _Julius Caesar_): How do the characters in _Julius Caesar_ respond to these situations? Do they make good decisions?

_____

_____

_____

_____

_____

Student Activity Sheet #6:
Julius Caesar Cast Party and Post-Party Posting

Applicable Portion of Play: Prereading, All

Objectives:　　1.　Students will interact as actors "in character" at a cast party for *Julius Caesar*.
　　　　　　　　2.　Students will be able to name characters and describe their relationships with other characters in the play.

Common Core Standard(s): 11-12.SL.1

Directions:　Your teacher will assign you a character from *Julius Caesar* and give you both a nametag and a short character description. You are to attend a "cast party" where your job is to meet as many people as possible and find out what you can about them. You are to look especially for characters with whom you have a connection. When the party is over, write notes on what you remember about the characters using the character sheet below. Then post your "post-party notes" online.

Post-Party Character Review

Character	What I know about the character
Julius Caesar	
Brutus	
Cassius	
Mark Antony	
Portia	
Calphurnia	
Casca	
Cinna	
Decius	
Ligarius	
Metellus Cimber	
Trebonius	
Cicero	
Publius	
Popilius Lena	

Character	What I know about the character
Flavius	
Marullus	
Lepidus	
Octavius	
Servant to Antony	
Servant to Octavius	
Lucius	
Lucilius	
Titinius	
Messala	
Varro	
Claudius	
Young Cato	
Strato	
Volumnius	
Dardanus	
Clitus	
Artemidorus	
Soothsayer	
Cinna the Poet	
Pindarus	
Another Poet	
Carpenter	
Cobbler	
Plebeians	
Messenger	

Character Descriptions for Cast Party

Julius Caesar: You are the popular leader of Rome, returned from war. The people want to make you king. You are married to Calphurnia. Your friend is Mark Antony, but you also like Brutus. You don't like Cassius.

Brutus: Roman Praetor, friend of Caesar, whom you will betray and kill. Co-conspirator with Cassius, Casca, Decius, Cinna, Metellus Cimber, Ligarius, and Trebonius. You are married to Portia. Your servant is Lucius and you are connected to the soldiers.

Cassius: Roman senator. Friend and co-conspirator with Brutus, Casca, Decius, Cinna, Metellus Cimber, Ligarius, and Trebonius. Master of Pindarus. You personally dislike Caesar, and you don't trust Mark Antony. Titinius is your friend.

Mark Antony: Friend to Caesar. You have a reputation for music, parties, and theater. You become enemies to Brutus and Cassius and stir the people to revenge. You are partners with Octavius and Lepidus, but you don't think highly of Lepidus.

Portia: Wife of Brutus. You are upset with your husband and nervous because he tells you of the plot to kill Caesar. Lucius is your servant. You also meet the soothsayer.

Calphurnia: Wife of Caesar. You are worried for Caesar's safety after having bad dreams. Decius reinterprets your dream in a way that you disagree with.

Casca: Co-conspirator with Brutus, Cassius, Decius, Cinna, Metellus Cimber, Ligarius, and Trebonius. You don't like the plebeians or Caesar. You are the first to stab Caesar.

Cinna: Co-conspirator with Brutus, Cassius, Casca, Decius, Metellus Cimber, Ligarius, and Trebonius.

Decius: Co-conspirator with Brutus, Cassius, Casca, Cinna, Metellus Cimber, Ligarius, and Trebonius. You flatter Caesar to bring him to the Capitol, where you and the others will kill him.

Ligarius: Co-conspirator with Brutus, Cassius, Decius, Casca, Cinna, Metellus Cimber, and Trebonius. You are sick, or pretending sickness, before killing Caesar.

Metellus Cimber: Co-conspirator with Brutus, Cassius, Decius, Casca, Cinna, Ligarius, and Trebonius. You will beg for your brother before killing Caesar.

Trebonius: Co-conspirator with Brutus, Cassius, Decius, Casca, Cinna, Metellus Cimber, and Ligarius. You will draw Mark Antony out of the way at the assassination.

Cicero: Famous Roman senator. You are not part of the conspiracy, but you witness it. You are not a friend of Caesar. You meet Casca during the storm. You are put to death by Mark Antony, Octavius, and Lepidus.

Publius: A senator. You prevent Artemidorus from getting a warning to Caesar. You are old and not involved with the plot to kill Caesar. You witness it, though.

Popilius Lena: A senator. You are present at Caesar's death, but you have no hand in it. You seem to know, however, that it will happen, and you hint to Cassius that you know.

Flavius: A tribune. You and Marullus scold the Cobbler and carpenter for honoring Caesar.

Marullus: A tribune. You and Flavius scold the Cobbler and carpenter for honoring Caesar.

Lepidus: A triumvir with Mark Antony and Octavius. You have a minor role. Antony doesn't think highly of you, but Octavius seems to like you.

Octavius: Nephew of Caesar. Triumvir with Mark Antony and Lepidus. You are an enemy to Brutus and Cassius and fight them.

Servant to Antony: You meet Brutus and Cassius after they murder Caesar. You speak for your master.

Servant to Octavius: You work for Octavius, but you also help Mark Antony carry Caesar's body to the marketplace.

Lucius: A boy. Servant to Brutus and Portia. You play a musical instrument. You know Cassius, also, and you follow Brutus to war, where you will meet the soldiers.

Lucilius: A soldier in Brutus's army. You pretend to be Brutus and are captured. You know the other soldiers and you know Octavius and Antony.

Titinius: A soldier for Cassius, so you know the other soldiers. You love Cassius and will die in grief for him.

Messala: Officer in Brutus's army. You know Brutus, Cassius, Antony, Octavius, and the other soldiers.

Varro: A soldier in Brutus's army. You are connected to Brutus, Lucius, and Claudius.

Claudius: A soldier in Brutus's army. You are connected to Brutus, Lucius, and Varro.

Young Cato: A soldier in Brutus's army. You are connected with Lucilius.

Strato: A soldier in Brutus's army. You are connected to Brutus, Volumnius, Dardanus, and Clitus. Brutus asks you to kill him, and you hold his sword while he runs on it.

Volumnius: A soldier in Brutus's army. You are connected to Brutus, Strato, Dardanus, and Clitus. Brutus asks you to kill him.

Dardanus: A soldier in Brutus's army. You are connected to Brutus, Strato, Volumnius, and Clitus. Brutus asks you to kill him.

Clitus: A soldier in Brutus's army. You are connected to Brutus, Strato, Volumnius, and Dardanus. Brutus asks you to kill him.

Artemidorus: A rhetorician who is against the conspiracy. You try to deliver a message to Caesar warning him of the conspiracy. Caesar, Decius, Publius, and Cassius prevent you.

Soothsayer: You deliver Caesar a warning to "beware the ides of March" twice in one scene and again in another. You also have a conversation with Portia. You are against the conspirators.

Cinna the Poet: You are a friend of Caesar. Following Caesar's death, you are mistaken for Cinna the conspirator and torn to pieces by the plebeians.

Pindarus: Slave to Cassius. You agree to kill him in the battle, then run off. You know Titinius.

Another Poet: You try to break into the tent where Brutus and Cassius are arguing. You know the soldiers, Brutus, and Cassius.

Carpenter: You are a plebeian, partying on the street at the opening of the play. You are with the Cobbler and others, and you are questioned by Flavius and Marullus.

Cobbler: You are a plebeian, partying on the street at the opening of the play. You are with the carpenter and others, and you are questioned by Flavius and Marullus.

Plebeian: You are present in the opening scene, possibly in other scenes, and certainly at the funeral speeches of Brutus and Cassius. You kill Cinna the Poet with the other plebeians.

Messenger: In the army of Mark Antony and Octavius. You deliver a message that Brutus and Cassius are coming for battle.

Name: _____   Date: _____

Student Activity Sheet #7:
When in Rome . . .

Applicable Portion of Play: Prereading, All

Objectives: 1.   Students will research social customs and historic events of Ancient Rome.
                  2.   Students will collaborate to build collective knowledge of the setting of *Julius Caesar*.

Common Core Standard(s): 11-12.W.8

Directions: Either in small groups or as a class, construct a large poster that has the title "When in Rome . . ." Using print and Internet resources, gather knowledge about social customs, fashion, etiquette, and contemporary events of Rome. Add your information to the poster. Be sure to include the specific century or centuries that apply to your information, and include the source of your information.

    When your classmates have posted information on the poster, try to find the same information from a source different from the source they used. If you can find a second source of the information, add your "corroboration" to their information. The table below (which includes examples) can help you organize your information.

Information	Source	Corroborated?
You may find graffiti on the walls.	http://www.roman-empire.net	Yes http://www.explore-italian-culture.com/ancient-roman-daily-life.html
Wear purple if you are in power.	http://www.explore-italian-culture.com/ancient-roman-daily-life.html	Yes http://www.vroma.org/~bmcmanus/clothing.html

"A vision fair and fortunate": Reading *Julius Caesar*

*I*n this chapter, we will walk through the script of *Julius Caesar*, and I will offer ideas to support student reading. It may be useful for you to have your script in hand, perhaps reading along with my commentary, or reading the scene and then consulting my commentary. I suggest that you do this prior to teaching the material, with as much lead time as is necessary to work the strategies/activities into your lesson planning. You may then want to refer back to the chapter as you read the script with your students, in whatever fashion works best for you. You may also skim the chapter for activities and discussion/journal ideas.

The nature of my comments is less interpretive than descriptive. What I try to do is notice details in the script and describe what I notice, translating those perceptions into possible class activities. Following this chapter, Chapters 6, 7, and 8 will offer additional discussion suggestions, performance ideas, and writing tasks associated with the study of *Julius Caesar*.

In order for students to get a reasonable foothold on the text, I suggest you read the first two or three acts in class with your students, also assigning the reading as homework in between sessions. When reading through the script for the first time with students, move at a reasonable pace, allowing the students to struggle with their impressions of what is happening, rather than stopping to explain every passage. The problem with walking through each scene, explaining every passage, is that you and your students will get bogged down. You will need to stop periodically to avoid utter loss of comprehension and resultant frustration, but remember that your students would experience the entire play in less than 3 hours in the theatre, so it is fine to move quickly through a first reading—as long as the experience does not stop there.

Shakespeare's scripts bear rereading, and changing the mode of reading between silent and aloud, individual and shared, is helpful. One of our goals is to move toward a performed "reading" of the script, where we examine what Rocklin (2005) referred to as what "the words do," as opposed to simply what the words say (p. xvi). As students' comfort level with the world of the play increases, they may be able to read independently with greater ease. Students will need several looks at the scenes in order to build interpretations of them, and the combination of quiet independent reading with supported in-class reading and concomitant informal, ungraded writing will prepare them for productive discussion and later interpretive activities such as performance and formal writing. How you distribute your students' attention in crafting your classes will affect their perception of the text. You can also show short clips from movie versions with individual scenes as a way to discuss directorial choices. Several clips from both the 1953 version (Houseman & Mankiewicz) and the 1970 version (Snell & Burge) are available on YouTube. You can mix in group activities (such as those suggested in this book) to engage more students in reading and speaking aloud. You can also use the suggestions in this chapter to focus your students' attention on small chunks of text for close reading and analysis.

As the scene is the basic division of the script (Rocklin, 2005), this chapter is divided into scene-by-scene descriptions, which I will separate into smaller chunks of dialogue, also called units or beats (Dakin, 2009; Rocklin, 2005). Typically, these conversational units in each scene can be further divided, or may be divided differently depending upon your interpretation. I will explain my logic in separating units of dialogue as I do, using the Folger Shakespeare Library edition of the script to mark line numbers. I will also frequently refer to actions of the actors rather than simply referring to characters to remind you that we are in the world of theater, not simply the world of individual quiet reading.

So without further ado, let us begin, and see what we notice.

Act 1

When we begin reading any Shakespeare script on our own or, more importantly, with students, the first questions we may ask are "Where are we?" and "What is it like there?" We may also ask "Who is there?" and "What are they like?" and "What are they doing?" Act 1 of *Julius Caesar* takes place entirely in public places, even though some of the conversations are private, even secretive. In the first scene, we meet two public officials, and perhaps more importantly, we meet the Roman public in the form of the plebeian workers on holiday to greet Julius Caesar, who is entering Rome in triumph. In the second scene, we meet all of the principal characters and experience the hierarchy of social status as illustrated by Caesar, the patrician senate, and the plebeians. We are very quickly introduced to the central conflict and are made aware of the possibility of a conspiracy to unseat Caesar as dictator. What follows is a scene-by-scene breakdown of Act 1, organized by units of dialogue, discussed in terms of what you as the teacher may notice with your students, with intermittent suggested journal/discussion topics and activities.

Act 1, Scene 1

The first scene in this script accomplishes a great deal regarding the first two W questions above, even though we do not meet any of the main characters. The scene establishes certain laws about the place we are entering, establishes the common people's (plebeian) view of Caesar, and shows us the tension among public officials who are worried that Caesar is growing too powerful. The scene may be broken down into three smaller units. They are:

1. Tribunes command commoners to go home, then question the carpenter and cobbler.
2. Reacting to the cobbler's admission that they are in the streets to see Caesar, Marullus delivers his rhetorical speech about why the commoners should not honor Caesar.
3. Following the departure of the commoners, Flavius and Marullus reflect on the situation and decide to remove decorations from Caesar's images.

The opening stage direction is "Enter Flavius, Marullus, and certain Commoners over the stage." Here we have an unusual stage direction, at least for Shakespeare, who rarely gives us anything approaching a specific reference to actor movement or positioning. The phrase "over the stage" indicates that the actors move across the stage before halting (Spevack, 2003, p. 76). Directors often modify these stage directions to suit their needs, but stage directions that do not appear in brackets appear in the First Folio, which is the authoritative text for all current versions of *Julius Caesar*. Stage directions that appear in brackets are added by editors of whatever edition one is reading such as the direction "[including a Carpenter and a Cobbler]" that appears after "Commoners" in the Folger edition. Stage directions provided by editors may be followed or ignored at will.

Shakespeare's scripts often begin with memorable lines and memorable scenes that serve to welcome the theatre patron into the world of the play and introduce the tone for action. For example, in *Hamlet*, two guards exchange a midnight greeting on a ghost-infested tower. In *Romeo and Juliet*, a prologue in the character of "Chorus" delivers a brief synopsis of the entire story to come, including the fate of the heroic couple. In *Twelfth Night*, a lovesick duke pines to hear the music that feeds his passion. *Julius Caesar* opens with an argument, fitting for a play that is characterized by rhetorical excess. As mentioned before, nearly every scene in this play contains an argument of some kind, and the tension between logic, persuasion, fear, and violence drives the action. Granted, the argument in the opening scene of *Julius Caesar* is one-sided and short, but it sets a tone of anger and frustration that is developed in pivotal points in the script.

The opening line in the play, "Hence! Home you idle creatures, get you home!" is spoken by the tribune Flavius. Tribunes were representatives of the plebeian class who had the role of protecting the plebeian interests and acting as magistrates. A couple of things to note about the tribunes is that they were not a part of the upper class (patricians) and that they were by law "inviolate," which meant they could not be personally harmed by anyone from either class.

Flavius questions whether the laborers know that they must not "walk / Upon a laboring day" without some sign of their profession (1.1.3–4). He and his fellow tribune, Marullus, interrogate two commoners until they reveal their identities, similar to a couple of ruffian police officers randomly asking people on the street for their identification. The carpenter states his profession immediately, but the exchange between the tribunes and the cobbler, who jokes with them and will not give a straight answer until they are both livid, gestures toward comedy, which will be virtually nonexistent in the rest of the play. The cobbler makes a series of double meanings (cobbler, mend) and puns on his profession (withal, with awl, all; souls, soles).

DISCUSSION/JOURNAL TOPIC: HOW DO THE COMMONERS FEEL?

Have students examine whether the commoners appear to be afraid of the tribunes at this point or whether they are at ease. You may even ask students to act out this opening scene to see what movements they might use to reinforce the language.

The tribunes refer to the cobbler alternately as "saucy," "naughty," and "knave," using the language of scolding. Ask your students what this choice of language says about the relative social positions of these characters. The choice of whether or not the cobbler is being willfully disrespectful to the tribunes is a performance choice, and your students may come back to this scene to discuss how they would stage it following their first reading of the entire script.

ACTIVITY: HISTORY SLEUTHS.

Find out about the social classes of Rome and the role of the tribunes. Find other terms, such as Senator and Praetor, and investigate those as well. Add facts to the "When in Rome . . ." poster in the classroom or online.

The first unit of dialogue transitions when the cobbler answers the question of why he is leading the men about the street: "But indeed, sir, we make holiday to see Caesar and to rejoice in his triumph" (1.1.33–35). At this point, we get our first argumentative speech. In this particular speech, the rhetorical tools of repetition and questioning are prefaced by an out-and-out insult. Marullus questions the workers' motives for rejoicing in Caesar's conquest, and then calls them "blocks," "stones," and "worse than senseless things" (1.1.39–40). Such insults would be hard to bear, especially when flung at a crowd, and your students might want to think about how the actors playing the roles of the commoners would react to these terms. If they react with the potential of violence, such a reaction would give occasion for Marullus's next line, "O you hard hearts, and cruel men of Rome, / Knew you not Pompey?" (1.1.41–42). He tones down his attack and ratchets up his rhetoric, reminding the plebeians that they had put forth the same kind of celebration for the fellow whom Caesar had overthrown. His speech crescendos with the repeated phrase (*anaphora* in rhetorical terms) "and do you now":

> And do you now put on your best attire?
> And do you now cull out a holiday?
> And do you now strew flowers in his way?
> That comes in triumph over Pompey's blood?
> Be gone!
> Run to your houses, fall upon your knees,
> Pray to the gods to intermit the plague
> That needs must light on this ingratitude. (1.1.53–60)

Flavius reiterates in softer language the command from Marullus and uses the phrase "good countrymen" when addressing the commoners. He tells them to "Assemble all the poor men of your sort" and to go weep into the Tiber River (1.1.62). The commoners leave, and though Flavius says to Marullus, "They vanish tongue-tied in their guiltiness" (1.1.67), it is unclear whether he is giving a legitimate stage direction to the actors playing the commoners, or whether the actors would just move on to get away from these two "killjoys" (Shapiro, 2005, p. 154).

Your students may have opinions about this scene based on their reading and on their own attitudes toward authority. Indeed, this scene contains a dynamic that will be very familiar to students who have been part of a group that has awakened the displeasure of an authority figure, like a teacher. One way to approach the opening scene is to treat it as though it is happening in a school hallway between classes, perhaps after the tardy bell has rung, with Flavius and Marullus in the roles of teachers or hall security personnel, and the commoners as students. It is telling that Shakespeare opens the script with two tribunes who clearly see themselves as superior in class to those they represent, and students instinctively know how power is distributed unequally in a school setting.

The final section of the opening scene, which begins with the exit of the crowd, shows the two tribunes revealing once again their disdain for the commoners they represent: "basest mettle," "vulgar," and "thick" are words used to describe them and their gathering. Flavius tells Marullus to "disrobe the images" that may have decorations (or the more religious term, "ceremonies," which are scarves) on them, and Marullus asks whether it is possible to do so, the day being the feast day of Lupercal (1.1.69).

If your students ask why the tribunes claim to the commoners that it is a working day when they know it is a holiday, you may smile, because that question will show you that your students are reading closely. The seeming contradiction is puzzling, and Shapiro (2005) has connected it (and other seeming oddities, such as the play's anachronisms) with contemporary changes in secular and religious holidays in Shakespeare's time. The Lupercal was a pagan holiday connected to fertility and purging (McMurtry, 2003). It is Marullus who mentions the holiday, and Flavius is the one who first claims it is a "laboring day" when addressing the commoners, so it is possible to perform this scene as though Flavius either doesn't know or has forgotten about the feast when he sees the people celebrating. The commoners certainly don't seem to be aware that it's Lupercal—they just want to see Caesar. When Marullus says to Flavius, "You know it is the feast of Lupercal," as though that would prohibit the two of them from disrobing images, Flavius responds, "It is no matter. Let no images / Be hung with Caesar's trophies." (1.1.72–74)

You may explore with your students how the actor playing Flavius would react to Marullus's news if he really doesn't know. One of the chief differences between treating Shakespeare's works as theatre scripts as opposed to simply reading texts is that there are silences during which actions may take place. One can imagine Flavius registering recognition of the holiday when he hears Marullus speak it, then processing how that affects what he has seen in the streets, then deciding, "It is no matter" (1.1.73). Or, if Flavius did know previously, he must either not acknowledge the Lupercal or believe that "the vulgar" have no rights to participate in it.

After deciding to disrobe images that celebrate Caesar's victory, Flavius ends the scene by claiming that undermining the celebration would be like plucking feathers from Caesar's wing: "who else would soar above the view of men / and keep us all in servile fearfulness" (1.1.79–80). The stage direction is simply, "They exit," though in the Folger edition, a bracketed addition to the stage direction includes "in different directions" (Shakespeare, 1623/1992b, p. 11). Talk to your students about why such stage directions are helpful, unnecessary, or limiting. We may presume that because Flavius tells Marullus to go toward the Capitol and that he will go another way (i.e., you go that way, I'll go this way), they may exit in different directions, but is exiting the stage in different directions necessary?

Reviewing the opening scene, we learn that we are in Rome, that Rome has a social class system regarding laborers and tribunes, and that the day is not an ordinary day. We discover that it is the Lupercal in Rome, that Caesar has returned, that people are out to celebrate his return, and that at least two tribunes don't like the celebration of Caesar's return. We learn that the tribunes are worried that Caesar may grow too powerful and keep them in "servile fearfulness" even though the tribunes themselves show disdain for the commoners. Finally, we learn that Rome has citizens and that public opinion may be fickle. According to Marullus, they had been converted from loving Pompey to loving Caesar, without much thinking, and if we believe the descriptions of the tribunes after the commoners leave, they have been persuaded again against Caesar. Indeed, public opinion is a major driving force in the pivotal events of this play.

Act 1, Scene 2

In this, the second longest scene in the play, we meet all of the major characters at once, all brought on stage by the procession of Caesar through the streets of Rome. This scene contains classic exposition in that we learn what relationships exist between characters, we learn of actions off stage through character witness reporting, and we learn of the central conflict. We learn that Cassius and Brutus are both, by varying degrees, worried about Caesar's power. The seeds of conspiracy are sown in Brutus's mind by Cassius. The scene may be separated into the following units, which may also be subdivided:

1. Caesar tells Antony to touch Calphurnia in the Lupercal race.
2. Caesar and the soothsayer confront each other, then Caesar moves on.
3. Cassius stays behind with Brutus and sounds him out regarding changes in Brutus's behavior.
4. Cassius praises Brutus and criticizes Caesar openly, comparing the two of them as equals. Cassius complains bitterly of Caesar's power and personal weakness. Brutus stops him at some point but gives him hope that Brutus will think about what he has said.
5. Caesar returns and warns Antony about Cassius.
6. Casca tells the story of Caesar being offered a crown by Mark Antony and having a seizure.
7. Brutus and Cassius resolve to meet again, and Cassius plans to forge letters praising Brutus, which will be put where Brutus will find them.

I suggest that you stage the first part of this scene (up until Caesar's exit) in class, even in the first reading, to get a sense of possible positionings and to teach your students how the words characters speak indicate directions for actors in the roles. Step-by-step instructions for a "scene lab" using this segment are provided in Chapter 7. Have students take notes, perhaps in a double entry journal, where on the lefthand side they record their first impressions of Caesar, Mark Antony, Brutus, Cassius, and Casca. They will then be able to return to their notes as you move further in the script to write on the righthand side their later reflections on how the characters develop.

Opening the scene, Caesar speaks first and calls for his wife, Calphurnia. The next person to speak is Casca, who bids everyone be quiet: "Peace, ho! Caesar speaks" (1.2.2). Casca later fills the same function of quieting everyone when the soothsayer calls out to Caesar. When you are finished reading the scene and your students have witnessed Casca's droll description of Caesar being offered a crown and having an epileptic seizure, compare Casca's attitude about Caesar with his role-playing in the beginning of the scene. Students may wonder how Casca transforms from one of Caesar's thugs into a witty, or "saucy," critic of Caesar.

The fact that Caesar has to call Calphurnia twice before she answers in the opening of the scene indicates that she is not standing next to him. Caesar then commands Mark Antony, who is running the Lupercal race, to touch Calphurnia with his leather thong as he passes her. As Caesar tells him, "The barren, touchèd in this holy chase, / Shake off their sterile curse" (1.2.10–11). So here we learn that Caesar and Calphurnia have been unsuccessful in producing a child. Although Caesar may blame it on his wife, listeners (or readers or playgoers) would have a broader picture. This exchange gives our first sense of possible physical weakness in Caesar, and we will very shortly become aware of more infirmities: deafness in one ear and epilepsy. Caesar's epilepsy is documented in Shakespeare's main source, Plutarch. Adding mention of partial deafness and sterility are Shakespeare's way of pointing out that the most powerful man in the world has physical limitations. These examples also anticipate Cassius's speech to Brutus later in the scene concerning Caesar's weakness.

The second and third sections of this scene, following the exit of Caesar, Antony, and the others, begin what is sometimes referred to as the "seduction" of Brutus, as Cassius works on him to join in what we will soon find out is a conspiracy to kill Caesar. In order to get your students fully oriented to the situation and the progress of the seduction scene, I suggest you start with a read-through without pause, followed by an "exposition jigsaw" activity. The read-through will take around 20–25 minutes. Entertain any questions students may have, or better yet, encourage them to write questions in their notebooks and save them for debriefing following the jigsaw exercise.

ACTIVITY: EXPOSITION JIGSAW.

As Shakespeare's plays are filled with exposition in the early scenes, students can act as detectives and share expertise by examining in groups small sections of expositional scenes in the first act of the script. Take Act 1, scene 2 of *Julius Caesar* and split it into six or seven roughly equal chunks of lines, and distribute the chunks to different small groups. Give each group class time to try to figure out what is being said in its chunk of text. Then reconfigure the groups so that each new group has one member from each of the previous groups and can piece together students' understandings. Debrief with the entire class and address remaining student questions.

Following the jigsaw, have students discuss their impressions of each character's motive for disliking Caesar's position. Cassius is the driving force in this scene, as the stakes are highest for him: He must win Brutus over to the conspiracy in order to also win the approval of the common people. We learn that Brutus is troubled by Caesar's growing power, but that Cassius harbors personal animosity toward Caesar. Casca's "blunt" nature and serious disregard for the commoners distinguishes him.

This scene also contains plenty of key passages you may want to explore in class. One of these is Cassius's opening statement in his speech on "honor," as he tells us:

I cannot tell what you and other men
Think of this life; but, for my single self,
I had as lief not be as live to be
In awe of such a thing as I myself. (1.2.100–103)

The third line of this statement may strike your students as a nonsensical statement, but if you teach them how to read the iambic verse, they will punch that first "be" and read it to mean "exist." Cassius would rather not exist than live under the rule of someone who is no greater than himself (see Chapter 2 for a discussion of iambic pentameter). But the line is all the more powerful by virtue of its monosyllabic structure. At key points throughout this script, characters deliver straight iambic pentameter lines that consist of 10 monosyllabic words, which lend them a martial and dramatic intensity. The line also hints at Cassius's inclination toward suicide, which will surface several times before he actually does kill himself in Act 5.

Another avenue you can take with your students in this scene is to examine the different means of persuasion Cassius uses to win Brutus to his cause, and particularly how he uses the words that Brutus and Casca speak to reflect back on their cause. Each time Brutus speaks, Cassius uses his language to persuade him. Cassius is brilliant in this scene. His clarity and motivation make him very compelling, in such a way that we will see again in the next scene, but then not see again for the rest of the script.

DISCUSSION/JOURNAL TOPIC: UNDERSTANDING CHARACTERS.

Have students journal on their understanding of the characters, Rome, and the actions of Cassius.

Act 1, Scene 3

This final scene of Act 1 is typically referred to as the "storm" scene. In it, Casca shows that he is greatly shaken by the strangeness and the intensity of the storm. Cicero makes his second cameo appearance and tries to calm Casca, then exits. Cassius continues his dominance as the moving force behind the conspiracy, and we first get the sense that the conspiracy is well underway. The scene can be broken into the following sections, which may be further separated into smaller units of conversation.

1. Casca and Cicero talk about the storm and the strange things seen on the streets.
2. Cassius confronts Casca and likens Caesar to the storm, then, through a series of arguments, wins Casca to the conspiracy.
3. Cinna enters and the three men discuss how to win Brutus to the conspiracy.

The opening of this scene shows us that nature is in upheaval, as this storm is apparently not your average Roman thunderstorm. The opening lines of the scene show us a wonderful example of how Shakespeare couches stage directions for actors in the dialogue itself. Cicero enters and says, "Good even, Casca. Brought you Caesar home? / Why are you breathless? And why stare you so? (1.3.1–2). For the actor playing Casca, the character Cicero just gave information for performance. The actor will appear out of breath and staring. Have your students think about how the storm might be represented on stage, as a way to reinforce the breathless and staring character of Casca, who is clearly, as we learn, frightened by what he has seen in the streets of Rome.

It is also worth noticing that Cicero first asks Casca whether he has brought Caesar home, which assumes a closeness between Casca and Caesar, or at least that Casca may have some responsibility for being with Caesar. Students will want to discuss the specific strange events that Casca describes (see activity below). They may also compare these events to what Flavius has said to the plebeians about the gods sending plague in return for their ingratitude toward Pompey. The strange disruption of nature represented here continues in descriptions of nature in Act 2. Casca clearly believes that humans are responsible when he says, "Or else the world, too saucy with the gods, / Incenses them to send destruction" (1.3.12–13). The theme of nature being out of balance as a result of human activity can be traced back to Sophocles's play of *Oedipus the King*, and Shakespeare's audience would have been well familiar with it. The storm also appears in Shakespeare's source, Plutarch, and Shakespeare is faithful to his source here. Shakespeare had used the notion of nature being out of balance in *A Midsummer Night's Dream*, relating it to the quarrels of Oberon and Titania, the king and queen of fairies. He would later make great use of a storm in *King Lear*.

ACTIVITY (SAS #8): IS IT REAL OR IS IT SUPERNATURAL?

Have students examine Casca's description of the storm and the things he has seen in Act 1, scene 3, which he interprets as unnatural. Have them construct possible rational explanations for the occurrences, and divide the sights described into two columns: those descriptions that may have natural causes, and those for which there are no rational explanations. For example, when Casca claims that this is the first time he's been through a tempest "dropping fire," could he be describing lightning? Have students discuss what those signs say about the events in the script.

Cicero tries to calm Casca by saying to him that men may often misinterpret signs by construing them "after their fashion, / Clean from the purpose of the things themselves" (1.3.34–35). This line, you will note, foreshadows the opposing interpretations of the storm and Calphurnia's dream in Act 2, scene 2, and some would say that this quote sums up the essential problem of the play.

HISTORY SLEUTHS: WHO WAS CICERO?

The character Cicero plays an interesting minor role in *Julius Caesar*, partly interesting because it is minor. Cicero was the most famous man in Rome at the time, with the exception of Caesar. Although he was not part of the conspiracy, he and Caesar were enemies, and Cicero, as we learn later in the script, will be put to death by the administration of Octavius, Mark Antony, and Lepidus. Have a student or group of students interested in history investigate the biographical information on Cicero to develop an explanation of why Shakespeare characterizes him as he does, and perhaps to explain why he is in the play at all. They may then present their findings to the class.

Because Cassius enters this scene as Cicero exits, directors have the choice of whether or not the two characters see each other. We will learn a little more about

Cassius's relationship with Cicero in the next act that may shed light on how this part of the scene would be staged, but if students know by now that Cassius is developing a conspiracy to kill Caesar, and that Cicero, a famous enemy of Caesar, is not part of the conspiracy, we have a number of options. The options provide a small example of what Rocklin (2005) said of silences and how they can be used to develop story.

1. What if Cassius sees Cicero, but avoids him? What if Cicero sees, but avoids, Cassius?
2. What if Cassius starts to approach Cicero, thinking perhaps to win him over to the conspiracy, then decides not to?
3. What if the two just miss each other?

These are options that are reasonable, even though there is no dialogue associated with them. Have students consider which staging works best for them.

Cassius is at his full height of power in this scene, as he is close to achieving his goal of forming the conspiracy. He comes bravely on, as we learn through the stage directions he gives himself, such as baring his "bosom to the thunder-stone" (1.3.52). In continuing your class analysis of forms of argument, have students study Cassius's train of reasoning through this encounter with Casca (starting with line 60). He starts by chastising Casca for his fear, and questioning his "Romanness," which he equates with courage or valor. He even uses the storm as a catalyst, likening it to Caesar. Following right on Cicero's statement that men may interpret things erroneously, Cassius offers an interpretation of the storm (which your students can contrast with Calphurnia's interpretation in the next act). Then he questions the courage of the Romans in general, and eventually introduces the idea that he would kill himself if Caesar became king. Students can trace how Cassius circulates these arguments until he knows he's won, and then suddenly acts as though he may have said too much:

> But, O grief,
> Where hast thou led me? I perhaps speak this
> Before a willing bondman; then, I know
> My answer must be made. But I am armed,
> And dangers are to me indifferent. (1.3.115–119)

This complicated and somewhat disingenuous bravado implies that Casca must either get on board with the conspiracy or fight Cassius. Casca not only joins him and swears to silence ("no fleering telltale" [1.3.121]), but claims that he will go as far as "who goes farthest" (1.3.124). Students may be reminded of this speech later on, when they see that Casca is the first to stab Caesar. What students may also note in Cassius's next speech is that he speaks of the "fearful night" (1.3.131).

He has achieved his goal, so there is, apparently, no more tempting the heavens for him. Cassius then lets Casca, and by proxy the audience, know that he has already gathered a group of conspirators. The final section of the scene begins as Cinna enters. The subject returns to Brutus and their need of him. The scene closes as we learn that the conspirators will pay Brutus a visit later that night.

> ## DISCUSSION/JOURNAL TOPIC:
> ## THE INFLUENCE OF FRIENDS.
>
> Have students discuss how being associated with certain people can help or hinder one's status, and why people, even teens, work to become part of a group, or to recruit certain people to the group. You may also have students look at current political situations, and ask why politicians like to be seen with certain famous or influential others. Have them compare these situations to what Cassius, Cinna, and Casca are discussing regarding Brutus in Act 1, scene 3, lines 145–169.

Act II

A few preliminary notes on Act II are appropriate. First, it is typical in Shakespeare that the second act of a play builds the conflict, increases tension, and further illuminates character personalities. *Julius Caesar* is no different in this regard, as we come to know Brutus through his private thoughts and his conversation with fellow conspirators. We meet the wives of the two principal figures in the play and witness how differently the husbands react to the wives' entreaties. Finally, and perhaps most importantly, we get a glimpse into Caesar's private life and witness how easily he can be swayed by flattery.

The first notable contrast between Act 1 and Act 2 is that Act 1 is set entirely in public spaces, and Act 2 is set entirely in private residences, save the brief encounter between Portia and the soothsayer outside Brutus's residence. In a play that mixes and melds the public and the private, this contrast points to the art of the dramatist who knows that his portrayal of these famous historical figures—his ability to humanize them for his audience—is part of what will make the play memorable. From the opening lines of Act 2, scene 1, when Brutus calls to his servant boy, Lucius, we see that we are in the domestic realm, and Shakespeare uses the domestic scene to emphasize that the very public and fateful actions of the conspirators are the result of individual soul searching on the part of the men, mixing talk of their personal viewpoints with their understanding of what Rome is and what it means to be a Roman. As with Act 1, I suggest that you allow your students to experience this act in "real time" the first time around, either through in-class reading or viewing, perhaps the 1953 movie version (Houseman & Mankiewicz). I suggest that you go through without too much stopping, having students use notebooks to jot down questions they have, comments, or other initial observations. They can use those notes as reference material for the second reading of the script. Instruct students, again, to look and listen for examples of stage directions in the dialogue that give actors choices for performance. As we work through this part of the chapter, I will point out some of those stage directions, although they can be found in any exchange of dialogue if you are alert to them.

Act 2, Scene 1

The first scene in Act 2, like the scene that precedes it, is one of the longest in the play. It establishes Brutus as the lead character in the conspiracy and humanizes him by showing him interacting with his servant and his wife. Perhaps more importantly, this scene shows us what Brutus thinks about Caesar's power and the prospect of killing Caesar to save Rome. The scene is broadly divided into seven sections as follows:

1. Brutus's short exchange with Lucius regarding light.
2. Brutus's soliloquy debating the question of assassination.
3. Brutus's reading the notes Cassius has forged.
4. The visit of the conspirators and Brutus's joining them.
5. Brutus's takeover of conspiracy: who shall live and who shall die.
6. Portia's interview with Brutus about the conspiracy.
7. Visit and transformation of Caius Ligarius.

Each of these sections can be broken down into smaller units of conversation. Sections 4, 5, and 6 are lengthy, and follow several conversational paths. As you begin reading this section with your students, have them note any parts of the conversations that puzzle them, so you can return to those sections for further study.

The first section (lines 1–9) is hardly a section at all, as it merely sets up Brutus's soliloquy, but one must wonder why the exchange with the boy Lucius and the command from Brutus for Lucius to put a taper (candle) in his study is necessary at all. Some directors may choose to cut these lines and open the scene with Brutus's soliloquy, but if they do so, they lose two things: a reference to the progress of time, which is very important in the play as a whole, and a glimpse into Brutus's domestic set-up. Lucius, a boy servant, is one of the few characters to appear in both the early part of the play, preassassination, and the latter part of the play, in the battlefield. Shakespeare had a reason for including this character, and the exchanges between him and Brutus can paint Brutus as a caring father figure or a harsh lord, depending upon the actor's choices.

The second section of the scene is important not only to this play, but to Shakespeare's career as a whole. As Bloom (1998) and Greenblatt (2004) pointed out, Shakespeare here shows us a man who is thinking out loud, thus allowing the audience into the thought process as it's happening. We get to overhear Brutus thinking about whether his reasons for murdering Caesar are legitimate, or, in the absence of real legitimacy, how he'll have to "fashion" his argument to make his reasons sound legitimate. Have a student read the soliloquy as though he is just thinking of the lines as he says them. Have students trace progressions or changes in Brutus's thinking within the speech.

An interesting sequence occurs at the end of the speech, which is the line, "and kill him in the shell" (2.1.36). As Lucius enters to let Brutus know that the candle is lit in his "closet," or study, another choice presents itself for your student directors. Should Lucius hear Brutus speak his last line? What would that imply about Lucius? Lucius also gives Brutus a letter thrown in (or set on) his window. Brutus asks Lucius whether the next day is the Ides of March, and sends him to check. It may be common that people would not know the date at that time, as the calendar itself was new, thanks to Caesar. The reference to a calendar being used by Caesar's assassin would not be lost on Shakespeare's audience (Shapiro, 2005), as the Elizabethan calendar was going through adjustments at the time of the play's first appearance. Brutus then notices the lights in the sky, "exhalations, whizzing in the air" (2.1.46), but seems moved only so far as to comment that they give him enough light to read the letter. Brutus, more so than all of the characters, seems unaffected by the strange storm, but he is affected by his own thoughts. He cannot sleep. The content of the letter calls upon Brutus to act on behalf of Rome. When Brutus claims, "Such instigations have been often dropped / Where I have took them up" (2.1.51–52), we see a time compression, realizing that Cassius has either been working on Brutus to join the conspiracy for some time, or that Cassius's letters are simply additions to what other Romans have written to Brutus. Ask your students which explanation for his line is more likely true. Brutus is reminded of his ancestors, who "did from the streets of Rome / The Tarquin drive when he was called a king" (2.1.56–57). Here we see an echo of one argument Cassius has used to bring Brutus into the conspiracy (1.2.167–170). Brutus is here succumbing to the flattery and the rhetoric of Cassius. He proclaims a private oath to Rome that he will act to preserve the republic: "O Rome, I make thee promise, / If the redress will follow, thou receivest / Thy full petition at the hand of Brutus" (2.1.59–61).

Lucius then returns to inform Brutus that "March is wasted fifteen days," meaning that it is, in fact, the Ides of March (2.1.62). Brutus answers, "'Tis good" (2.1.63). Ask your students to explore reasons why Brutus would comment that it is good. How does that comment fit with the resolution Brutus has just made? Does he now see his actions as part of the fateful prediction of the soothsayer? Certainly, Brutus has heard the soothsayer's warning to Caesar. His speech to himself that follows shows the extent of his nervous excitement:

> Since Cassius first did whet me against Caesar,
> I have not slept.

Between the acting of a dreadful thing
And the first motion, all the interim is
Like a phantasma or a hideous dream.
The genius and the mortal instruments
Are then in council, and the state of man,
Like to a little kingdom, suffers then
The nature of an insurrection. (2.1.64–72)

Notice that Brutus is not only describing his own state, but also theorizing on it as a common principle, perhaps a feeling he himself has suffered before. The body revolting against the mind during stress is commonly known today, but Shakespeare's characters knew it as well. You can discuss with your students why there is a short, two-beat line early in this speech. An actor may take that as a signal to breathe for three beats before going on, or to somehow communicate the bodily stress. Furthermore, perhaps Brutus needs those few seconds to take his own anxiety and transform it into the logical principle that follows in his explanation.

DISCUSSION/JOURNAL TOPIC: BRUTUS'S TRANSFORMATION.

Have students discuss how Brutus has changed between Act 1, scene 2 and Act 2, scene 1. What role did his soliloquy play in that change?

The next section of the scene begins with the entrance of the conspirators, and this section is notable for a few reasons. First, the conspirators are named, one by one, as they greet Brutus, thus giving us a roll call, so to speak, of the men who will murder Caesar. As Cassius draws Brutus aside for private conversation, the conspirators make small talk about the astronomical position of the sunrise, which may be staged as cover talk while Brutus and Cassius seal the deal of Brutus's involvement, or it may be a legitimate argument that ends with Casca pointing his sword at Brutus, saying, "Here, as I point my sword, the sun arises, / Which is a great way growing on the south, / Weighing the youthful season of the year" (2.1.116–118). The second and perhaps most notable aspect of this scene is the immediate shift in power as Brutus takes control of the conspiracy from Cassius. Shakespeare is so artful in his presentation of the shift that the very first exchange following Brutus's acknowledgment of his participation, "Give me your hands all over, one by one" (2.1.123), shows him contradicting Cassius.

| Cassius: | And let us swear our resolution. |
| Brutus: | No, not an oath. If not the face of men, |

The sufferance of our souls, the time's abuse—
If these be motives weak, break off betimes,
And every man hence to his idle bed. (2.1.125–128)

Brutus goes on for another 27 lines explaining in high tones his reasoning for not taking an oath, establishing dominance over Cassius and the others. You may remember that just a few lines earlier, before the conspirators entered, Brutus himself had sworn an oath to Rome. Have your students study Brutus's speech rejecting Cassius's oath and have them discuss why he goes to such lengths to dissuade his fellow conspirators from engaging in what seems like a solidifying ritual. Have them also trace the conversation that follows regarding other possible conspirators, and see how Brutus gets his way in each circumstance. Most notable is the argument regarding Mark Antony. As the play develops, we will see that Brutus is wrong with every decision he makes in contrast to Cassius's arguments. This scene is crucial for setting up that pattern.

The final notable aspect of this section of the scene is Decius's claim that he can convince Caesar to come to the capitol even if he decides against it.

If he be so resolved,
I can o'ersway him, for he loves to hear
That unicorns may be betrayed with trees,
And bears with glasses, elephants with holes,
Lions with toils, and men with flatterers.
But when I tell him he hates flatterers,
He says he does, being then most flatterèd.
Let me work,
For I can give his humor the true bent,
And I will bring him to the Capitol. (2.1.219–228)

This passage is notable not only for what it says about Caesar as an easily duped authority figure, but also what it reveals about Brutus, who has also just been flattered into joining the conspiracy. Students may be able to discuss how they have used similar tactics on parents or teachers.

The conspirators agree to accompany Caesar to the capitol, but not before introducing another possible conspirator, Caius Ligarius. Why does Shakespeare include this conspirator? First, Ligarius is in Shakespeare's source, Plutarch, so Shakespeare's audience may expect this addition, but also, the introduction of Ligarius sets up Brutus, newly joined in the conspiracy, as a recruiter for new conspirators, further assuming what had been Cassius's role. Brutus asks each man to "look fresh and merrily" and calls on them to remember the Roman actors who demonstrate "untired spirits and formal constancy" (2.1.243, 246). One can't help but believe Shakespeare is giving a wink and a nod to his profession.

We might think of the exit of the conspirators as a fitting end to the scene, but Shakespeare doesn't let Brutus off the hook so easily. Brutus finds his servant Lucius asleep (what did Lucius hear of the conversation, if anything?), and as Brutus muses on the boy's ability to sleep peacefully, his wife, Portia, enters, shifting the scene.

The section of the scene with Portia is one of the most memorable in the play, and provides great material for an actress. Brutus, who has just dominated the company of his fellow conspirators, is put on the defensive by his wife, who dominates the entire scene in terms of rhetoric and number of lines spoken (Portia–63 lines, Brutus–17 lines). She tells a story of Brutus's unnatural behavior, then asks him what ails him. When Brutus attempts to brush her off with, "I am not well in health, and that is all" (2.1.277), she steps up her inquiry.

ACTIVITY: LITERATURE WORKSHOP WITH ACT 2, SCENE 1, 253–333, PORTIA AND BRUTUS.

This activity, based on Sheridan Blau's *The Literature Workshop* (2003), will follow an impressionistic path to textual analysis following six steps: silent reading, jump-in reading, pointing, writing about a line, sharing in writing groups, and reporting out/ publishing. Students will take a full class period to consider Portia's scene through a shared reading experience. The activity moves from private encounter with the text through shared processing and, ultimately, individual reporting of gained understanding and perspective.

Silent Reading (5 minutes)

First, provide students with a clean copy of the scene (Act 2, scene 1, lines 253–333), so that they can feel free to write on it as they see fit. After a brief conversation about the context of this scene, ask the students to read the scene silently, paying special attention to any lines or expressions that they find confusing, interesting, or disturbing. Ask students to mark those lines as they go. Note: It will be beneficial for the teacher to model these individual steps along with the students, acting not only as a facilitator but also as an equal participant.

Jump-In Reading (5 minutes)

Having read the scene silently and marked lines that were confusing, interesting, or disturbing, students are ready for their second reading. It is important to *not* engage in any extended discussion of the scene prior to this step, other than to clarify word meanings for students who ask. Jump-in reading involves one student beginning to read for a few lines, then stopping whenever he or she sees fit. Then another student jumps in and continues without raising a hand or waiting for a teacher prompt. If two students start reading at the same time, one backs off so that one voice is heard. Continue until the scene is completed, noting the number of students who read aloud. Students may not worry that they stop in the middle of one of Portia's speeches or that Brutus has lines, too. The randomness of the voices reading aloud adds a touch of anticipation and focused listening to this second reading. Jump-in reading is not the same as popcorn reading in that students will not assign the succeeding reader. Have students again note any lines that are powerful to them or interesting in another way. Have them keep their interpretations private for the time being, but allow for short discussion of the sound of the speech as they heard it.

Pointing (5 minutes)

This section of the activity will constitute a third "reading" of the soliloquy with a dramatic flavor, in that students will not encounter the text in a linear way. They will instead hear selected lines read randomly and repeatedly by their classmates. This part of the activity may be audiotaped for review. Have students look back at the lines and phrases they have marked through their first two readings. Once you start the pointing activity, students are to read aloud only the lines or phrases they wish to read. Three rules apply: (1) a student may repeat a line as many times as the student wishes, (2) no student "owns" a line, meaning that more than one student may read the same line, and (3) if two students start saying their line or phrase at the same time, one backs off so that they don't "clutter" each other. Have no concern over whether every line of the scene is represented, as students are engaging (albeit unconsciously) in selecting main ideas and hearing the sounds of the speech that have resonance. The exercise might sound like this:

"Brutus is wise"
"I charm you, by my once commended beauty"
"Kneel not, gentle Portia"
"It will not let you eat nor talk nor sleep"
"Is Brutus sick?"
"Some six or seven who did hide their faces"
"Portia is Brutus's harlot"
"It will not let you eat nor talk nor sleep"
"You are my true and honorable wife"
"I have made strong proof of my constancy"
"I grant I am a woman"

"Tell me your counsels; I will not disclose 'em"
"Good Portia, go to bed."
"Am I your self"
"Y' have ungently, Brutus, stole from my bed"
"I am not well in health, and that is all"

The pointing activity can last as long as the students continue reading out lines from the speech, but I suggest you give it a little time to get started and gain momentun, then cut it off before it dies completely. Short discussion of the experience may ensue, but further discussion will come later. Move on to the next step.

Writing About a Line (10 minutes)

Now students should be primed to write about the scene in a way that is focused yet informal. Have them pick a line or phrase that they chose earlier, or perhaps one that they heard that fascinated them, and write about it silently for several minutes. Tell them to feel free to explore what the significance of the line or phrase is for the scene and for the play. They may even explore in their writing how the line relates to their own experience and understanding of the world, or compare their understanding of the line with what Portia is experiencing. Students may refer to more than one line in their writing, but the emphasis is on exploration rather than formal analysis. It should be clear to the students that what they write here won't be graded or critiqued. The idea is to keep writing for the allotted time.

Sharing in Writing Groups (10 minutes)

Have students get into groups of three in order to share with their peers their writing. Students should actually read what they wrote rather than tell about what they wrote. Hearing what they wrote will help them process their thoughts and will help their peers recreate their thinking accurately. Following each reading, students should freely discuss in their groups what they have heard as a way of sharing interpretations and thoughts. The teacher should stay out of these discussions as much as possible, simply joining one of the groups as an equal participant.

Reporting Out/Publishing (12+ minutes)

After the groups have discussed their readings and writing about specific lines, the room will be full of energy and students will have developed a stake in their thoughts regarding the scene. At this point, gather the class together again as a whole group and ask for groups to report what they have discussed. The best way to approach this is to have individual members of the groups either volunteer to read what they wrote to the larger group or to nominate another member of their group to read (e.g., "Have Lisha read hers; it's really good!"). Sample several readings from different groups, and if discussion is brisk or differences in interpretation come up, facilitate follow-up discussion. Make sure anyone who wants to share gets the opportunity to do so, but don't force reluctant students.

Follow-Up

This reading/discussion activity incorporates several research-based reading strategies without the students ever needing to be explicitly instructed in the strategies. For example, the activity incorporates rereading, reading out loud, small-group guided discussion, response writing, and analytical discussion, all of which are supported by research. Furthermore, when you advance to Chapter 8 and start to consider critical perspectives for interpreting *Julius Caesar,* this activity can be revisited so that students may try to put critical labels on their readings of the scene that grew out of the activity. Students engage in focused discussion without the teacher dictating interpretations or bearing the burden of trying to keep discussion going by throwing out one predetermined analytical question after another. The series of readings here may be applied to scenes with several characters and may lead to other extension activities.

The knocking at the door (line 327), a frequent plot device in Shakespeare, allows Brutus to direct Portia to go inside, but not before he promises to share his secret with her. Thus, we see that Portia has persuaded her husband to tell his secret, and given the strength of her spirit as shown in the scene, we can bet that she'll hold him to his promise. When we get to Act 2, scene 4, we will see the anxiety that attends her after Brutus goes to the capitol, indicating that he did, indeed, keep his promise. Your students will be able to compare this husband/wife scene with the husband/wife exchange that follows in Act 2, scene 2.

Following Portia's exit, the final section of Act 2, scene 1 begins with the entrance of Caius Ligarius. In a strange little unit that offers a variety of choices for actors, Ligarius comes in as a sick man, and when Brutus laments his sickness, Ligarius claims he can be made better if "Brutus have in hand / Any exploit worthy the name of honor" (2.1.342–343). Brutus replies that he has, and Ligarius casts off his "sickness":

Ligarius: By all the gods that Romans bow before,
  I here discard my sickness. Soul of Rome,
  Brave son derived from honorable loins,
  Thou like an exorcist hast conjured up
  My mortifièd spirit. Now bid me run,
  And I will strive with things impossible,

	Yea, get the better of them. What's to do?
Brutus:	A piece of work that will make sick men whole.
Ligarius:	But are not some whole that we must make sick? (2.1.346–355)

Notice the language of sickness and health, and the sense Ligarius has that they will do something to at least injure someone. It seems odd, then, that just a few lines later, Ligarius says, "And with a heart new-fired I follow you / To do I know not what; but it sufficeth / That Brutus leads me on." (2.1.361–362). Does Ligarius really not know what is being planned? What is the function of this scene? How does Ligarius's sickness contrast with the sickness Portia attributes to Brutus? Students may offer ideas.

DISCUSSION/ JOURNAL TOPIC: IS LIGARIUS SICK OR NOT SICK?

If Ligarius is truthfully ill, then two interpretations are possible: that he will ignore his illness to follow Brutus or that Brutus has actually "cured" him simply by calling him to join in the conspiracy. Another possibility is that Ligarius is feigning illness and that he springs forth from his feigned illness to provide further inspiration for Brutus. Certainly, Ligarius's rhetoric fits with the personal praise for Brutus that Cassius used to win him to the cause. Either Cassius has sent Ligarius to further "whet" Brutus against Caesar, or Brutus has powers of leadership (or healing powers) that we previously have not seen. In any sense, this long scene ends with the men heading toward Caesar with destiny in their minds.

Act 2, Scene 2

This scene is a mirror of the section of the previous scene that involves Portia and Brutus. Here we see Caesar and his fearful wife, Calphurnia, arguing whether or not Caesar should go to the Capitol. How might a director stage these two scenes to show that they mirror each other? Notice that the balance of lines is far different from one scene to the other, with Calphurnia unable to dominate discussion with Caesar as Portia has done with Brutus.

ACTIVITY (SAS #9): THE WOMEN: SIMILARITIES AND DIFFERENCES IN THEIR TACTICS.

Cohen (2006), influenced by Knight (1931), has remarked that this play contains a lack of feminine energy, and that the imbalance of gender influence is a central aspect of the tragedy. Have students construct a Venn diagram or other visual representation through which to compare and contrast the scenes between Brutus and Portia and Caesar and Calphurnia. What similarities and differences in the two marital relationships are evident in the scenes? Have students compare their findings with each other.

Act 2, scene 2 is also important in that it shows us a full picture of Caesar's private and public personalities: his ego, sense of self, and superstition, all in concert, but overridden by his vulnerability to flattery. Remind your students that every scene in the play contains at least one argument, and they can learn a great deal about persuasion by tracking who persuades whom to do what in each circumstance, and by what means. I divide this scene into the following three sections:

1. Caesar alone and with Calphurnia.
2. Decius changes Caesar's mind.
3. Conspirators come to accompany Caesar to the Capitol.

Section one of this scene shows us Caesar alone for the only time in the script. He has not even three full lines of soliloquy before a servant enters, and we never see him alone on stage again.

> *Caesar:*   Nor heaven nor earth have been at peace tonight.
> Thrice hath Calphurnia in her sleep cried out
> "Help ho, they murder Caesar!"—Who's within? (2.2.1–3)

When compared to the amount of time we see Brutus, and even Cassius, speaking in soliloquy, we see that Shakespeare does not allow the audience to get emotionally close to Caesar. The nature of Caesar's short speech is telling. He explicitly mentions that Calphurnia had cried out in her sleep, "Help, ho, they murder Caesar" (2.2.3). He notices the strange celestial events and is sufficiently impressed by these events to have his augurers do sacrifice to bring their "opinions of success" (2.2.6). Have students read this entire scene to learn how Caesar's mind changes, and what causes those changes. Then students can discuss how the opening three lines of the scene may be staged, either showing Caesar as curious, concerned, amused, or frightened by what he describes. The question, "Who's within?" (2.2.3) may provide a glimpse at Caesar's worry or lack thereof for his own safety. If the actor flinches when he hears the noise, or if he takes an aggressive posture, as though the noise may be an attacker, that will produce a certain interpretation of his personality that a casual demeanor would not.

DISCUSSION/JOURNAL TOPIC: CAESAR'S LOGIC.

Have students trace Caesar's decision making in this scene from beginning to end. A good way to do this is to remove Calphurnia's lines and just listen to Caesar's responses.

Calphurnia enters with a command to Caesar: "You shall not stir out of your house today" (2.2.9). No other person in this play would dare issue a command to Caesar. One difference between Calphurnia's unsuccessful argument to persuade

Caesar to stay home and Portia's successful argument to hear what Brutus has in his mind is the nature of what they are seeking. One is seeking information, the other action. In the exchanges in lines 8–60, notice how Caesar mixes references to himself in third person with references in the first person:

> *Caesar:* Caesar shall forth. The things that threatened me
> Ne'er looked but on my back. When they shall see
> The face of Caesar, they are vanishèd. (2.2.10–12)

Even in private conversation with his wife, Caesar is distancing himself, and others, from himself, as though aware of his otherness as Caesar. Furthermore, what Caesar says here has already been contradicted in an earlier scene (1.2) with the soothsayer. When Caesar brought the soothsayer forth to look him in the face, the fellow did not vanish; rather, he repeated his warning.

Calphurnia is not without skill as a rhetorician. She starts with a self-reference reminiscent of Cassius: "I never stood on ceremonies, / Yet now they fright me" (2.2.13–14). In other words, she doesn't see herself as a superstitious person, but she's changing her mind. Her argument depends on Caesar agreeing that she's not normally superstitious; otherwise, he would laugh at her statement. Calphurnia's argument tells us all of the strange and supernatural events that have happened that night, such as we have seen in the final scene of Act 1. Calphurnia has sufficient reason to believe her husband's life is in danger. The sights she recounts of what she has seen and heard are extraordinary, from a lioness giving birth in the street to graves opening and yielding "up their dead" (2.2.18).

Caesar's response to her fears is curiously fatalistic:

> What can be avoided
> Whose end is purposed by the mighty gods?
> Yet Caesar shall go forth, for these predictions
> Are to the world in general as to Caesar. (2.2.27–30)

Calphurnia's response is perhaps the most famous speech she makes in the play:

> When beggars die there are no comets seen;
> The heavens themselves blaze forth the death of princes. (2.2.31–32)

Notice that Calphurnia is the first to use the word "death" in this scene. In effect, she has raised the stakes in the argument and forced Caesar to confront the specific threat to his life. Caesar's following speech is equally fatalistic to his previous lines.

> Cowards die many times before their deaths;
> The valiant never taste of death but once.
> Of all the wonders that I yet have heard,
> It seems to me most strange that men should fear,
> Seeing that death, a necessary end,
> Will come when it will come. (2.2.34–39)

Notice the use of the word "cowards" and the self-reference, all in the first person. Caesar is thinking from his heart, rather than as the public "Caesar." Have students replace the personal pronoun "I" in these lines with "Caesar" to see how the tone of the speech changes. Then have them do the opposite in Caesar's next speech in response to the report of the augurers. When the servant enters and delivers the news that the augurers would not have him stir forth, Caesar is back to his lofty, distant, and perhaps overly arrogant self, saying, "The gods do this in shame of cowardice" (2.2.44).

Caesar will go forth, even though there is strong evidence (in the terms of his own belief system) that he should not go. Calphurnia sees through Caesar's facade and brings him to his senses:

> Alas, my lord,
> Your wisdom is consumed in confidence. (2.2.52–53)

Going down on her knees (as the stage signal in line 58 tells us), she prevails upon him to stay at home. We may believe she has won the argument and saved her husband's life until Decius enters, the same Decius who has told the audience earlier that he may persuade Caesar to go to the Capitol. Caesar immediately shifts back to his "I am Caesar" rhetoric. Ironically, it is Caesar's acknowledgment of his love for Decius, as a friend, that opens the way for Decius to change Caesar's mind. Caesar tells Decius about Calphurnia's dream, which not only extends the imagery we have already seen as described by Calphurnia, but introduces a new level of blood imagery, with Caesar's statue spouting fountains of blood (2.2.81–85). Caesar's speech also informs us that the argument we have just heard between Caesar and Calphurnia must have started earlier, off stage, for Caesar to know what her dream was. But Decius offers an alternative "reading" of the dream (2.2.88–95) that immediately persuades Caesar to change his mind, thus fulfilling Decius's earlier claim that Caesar is easily duped. Decius then plays upon Caesar's ambition and his desire not to appear vulnerable or afraid (2.2.97–109) to convince him to go forth.

Also important in the last part of this section of the scene is that Calphurnia does not speak again. What she may be doing on stage is another issue. Does she get pushed aside? Does she fall to her knees again? Does she try to speak? Have students discuss the lengths Calphurnia goes to in order to keep Caesar at home and compare that to Portia's willingness to stab herself in the thigh. Also, have them compare the way Caesar addresses his wife as compared to the way Brutus addresses his wife:

> How foolish do your fears seem now, Calphurnia!
> I am ashamèd I did yield to them.
> Give me my robe, for I will go. (2.2.110–112)

The wheels are set in motion for Caesar's fateful day. The final section of the scene shows all of the conspirators coming to accompany Caesar to the capitol. This short unit of dialogue shows a gregarious and affable Caesar greeting the very men who will take his life, treating them as friends, and even inviting them into his house to enjoy a cup of wine before heading for the capitol. The entrance of Antony is notable here, as in his absence, the conspirators may have been able to kill Caesar right then and there at his home. Caesar even comments on Antony's reputation for partying and is surprised at his early arrival.

Have students discuss how Caesar and his friends would behave toward each other in this scene. Is there hugging or other genuine signs of affection? Does Caesar sense the menace in these men's hearts? Caesar notes Ligarius's sickness, and the fact that Ligarius is "lean" (2.2.119), which brings to mind what Caesar said earlier about lean men. Also worth noting in this meeting of men who will accompany Caesar to the senate house is the absence of Cassius. Ask students why Cassius should be absent from this scene.

Act 2, Scene 3

This is a curious little scene that shows a possible survival route for Caesar. We see Artemidorus, a rhetorician, reading a letter he has penned warning Caesar of the conspiracy. He mentions the names of all the conspirators, indicating that he knows details of the conspiracy. Shakespeare takes this element of the plot from Plutarch, too, and while we know what is going to happen to Caesar, showing on stage the possible salvation through Artemidorus's warning helps increase dramatic tension. But Shakespeare's inclusion of this scene also serves another function. As readers, or more importantly, as audience members, we may have developed some sympathy for Brutus and the other conspirators, especially if Caesar is portrayed as aloof and self-centered in the previous scene. In this scene, however, we are introduced to a neutral character, someone we have no reason to disbelieve, using the word "virtue" (2.3.13) in association with Caesar and "traitors" (2.3.16) to describe the conspirators. Artemidorus believes his little letter "mayest" (2.3.15) save Caesar, but he also worries that "the fates with traitors do contrive" (2.3.16). In Act 3, scene 1, we will see that Artemidorus does indeed try to get Caesar to read his letter, but without success.

Act 2, Scene 4

This scene is notable for two reasons. It reintroduces Portia, and it humanizes the soothsayer. The scene has two sections and a short coda.

1. Portia commands Lucius to go to the Capitol, but won't tell him his mission.
2. Portia engages the soothsayer in conversation.
3. Coda: Portia's tortured final speech.

In the opening of this scene, Portia wants Lucius to run to the Capitol to report what is happening there, but she cannot tell him what she knows is going to happen. She comments on her womanhood and how difficult it is for women to remain constant. There are many option for an actress playing the part here: to move around the stage, to measure her comments, thinking about what she wants Lucius to hear and what she fears he will hear. In a play that functions through the keeping of secrets, Portia's comments anticipate the panic of the scene that will follow, where the fear of the conspirators that their plot has been discovered is very real.

DISCUSSION/JOURNAL TOPIC: KEEPING SECRETS.

Give students the following prompt: Who keeps secrets better, boys or girls? Why do you think this is so? How would you portray Portia in this scene?

In the second section of this scene, the soothsayer happens to stroll past Brutus's house, and Portia engages him in conversation. This little scene between Portia and the soothsayer is sometimes cut in production, because it doesn't forward the plot and it also presents a logistical problem. The soothsayer wants to move to a less-crowded street to see Caesar, which would indicate that Caesar will be going right past Brutus's house,

> Here the street is narrow.
> The throng that follows Caesar at the heels,
> Of senators, praetors, common suitors,
> Will crowd a feeble man almost to death. (2.4.39–42)

Yet Portia still sends Lucius away to the Capitol to find Brutus. She seems unaware of the possibility that Caesar and everyone else, including Brutus, would parade right past her door.

Another function of this exchange is to humanize the soothsayer. When he first enters and Portia waves him over to her, she asks him where he has been and what time it is, both common conversational elements. When the soothsayer tells her that he is on his way to see Caesar "pass on to the Capitol" (2.4.30), Portia guesses that he "hast some suit to Caesar" (2.4.31). The soothsayer's response demonstrates what could be interpreted as a genuine concern for Caesar: "That I have, lady. If it will please Caesar / To be so good to Caesar as to hear me, / I will beseech him to befriend himself" (2.4.32–34). Portia's blood pressure shoots up immediately, as she responds, "Why, know't thou any harms intended towards him?" (2.4.35–36). The soothsayer's response, "None that I know will be, much that I fear may chance" (2.4.37–38), tells us something of the nature of soothsaying. Have students discuss how they would portray the soothsayer, and what they think of his role in this play. When Act 3, scene 1 opens, we will see that the soothsayer, face to face with Caesar once more, does no beseeching whatsoever, only giving a short, ominous warning:

> *Caesar:* The ides of March are come.
> *Soothsayer:* Ay, Caesar, but not gone. (3.1.1–2)

After the soothsayer says goodbye to Portia, she delivers a coda to Act 2, scene 4, returning to her earlier agony in the first section of the scene, lamenting the weakness of women and sending Lucius to the Capitol, with no better errand than to report on what he sees of Brutus there. Her anxiety (she grows "faint" [2.4.50]) ends this second act that has been played out in the private residences of the two principal characters. Shakespeare has set the stage for the fast-moving, pivotal third act.

Act 3

Act 3 of *Julius Caesar*, as with so many Shakespeare plays, gives us the climax or turning point of the action and changes the reality that has been building throughout Acts 1 and 2. We can assume that Caesar is going to be assassinated in this act, as we know it happened historically and everything in the play thus far has prepared us for it. That being said, critics argue about what particular event in the play actually stands as the climax. Although it is easy to see Caesar's assassination as the climax, other possible events in the play that have climactic impact are the entrance of Antony's servant following the assassination, Antony's funeral oration in Act 3, scene 2, and the mob killing of the innocent poet, Cinna, in Act 3, scene 3.

Act 3, Scene 1

This scene moves us back to public space, as we are on a Roman street, approaching the Capitol. The scene is crowded, chaotic, and intense. I suggest that you read the scene aloud in class with your students, and that you position students to act out or reconstruct the scene to get a sense of the movement. The scene may be divided into any number of smaller units, but I prefer to think of it as having seven distinct sections as follows:

1. Caesar and retinue approach Capitol with suitors following.
2. Caesar's confrontation with senators and assassination.
3. Immediate aftermath with Caesar's assassins.
4. Antony's servant and assassins.
5. Antony and assassins.
6. Antony's soliloquy.
7. Antony and Octavius Caesar's servant.

The longest of these sections, Antony and the assassins, is 116 lines long, and the shortest, Antony's soliloquy, is only 21 lines, but your students will negotiate the scene more successfully if you point out to them the distinct segments in the scene. Students may take these sections and divide them further as an in-class writing or discussion exercise, which is a good way to assess their understanding of what might be happening on stage or, at least, what is happening in the dialogue.

The scene opens with Caesar and the "throng of suitors" that the soothsayer had mentioned in the previous scene. The first exchange of dialogue in this act is between Caesar and the soothsayer, and it can be compared to their first exchange in Act 1 (1.2.15–29). For some reason, the soothsayer does not issue any further warnings to Caesar, even though he has told Portia that he will "beseech him (Caesar) to befriend himself" (2.4.34). Immediately after the opening exchange between Caesar and the soothsayer, Artemidorus attempts to get Caesar to read his letter (see Act 2, scene 3 discussion above), but he is overwhelmed by Decius, who steps in with a different (probably invented) suit. Artemidorus tries to command Caesar's attention to read his first, which would, of course, expose the conspiracy, but Caesar brushes him off with, "What touches us ourself shall be last served" (3.1.8).

Students may wonder why Caesar is being so dismissive of both the soothsayer and Artemidorus. In fact, according to Shakespeare's source, Plutarch, by some reports, Caesar does take the letter of Artemidorus and attempts many times to read it, but is prevented by the crowd (Spevack, 2003, p. 183). In Shakespeare's play, Artemidorus doesn't give up, and there is a great stage signal that indicates physical action when Caesar says, "What, is the fellow mad?" (3.1.10). Publius and Cassius apparently move poor Artemidorus out of the way, and that's the last we hear of him. One may also wonder why Artemidorus doesn't just shout to Caesar what he knows of the conspiracy. Discuss with your students how this part of the scene could be staged so that Artemidorus can only hope Caesar reads the letter, with no opportunity to actually say out loud what he knows.

As Caesar's entourage reaches the Capitol, a new character is introduced, Popilius Lena, who cryptically wishes Cassius success with his enterprise, setting off a small panic attack for Cassius. The dramatic tension builds as Brutus and Cassius watch Popilius approach Caesar, and Cassius makes his third reference in the play to the possibility of killing himself, the first two references being philosophical (1.2.102 and 1.3.92–103), but this reference being very real. Shakespeare is again borrowing directly from his source, Plutarch, who tells the same events twice, once in his portrait of Julius Caesar and again, with different details provided, in his life of Marcus Brutus. In Plutarch's account, all of the conspirators have their swords out, ready to kill themselves if the plot has been discovered. The effect of Popilius Lena's role is to increase tension and hurry the action. When Cassius reports that Trebonius has drawn Antony out of the way, the next section of the scene begins with Caesar addressing the gathered senators.

Caesar wonders what is going on, and Metellus Cimber kneels, starting the sequence that leads to the assassination. Have students read the section from lines 34–85 in class, then have them act like crime scene investigators to relive it as though they are on stage themselves, and they are trying to recreate what happened to Caesar. Certainly, they will be in line with the action of the play itself, wherein the characters are acting their suit to Caesar as a mere pretense to get him isolated and surrounded so that they can kill him. Caesar then delivers his speech about constancy, a major theme in the play (Spevack, 2003). Have students analyze Caesar's final speech (3.1.64–79) to determine what Caesar says about himself (see Chapter 1 for commentary). One thing they may notice is that Caesar has completely abandoned the third person reference, using the word "I" seven times. Why? Is Caesar pleading? Is he angry beyond the bounds of his usual, cool decorum? In any case, he will be dead in a moment. Have students, in their CSI investigation, construct a sequence of the stabbing that begins with Casca's "Speak, hands, for me" (3.1.84) and that ends in Caesar's *Et tu, Brutè?*—Then fall, Caesar" (3.1.85). Discuss with students the difference between the script, which only gives us these few words, and the staging, which might draw out the stabbing scene over several seconds without words. View the scene in the most accessible film versions (Houseman & Mankiewicz, 1953; Snell & Burge, 1970) to show the sequence and talk about how we must provide visual details to read the script. Compare Shakespeare's version of the events to the description of the killing found in Plutarch.

ACTIVITY (SAS #11): COMPARING ACCOUNTS OF CAESAR'S ASSASSINATION IN SHAKESPEARE AND PLUTARCH.

Students can access the text of Plutarch's "The Life of Julius Caesar" online at http://penelope.uchicago.edu/Thayer/E/Roman/Texts/Plutarch/Lives/Caesar*.html, thanks to Bill Thayer and the University of Chicago. Have students chart the progression of events related to Caesar's assassination in Plutarch, then compare those to Shakespeare's script.

The next section of the scene begins immediately, and we may imagine a public spectacle on stage. There are modern parallels to discuss, such as the public assassination of President John F. Kennedy or the televised assassination of former Egyptian President Anwar Sadat. The effect of the event on the citizens is told by the characters themselves: "Men, wives, and children stare, cry out, and run / As it were doomsday" (3.1.107–108).

Brutus and Casca have a bizarre exchange of dialogue on the benefits of death over fearing death, and then Brutus asks the conspirators to dip their hands into Caesar's blood. He is joined by Cassius. Once more using the metaphor of acting, Brutus and Cassius, in their one postconspiracy moment of complete agreement, initiate a ceremony that they imagine will be "acted over / In states unborn and accents yet unknown" (3.1.125–126). The section ends with Cassius stating that "Brutus shall lead, and we will grace his heels / With the most boldest and best hearts of Rome" (3.1.135–136).

Have students discuss their gut feeling at this point in the script about who is morally right. The violence of the assassination may be something you want to address with your students, some of whom may have experienced violence in their own lives. A debate (see Chapter 6) over the justification of the assassination may be started here, and continued after students have read the arguments of Brutus and Antony in Act 3, scene 2.

The fourth section of this scene begins with the entrance of Antony's servant. The servant shows himself to be an articulate actor, speaking his own stage directions as he says what Antony directed him to say. As we see in many portions of this play, we have actors portraying characters who are acting. The servant's speech is a brilliant piece of theater and rhetoric on Shakespeare's part, and your class can workshop the servant's speech for rhetorical strategy. One thing to note with your students is that Antony apparently addresses only Brutus through his messenger, without mention of the other conspirators, including Cassius. Students may keep this in mind when the men meet in the next scene. Antony knows who his greatest rival is, although he eventually shows great contempt for all of them.

What the servant wants, and what Antony himself will request, is an explanation of why Brutus and the others killed Caesar. Brutus makes promises several times, first in his exchange with the servant and again with Antony. But notice in the remainder of the scene how he fails to follow through on that promise, to his own detriment. After the servant exits to "fetch" Antony (3.1.158), Cassius speaks his concern about Antony to Brutus, a concern that Brutus ignores again and again.

The next section of the scene begins with the entrance of Mark Antony. Have your students trace Antony's speeches from his entrance until the end of the scene, describing how he changes and how he persuades the conspirators to give him what he wants. He switches between addressing the assassins and speaking directly to the body of Caesar. What are his reasons for speaking to Caesar's body? Note the following lines: "O mighty Caesar, dost thou lie so low? / Are all thy conquests, glories, triumphs, spoils / Shrunk to this little measure?" (3.1.164–166). Antony here reminds the audience that Caesar really was the "colossus" that Cassius complained of in Act 1.

DISCUSSION/JOURNAL TOPIC: ANTONY'S ADDRESS.

How does Antony address the body of Julius Caesar in the presence of others, and how does he address it when on stage alone? What is the tone of each address? What do his addresses to Caesar's body tell us about Antony and his relationship to Caesar and to Brutus?

In his address to Brutus and the others, Antony first offers himself for them to kill. Note the specificity and graphic description he provides of the post-murder scene: "whilst your purpled hands do reek and smoke" (3.1.174). Remember that Brutus, Cassius, and the others have recently "bathed" in Caesar's blood, which could be staged to look grisly in the theatre. You may point out to your students that only Antony, Brutus, and Cassius speak in this part of the scene, and your students can explore how each man's lines fit with his character. While Brutus talks of love and pity and "the general wrong of Rome" (3.1.186), Cassius appeals to Antony's promotion to a level as high as the highest among them. But Antony's request, again, to be given reasons why "Caesar was dangerous" (3.1.243) is not satisfied, only promised, by Brutus.

ACTIVITY: LET ME SHAKE YOUR HAND.

Notice that in Act 3, scene 1, lines 201–208, Antony makes a point to name each of the men who killed Julius Caesar as he shakes their bloody hands. Have students discuss his reasons for shaking and naming, then have students develop options for how these handshakes might look on stage, and what nonverbal communication is possible. He starts with Brutus and ends with Trebonius. Why Brutus first? Why Trebonius last, and why does he say to Trebonius, "Though last, not least in love, yours, good Trebonius" (3.1.207–208)? Have students write informally about how they would stage each of the handshakes and why, related to what they know of each of the characters.

What is the role of Cassius in this scene? When Antony addresses the body of Caesar again (3.1.213–230), he calls them "foes" and "hunters" and begs Caesar's forgiveness. It is Cassius who pulls him back to the living and questions his motives. Antony's famous line, "Friends am I with you all and love you all" (3.1.241), memorable not only for being a string of 10 monosyllables, but also as a great lie, is followed again with a request that Brutus and the others show just cause.

DISCUSSION/JOURNAL TOPIC: BRUTUS'S REASONS.

Why doesn't Brutus give Antony reasons for killing Caesar right then and there? Why does he need to wait until the public has been satisfied? Could it be that the reasons are too vague? Or is Brutus still visibly shaken by the violence he has committed?

In the remainder of the scene, Brutus again ignores Cassius when he voices concern over Antony speaking at the funeral. Cassius has said earlier that his "misgiving still / Falls shrewdly to the purpose" (3.1.161–162). What does Cassius mean, and is he accurate in his portrayal of himself and his concerns about Antony? Brutus assumes that by speaking himself before Antony, there will be no harm that Antony can cause. What does this assumption tell us about Brutus? Note in lines 270–274 that Brutus prescribes the rhetoric that Antony must use in his funeral oration. Brutus and company leave Antony alone with Caesar's body by Brutus's order; Antony's tone changes immediately, and we see him grow before our eyes into a prophet of destruction.

The final section of this scene introduces a new character who will, ironically, deliver the final lines in the play, and who will emerge as the foremost man in succession to his uncle, even though we don't actually meet him until the next act. The servant of Octavius Caesar enters and grieves with Antony when he sees Caesar's body. This tag on the pivotal murder scene demonstrates a familiarity between servants and masters in Shakespeare's portrayal of Roman society. Have students focus on how Antony speaks to the servant in this scene, and the personal compassion he shows right after prophesying devastating war and destruction for Rome. Antony also depends upon the servant to be literate enough to witness the funeral and then report events accurately to Octavius. The scene ends with Antony preparing the audience for the speech he will give in Caesar's funeral:

> There shall I try,
> In my oration, how the people take
> The cruel issue of these bloody men,
> According to the which thou shalt discourse
> To young Octavius of the state of things.
> Lend me your hand. (3.1.319–324)

Act 3, Scene 2

Act 3, scene 2 signifies the climax not of the action so much as the rhetoric of the play. As we have seen thus far, every scene in the play contains an argument of one type or another. In Act 1, the rhetoric is controlled by Cassius, who needs to win Brutus and others to the conspiracy. In Act 2, the primary rhetorical struggles are between Brutus and himself, Brutus and Portia, Caesar and Calphurnia, and Calphurnia and Decius. Act 3, scene 1 contains the argument of Caesar regarding his constancy, but his argument is lost through violence. This scene, following the assassination, contains what may be described as the most famous debate in all of Western literature. It is easy for students and teachers to focus on the two rival orators, Brutus and Mark Antony, and their rhetorical strategies, but students should not forget the "character" of the plebeians in this and other scenes. Also, students should note that one bizarre characteristic of this most famous of debates is that neither rival debater attends the other's speech. Mark Antony seems to know the gist of Brutus's speech, but he is not on stage while Brutus delivers it. Brutus, as we will see, consciously leaves the scene before Antony speaks, though we know by this point that if Cassius were not speaking himself at another location, he would have cautioned Brutus not to be so trusting.

This scene may be divided into the following sections, which can be further segmented by you and your students.

1. Prefatory to Brutus's speech to plebeians.
2. Brutus persuades the plebeians to accept Caesar's death.
3. Mark Antony sways the plebeians to mutiny.
4. Servant of Octavius delivers update on situation.

The scene opens with a short exchange between Brutus and the plebeians, who are clamoring to be satisfied with reasons for the death of Caesar. Two things to note are that Brutus tells Cassius to split the crowd and go to deliver reasons in another location, while Brutus will do the same in his current location. Thus, we have reference to a speech we will never hear, Cassius's explanation of the assassination. The second and related detail to notice is that Cassius does not speak, even to agree with Brutus. He is effectively silenced by Shakespeare, furthering the disconnect between Cassius and the outcome of events.

DISCUSSION/JOURNAL TOPIC: THE LOST SPEECH— CASSIUS'S ADDRESS TO THE CROWD.

At the beginning of Act 3, scene 2, Brutus and Cassius split up so that each may make a speech explaining the assassination of Caesar to the Roman public. We never hear Cassius's speech. Ask students what they think Cassius would say based on what they know of him. A student may want to draft a speech for Cassius or invent the scene.

The second section of the scene is Brutus's argument to the plebeians. Have students mark how the plebeians respond to Brutus through his speech, but also have them trace Brutus's rhetoric (see activity below). One structural signal to an actor playing Brutus is that Shakespeare breaks his pattern of iambic pentameter poetry for Brutus's speech. Typically in this play, only the plebeians speak in prose, so we could argue that Brutus is anticipating his crowd and thus speaking to them in language that they understand, but on closer analysis, your students will find that Brutus's speech is complicated, even if it has the desired effect in the short run. Ask students if they would be persuaded by listening to Brutus. What evidence does Brutus give to support his argument that Caesar was ambitious? What does his argument lack that makes it a good straw man argument for Antony to dismantle?

ACTIVITY (SAS #13A): COPYING BRUTUS'S RHETORIC.

Brutus uses what we call "parallelism" in his argument. Have students model Brutus's parallelism in an argument of their own creation. For example, "As I was busy, I forgot about the assignment; as I was confused, I left some questions blank; as I was hurried, I wrote sloppily; but as I was worried about my grade, I cheated."

By the end of his speech, Brutus has satisfied his listeners, who want to build a statue of him and make him Caesar, indicating that the family name would become a title in itself synonymous with "ruler." Ask your students what they think of the plebeians' response to Brutus, comparing their attitudes to the opening scene of the play. Why are they so easily persuaded? Although Brutus has appeased their minds and given them satisfaction, he hasn't stirred their hearts.

The third section of this scene, Antony's funeral oration, can be dissected into stages of persuasion, and will merit a full day's attention in your class. Students should keep in mind a picture of staging and the relationship between what is happening on stage and what effects a director would want an audience to feel. The audience may even become an extension of the Roman public in this sequence, as Antony dismantles Brutus's argument and stirs the minds and hearts of his listeners. There are several key differences between the arguments of Brutus and Antony, but the first to notice is in the structure of the lines. Antony has poetry on his side. Indeed, no sooner has Brutus finished his prose speech that the plebeians begin speaking in verse. Brutus, when he is not making an argument, returns to poetry as well. But Antony has more than just poetry on his side. He has the advantage of knowing Brutus's argument and knowing also what Brutus has demanded of him: that he speak no ill of the assassins, but only good of Caesar (3.1.271–272). Antony uses the rhetorical devices of irony, antithesis, and the rhetorical question. He demonstrates a command of ethos, pathos, and logos to convert the plebeians and to stir them to violence.

ACTIVITY (SAS#13B): ETHOS, PATHOS, LOGOS.

Have students compare the speeches of Brutus and Antony using the classical strategies of ethos, pathos, and logos. In other words, have them chart when and how each speaker appeals to the crowd's sense of the speaker's integrity, the crowd's emotions, and the crowd's sense of logic. Students may consult the University of Kentucky's rhetorical strategies web page at http://www.uky.edu/AS/Classics/rhetoric.html for help with this and other persuasive speeches in the script.

What is perhaps most amazing about Antony's speech is that it is a conscious performance, something we see in Shakespeare again and again, particularly in this play. Antony has told us in the previous scene that he will "try, / In my oration, how the people take / The cruel issue of these bloody men" (3.1.319–321). As soon as Antony has achieved his goal of turning the plebeians against Brutus and the others, he comments on the success of his performance, saying of Brutus and Cassius, who have been driven out of Rome, "Belike they had some notice of the people / How I had moved them" (3.2.286–287).

Antony's speech can be separated into segments that correlate to his strategies. When he introduces a new strategy, he does not abandon his previous strategies, but reinforces them from time to time. Once Antony gains the crowd's attention, the structure of the speech runs something like this: two long speeches punctuated by plebeian commentary and followed by a dialogic exchange with the plebeians, then the same structure repeated, with two more speeches separated by plebeian response, and a final dialogic exchange with the plebeians leading to their uprising.

It takes Antony a moment to get the crowd's attention, which allows Shakespeare to establish the crowd's possible antagonism toward Antony following Brutus's speech. Then Antony gives his first long speech on Caesar's ambition ("Friends, Romans, countrymen . . . ," 3.2.82–117), dismantling Brutus's argument with logical evidence contradictory to Caesar's alleged "ambition." This first speech, however logical (logos), ends with Antony weeping, thus introducing pathos into the argument. Antony is interrupted by the plebeian commentary (3.2.118–129), then begins his second long oration ("But yesterday the word of Caesar . . . ," 3.2.130–149), reinforcing the ironical approach to "honorable men" and introducing what will be his trump card: Caesar's will. The next segment is a conversation between Antony and the plebeians (3.2.150–180) as he baits them to make him read Caesar's will. One interesting comment Antony makes here is to tell the crowd, "You are not wood, you are not stones, but men" (3.2.154). Your students will remember that Marullus had said the exact opposite to the plebeians in the opening scene of the play (1.1.39–40). Ask your students who they think is right, Antony or Marullus, as a way of focusing their attention on the crowd. By this point in Antony's address, the plebeians are calling Brutus and Cassius traitors and have comprehended the irony of "honorable men" in Antony's argument. Lines 169–180 offer the opportunity for a good bit of stage business as Antony descends to the crowd. Have students trace the stage directions in the dialogue and perhaps give directions for performance.

At line 181, Antony begins his third speech ("If you have tears, prepare to shed them now"). This speech focuses on the cloaked body of Caesar, as Mark Antony describes individual wounds in Caesar's mantle and connects each with the person who made the wound, culminating with Brutus's "most unkindest cut of all"

(3.2.195). As Antony notices the emotional effect he's having on the crowd, he punctuates the spectacle by removing Caesar's cloak and showing the body itself. In a speech attributed in the Folger edition to the crowd, we see their emotions running hot: "Revenge! About! Seek! Burn! Fire! Kill! / Slay! Let not a traitor live!" (3.2.216–217). You may want to remind your students that these are the same citizens who but 10 minutes earlier wanted to set up a statue of Brutus in his honor. Antony is then in the enviable position of having to calm (though not seriously) the crowd in order to play his trump card. His fourth speech ("Good friends, sweet friends, let me not stir you up . . . ," 3.2.222–244) allows Antony to reinforce each of the rhetorical strategies he has used in the scene and introduce his own ethos as "a plain blunt man" (3.2.230), "no orator, as Brutus is" (3.2.229), comparing the two speeches and men. The final segment of his persuasive argument is an extended dialogue with the plebeians revealing the contents of Caesar's will. After discovering that they are heirs to Caesar's fortune, the crowd can no longer control themselves, and they depart, mob-like, carrying Caesar's body, intending to burn the houses of Caesar's assassins. Left alone, Antony comments on his successful performance: "Now let it work. Mischief, thou art afoot; / Take thou what course thou wilt" (3.2.275–276).

The scene ends with a short section between Antony and Octavius's servant (just as Act 3, scene 1 ends). It may seem odd that Antony had told the servant to stay to hear his speech then report it to Octavius and that the servant was able to do so in the space of two spoken lines and perhaps 5–10 seconds of stage time. Students can discuss possible ways to address this problem in performance. Perhaps the servant left earlier in the scene when he saw that the people were stirred against Brutus and Cassius, or perhaps this is another servant. A third option is to acknowledge what is often referred to as time compression in Shakespeare, for the sake of stage movement. We simply suspend our disbelief and accept that events that would take perhaps take hours or days can be addressed in a few seconds of stage time. The plebeians have left the stage only seconds before, but Brutus and Cassius are already "rid like madmen through the gates of Rome" (3.2.285). Here we can see the beginning of the "civil strife" that Antony has prophesied.

Act 3, Scene 3

This scene is very short and features none of the principal characters, unless we conceptualize the Roman mob as a major character in this play (as I do). This is the last public scene in the streets of Rome. (Indeed, following the short proscription scene at the beginning of Act 4, the rest of the play will take place away from Rome itself.) We could argue that this scene, the senseless mob murder of the poet Cinna, is the real turning point of the play. In this interpretation, the play that has focused from its opening scene on the rhetorical battle to win over public opinion culminates in an act of violence by a Roman crowd that has lost its ability to reason. They tear a man to pieces simply because he shares the same name as Cinna the conspirator. When the man offers a reason for them not to kill him, "I am Cinna the poet!" (3.3.30), they dislodge themselves from the restraints of reason as they fall upon him: "Tear him for his bad verses, tear him for his bad verses!" (3.3.31-32). If you have a copy of Plutarch, you can show your students what Shakespeare adds to the source. In Plutarch, Cinna is brutally murdered because the crowd mistakes him for Cinna the conspirator. In Shakespeare, even when the crowd is told they have the wrong man, they murder him anyway. Ask students to discuss why Shakespeare would make such a change. That being said, however, the scene may also be staged with humor, as suggested by Holmes (2001). The exchanges between the crowd and the poet seem to support a humorous reading, although the actual death of the poet would be incongruous with such a reading. As Bate (2008) pointed out, Shakespeare first showed a character (clerk) being killed (lynched) simply for being literate in *Henry VI, Part 2*. Students can argue the importance of this scene and what it contributes to the overall play in performance. Students can read this scene out loud and compare it to other scenes they may have encountered of mob violence such as Shirley Jackson's "The Lottery" or the killing of Simon in *Lord of the Flies*. See the discussion questions at the end of Chapter 6 for more ideas related to this scene.

DISCUSSION/JOURNAL TOPIC: ACT 3, SCENE 3. CUT IT OR KEEP IT?

Have students argue why, in a stage production of *Julius Caesar*, they would include the scene with Cinna and the mob or cut it. Have them give reasons supporting either case, and then have them discuss whether, if it were to be included, it would result in the poet's death (as in Shakespeare's source, Plutarch).

Act 4

Act 4 marks a shift in the play, not only because Caesar is no longer living, but also because Rome has seen a complete breakdown in its power structure. A triumvirate of rulers has taken command, composed of Antony, Lepidus, and Octavius. This act in the play shows the new leadership of Rome and what may be called the rebel camp of Brutus and Cassius. None of the other conspirators from Acts 1–3 will appear again, and the audience may assume that they have either fled or been killed. The most notable death mentioned in the remainder of the script is Cicero, who has no part in the assassination in either Plutarch or Shakespeare.

Act 4, Scene 1

Commonly referred to as the "proscription scene," Act 4, scene 1 is a short scene with two sections.

1. Triumvirs discuss proscription list of condemned men.
2. Antony and Octavius discuss Lepidus and their enemies.

The scene shifts us again from the public streets of Rome to a private room. It opens with Mark Antony, Octavius, and Lepidus, the new leaders of Rome, perhaps sitting around a table, developing a list of men who shall be put to death. The reasons for their deaths are not given, but we may suppose that the men pose threats real or imagined, enough to warrant their disposal in the minds of the triumvirs. Within 11 lines of dialogue, the same Antony who thrilled us with his passionate and effective oratory before the Roman public in Act 3, scene 2 shocks us with his nonchalance over the condemnation of his own nephew and disgusts us with his desire to cheat the Romans out of their inheritance from Caesar. I would suggest that you start study of this scene by first asking students what they think of Antony following the funeral oration. Do they like him as a character? Do they admire his loyalty to his friend Caesar? Then have them read this scene in class and determine how and whether the Antony presented matches the Antony they have in their minds. Shakespeare gives us a little twist by having Antony send Lepidus to "fetch" the will of Caesar and discuss how they may "cut off some charge in legacies," or reduce the amount of money the citizens shall inherit (4.1.11). One may wonder why a servant isn't sent on such an errand. Is it simply a way to get Lepidus out of the room, or is the will of Caesar of such import that only one of them may handle it safely?

Once Lepidus leaves, Antony begins a long and detailed criticism of Lepidus to Octavius, questioning his worthiness to be an equal to the two of them. Students will enjoy the parallels Antony makes between Lepidus and an ass and then a horse. Octavius, for his part, will not participate in the criticism, and we see here the very beginning of a rivalry between Antony and Octavius that will resurface in later scenes and, a few years later in history and in Shakespeare's career, form a central conflict in *Antony and Cleopatra*. Also notable in Antony's criticism of Lepidus is the complaint about his taste in the arts (4.1.40–43). Have students compare and contrast these lines with Caesar's critique of Cassius as told to Antony in 1.2.208–220. The scene continues Shakespeare's depiction of these great and powerful men subject to the most basic of human jealousies.

The scene ends with a short dialogue about Brutus and Cassius, who have raised armies against the triumvirate. Notable here, again, is the compression of time. Octavius portrays their situation as unfavorable, comparing them to a bear tied to a stake and surrounded by dogs. Historically, just a short walk from

Shakespeare's Globe Theatre, where this play may have been the first one performed, were bear-bating arenas. This scene has introduced us to Octavius, who has far fewer lines than Antony. Have students try to develop a preliminary character sketch of Octavius based on what he says in this scene. Later, they will be able to compare their first impressions with Octavius as he appears in Act 5. Ask students why Octavius ends the scene with the line, "And some that smile have in their hearts, I fear, / Millions of mischiefs" (4.1.54–55).

Act 4, Scene 2

This short scene prefaces the scene that follows. The scene does, however, have three distinct sections.

1. Brutus greets Cassius's man Pindarus.
2. Brutus questions Lucilius regarding Cassius's temper.
3. Cassius enters and starts his complaint to Brutus in front of troops.

In this scene, we are no longer in Rome but in a military camp in Sardis, far to the east of Rome in what is now Turkey. The change from the Roman streets we encountered in the beginning of the play is stark, telling us that the actions of the conspirators have resulted in a civil war. In fact, the remainder of the stage action is remote from Rome, and nearly 2 years have passed in historical time, although Shakespeare compresses the time to give a sense that events are unfolding quickly. The scene also gives the impression that entire armies of men are present or nearby, so extra actors may be added to the stage to create the sense of armies. The first section opens with army commands:

Brutus: Stand ho!
Lucilius: Give the word, ho, and stand! (4.2.1–2)

These lines may make no sense to your students if you do not imagine an army in a camp, milling about. The effect on stage, though, if well done, can paint a clear picture of military commands and bearing. "Stand" means "stop," so the signal to the actors is to stop, perhaps to form lines, to allow Pindarus to enter, and eventually to allow Cassius to enter as a commander. The scene also introduces several new characters. It is not uncommon for Shakespeare to bring in new characters in the later stages of a play, but there are four here, and there will be another handful of soldiers in speaking roles introduced in the final act. Students may want to diagram the relationships between the soldiers, servants, and generals. In Act 4, we meet for the first time Lucilius, Pindarus, Messala, Titinius, a poet, Varro, and Claudius.

The first conversational unit between Brutus, his soldier Lucilius, and Cassius's soldier Pindarus works as a short prelude to the action to come. Brutus informs Pindarus that he is displeased with Cassius. The scene paints Brutus and Cassius as rivals, even though they are allies. When Brutus says, "Your master, Pindarus / In his own change or by ill officers, / Hath given me some worthy cause to wish / Things done undone" (4.2.6–9), what is he referring to? Use this guiding question as a preface to the conversation that Brutus and Cassius will have in this and the following scene. Is Brutus referring to the actions of Cassius or to something greater, such as the assassination of Caesar?

The second section of the scene is often interpreted as a private conversation between Brutus and Lucilius, even though Pindarus is present. Brutus questions Lucilius for information on Cassius's treatment of Lucilius, wanting to gain a sense of Cassius's demeanor. When Lucilius describes a change in Cassius's behavior, Brutus issues his first personal criticism of Cassius. Have students read Brutus's speech in lines 21–30 regarding Cassius's attitude and Cassius's behavior in the scene that follows. Ask students to describe why Brutus might call Cassius a "hollow" man.

ACTIVITY: WE ARE THE HOLLOW MEN.

Analyze the T. S. Eliot poem "The Hollow Men" in comparison to *Julius Caesar*. How is the poem apparently connected to Shakespeare's text?

The final section of this scene is a preamble to the next scene, which is the longest in the play. Cassius minces no words as he approaches Brutus and immediately states, "Most noble brother, you have done me wrong" (4.2.41). Your students will notice that this scene combines the public and the private and reminds us of the continual movement between the two. Brutus makes the difference explicit as he tells Cassius to save his argument until they are in Brutus's tent, away from the armies. Cassius agrees, and we are set for the famous quarrel scene.

Act 4, Scene 3

I divide this scene into eight sections or conversational units. They include the following, which will be discussed further below:
1. Brutus and Cassius argue.
2. Brutus and Cassius make amends.
3. Poet bursts into the tent.
4. Brutus tells Cassius of Portia's death.
5. Titinius and Messala enter and give news of armies.
6. Brutus and Cassius argue tactics.

7. Brutus dismisses Cassius and others and retires.
8. Brutus is visited by Caesar's ghost.

I encourage you to keep in mind a couple of things while reading this scene with your students. First, by this point in their reading of the script of *Julius Caesar*, your students will be familiar enough with the language and the characters that they may be comfortable reading on their own. Second, this scene provides an outstanding performance piece for classroom workshopping (see Chapter 7 for a variety of ideas). What I suggest, then, is that you assign students to read the scene for homework, but with the understanding that they come to class with some ideas for how the scene should be staged. You may even divide the class into groups and give each group a chunk of the scene, having them develop stage directions for actors.

ACTIVITY (SAS #14): STAGING THE QUARREL SCENE.

Have students read on their own Act 4, scene 3, lines 1–119 and make notes for performance based on suggestions for action (signals) in the dialogue. Have them bring their staging ideas to class and then share in groups, taking the most interesting ideas and combining them to create an effective description of stage action.

The first section of the scene, the argument, runs from lines 1–119. The argument follows a series of arcs in intensity. As the scene opens, Cassius is already upset, and an actor will need to decide whether to make that anger explicit or keep it under the surface. Cassius critiques Brutus for disciplining a man for taking bribes, despite Cassius's letters written in his favor. The hint of possible physical violence between the two surfaces early on, spoken by Cassius: "You know that you are Brutus that speaks this, / Or, by the gods, this speech were else your last." (4.3.14–15). Brutus reminds Cassius of the original reasons for the conspiracy against Julius Caesar (4.3.19–29). What is odd about the speech is that "supporting robbers" is never mentioned in Acts 1 and 2 in the arguments laid out by Brutus and Cassius for killing Caesar. You and your students may note that in a play that is filled with highly rhetorical arguments, this most intense argument scene degenerates into almost childish antithesis, as shown here:

Cassius:	Brutus, bait not me.
	I'll not endure it. You forget yourself
	To hedge me in. I am a soldier, I,
	Older in practice, abler than yourself
	To make conditions.
Brutus:	Go to! You are not, Cassius.

Cassius:	I am.
Brutus:	I say you are not.
Cassius:	Urge me no more. I shall forget myself.
	Have mind upon your health. Tempt me no farther.
Brutus:	Away, slight man! (4.3.30–40)

This line, "Away, slight man!" may provide a stage signal for the actor portraying Brutus to establish physical intimidation because Cassius backs off, and Brutus presses his advantage. When Cassius suggests that Caesar himself would not have dared to upset him, Brutus soundly rejects his claim, indicating that Brutus saw Caesar clearly as Cassius's better. After Brutus lays out his complaint in lines 78–86, he stakes his honor against his life by stating that the gods should "dash him to pieces" if he grows "covetous" (4.3.88–91). The argument again degenerates into "I denied you not." / "You did." / "I did not" (4.3.92–94) until Cassius, in dramatic fashion, calls on the enemies, Antony and Octavius, to kill him. Cassius's speech marks the fourth point in the play that a character has offered himself up to be sacrificed, and also the fourth point in the play that Cassius has mentioned a willingness to die. Your students, if they are reading well, will see a pattern in the character and the story.

ACTIVITY (SAS #15): "THERE IS MY DAGGER, AND HERE MY NAKED BREAST."

Each of the four leading characters in this play offers himself up to be killed. Have students find and compare the situations and the effects of the offers of self-sacrifice made by Caesar, Antony, Brutus, and Cassius. When students read Act 5 and see the manner in which both Cassius and Brutus die, they will see the culmination of this pattern.

For Cassius, apparently, the principal reason to die is that Brutus loved Caesar more than he loves Cassius (4.3.117–119). Ask your students to consider the legitimacy of Cassius's reasoning. The second section in the scene, which follows from Brutus's "Sheath your dagger" (4.3.120–121), shows two men speaking more like lovers than military giants and co-conspirators. Students may notice the emotional tenor of the exchanges, and may find the scene almost farcical if viewed only as an argument between friends. Both men speak in terms of possession, such as "his Brutus," (4.3.129) and "your Brutus" (4.3.141) and give their hearts and love to each other. Humphreys (1984) commented on how this scene presents emotional vulnerability in Cassius while Brutus appears somewhat harsh, thus increasing our sympathy for Cassius.

The entrance of an unidentified poet, who oddly bursts in to make sure the generals are getting along with one another, interrupts the moment of reconciliation between the two men. Although the interruption is found in Shakespeare's source, this man, Favonius, is referred to in Plutarch (2003) as a "philosopher" (p. 197). Why Shakespeare portrays him as a poet may be worth discussion. The last poet seen on stage in this play (Cinna) didn't fare too well. This one is not treated much better, as Brutus and Cassius dismiss the man without acknowledging the veracity of his concern. Brutus's reaction to him, for some reason, is more harsh than Cassius's reaction. Does Brutus's treatment of the poet fit with our sense of him? Ask your students why Shakespeare would insert this short interlude into the script.

In the fourth section of the scene, Brutus shares the most intimate detail of all. He tells Cassius that Portia is dead. Coming right behind the pseudo-lovers' quarrel of Brutus and Cassius, the news effectively ends all feminine influence in the story. Brutus shows his "stoicism" in receiving the news, and turns to matters military. Beginning the fifth section of the scene, Messala and Titinius enter. Messala gives the news regarding the powers of Octavius and Antony, and the death of the senators. When Messala also delicately leads into the news of Portia, we have an odd moment. Why does Brutus let Messala deliver news that we already know Brutus has? Ask students how they think the actor playing Brutus should act through the two points when he speaks about Portia. Eventually, he says, "Well, to our work alive" (4.3.224), and thus the scene enters its sixth section, the military strategy session.

This sixth section will mark the final time that Brutus overrides Cassius's advice, and you may want to recount with your students each time in the script that Cassius has advised Brutus to no avail, beginning back in Act 2, scene 1, when Brutus first joins the conspiracy. Every decision Brutus has made over Cassius's objections has proven to be wrong, and students will note the sadness of this last attempt by Cassius to persuade Brutus not to march to Philippi. In other words, in a play that highlights powers of persuasion, Cassius succeeds in persuading Brutus to join the conspiracy against Caesar, then fails miserably to persuade Brutus to follow his advice thereafter. When Cassius says to Brutus, "Hear me, good brother—" (4.3.243), only to be cut off, his resolution fails, and he listens to Brutus go on about the "tide in the affairs of men" (4.3.249), accepting a battle tactic he believes is wrong. Indeed, in Act 5, Cassius will ask Messala to bear witness that Cassius goes to battle against his will (5.1.81–83), thus, in essence, asking Messala to report rightly the error in judgment shown by Brutus. At the end of this section, the men depart as brothers, each pledging no more division between them.

> ## ACTIVITY (SAS #16): BRUTUS VS. CASSIUS.
>
> Have students list each disagreement Brutus and Cassius have about the right action to take, beginning with Act 2, scene 1, line 124 and continuing through the end of Act 4. Place Cassius's advice and Brutus's decision side by side, then list the outcome of each situation. Finally, consider who is right. Answers students give may depend upon the outcome of the situation or the morality of the decision. This will give students the opportunity to discuss whether bad means can lead to good ends in politics.

The seventh section of the scene shows a return to the tenderness Brutus has shown to the boy Lucius, showing the audience the closest thing to a domestic situation that is possible in a military tent. The boy is asked to play a tune, and he falls asleep at his instrument. Ask your students to consider why Shakespeare would include such a sequence after the intensity of what has just happened in the scene.

This short sequence sets up the final section in the scene, which is the appearance of Caesar's ghost. Students may do research on other Shakespeare plays that contain ghosts and will discover that it is a frequent plot device, something that Elizabethan theatre-goers would love. And why not? Today's audiences still love to see ghosts used in stories and movies. But Shakespeare is merely reflecting Plutarch in this sequence, and even gives the ghost the same quotes from North's translation of Plutarch, "Thy evil spirit, Brutus" (4.3.325) and "thou shalt see me at Philippi" (4.3.327). Have students consider Brutus's reaction to the ghost and his actions of waking the others in his tent when the ghost disappears. Does Brutus seem surprised or worried that the ghost has appeared? Why or why not? How should an actor play this sequence?

Act 5

The final act of *Julius Caesar* moves quickly. A script and a story that has exploited various means of argument and persuasion at last ends in war. Students will want to read the five-scene act with whatever predictions or unanswered questions they have handy, looking for signs of resolution, not only of the greater revenge tragedy, but of previously identified themes and tropes.

Act 5, Scene 1

This scene has four sections, each of which can be further analyzed for shifts in focus.

1. Octavius and Antony discuss strategy.

2. Parley between the generals.
3. Cassius hints at his own coming death with Messala.
4. Brutus and Cassius bid each other farewell.

The first section of the scene offers us an opportunity to see the dynamic between the young Octavius and Antony. Although in retrospect it is tempting to see this scene as a prelude to the conflict between the two men in *Antony and Cleopatra*, Shakespeare had not yet written that play and would not for several years. But perhaps he already was thinking about it when he showed how Octavius, the nephew of Julius Caesar, coolly and authoritatively exercises the same veto over Antony that Brutus has exercised over Cassius. While we have just seen Brutus rejecting Cassius's desire to wait for the opposing army to march toward Sardis, here we see that Brutus once again has played into the enemies' hands and shown poor judgment. Octavius indicates their advantage in his first speech, but also points out that Antony has predicted otherwise. When Antony tells Octavius to take the "left hand of the even field" (5.1.17–18) with his troops, Octavius simply responds, "Upon the right hand, I; keep thou the left" (5.1.19), Antony questions his disagreement, and Octavius says, again simply, "I do not cross you, but I will do so" (5.1.21). The line has an ambiguity in the phrase "I will do so." Is Octavius simply repeating that he will take the right side, or that he will cross Antony at a later time? Ask students to compare this exchange with the dialogue between the two men in Act 4, scene 1 to determine the balance of power between them and to also listen to how the two of them speak with Brutus and Cassius in the second section of the scene.

The meeting between the two "powers" in the second section of this scene represents the complete breakdown in what we would call diplomatic relations today. If the argument between Brutus and Cassius in Act 4, scene 3 represents a deterioration in the high rhetoric prevalent in the first three acts, this scene shows it disintegrating further into personal bitterness and insult. To believe that such an exchange as the one that occurs between lines 28 and 68 involves the rival leaders of a great republic is to acknowledge that all politics, all power, is subject to the frailties and jealousies of human individuals.

ACTIVITY: WHO IS MORE BELIEVABLE?

Choose student actors to split into two "camps" to read Act 5, scene 1, lines 28–68 and perform the segment so that it makes their chosen side look favorable. Have students discuss their gut reactions as to whom they favor in the battle.

Notice in reading the exchange that Brutus and Cassius are clearly aware that Antony's words have changed the situation in Rome. Brutus and Cassius appear to feel as though Antony has double-crossed them, while Antony and Octavius stick to the theme of Caesar's death. Cassius reminds Brutus that his leniency toward Antony in the conspiracy has led them to this place. Brutus talks of honor and Cassius rails against the "peevish schoolboy" (Octavius; 5.1.65) and the "masker and a reveler" (Antony; 5.1.66).

A telling line, and one of my favorites, is Antony's response to Cassius's insult: "Old Cassius still" (5.1.67). Antony knows Cassius's personality well and perhaps remembers Caesar's earlier warning to him about how dangerous Cassius is. Could Antony smile in recognizing that Cassius, at least, is consistent in his character? The complaint against Antony's love of the arts (masker and reveler) demonstrates the extent to which Cassius's personal intolerance fuels his actions. Perhaps most important in this scene of hurled insults in the place of cool argument is that Octavius speaks more than we have seen before, and it is Octavius who breaks off the parley and calls for the battle, establishing himself as the leader of the Roman army.

The exit of Octavius and Antony leads to the next section of the scene, which I call Cassius's lament. He questions his philosophy and, as mentioned before, he asks Messala to "witness" that he is entering the battle against his will. Even though he loves Brutus and in the final section of the scene will part with him as a brother, Cassius is still very conscious that Brutus's inability to listen to his advice has led to the situation they are in. It is sad on the one hand and self-vindicating on the other. He also explains a portent that worries him, regarding the birds that are following their armies. Have students read his speech here (5.1.78–96), then go back and read Cassius's speech to Casca in Act 1, scene 3, during the storm (1.3.60–81). Have students examine how Cassius has changed.

The final section of this scene shows the last meeting between Brutus and Cassius. Have students read this scene for both tone and content. Cassius wants to know from Brutus whether he will kill himself if captured by the opposing side, and he gets a mixed response. Brutus deplores suicide, yet he will not "go bound to Rome" (5.1.122). His lines foreshadow how he will die in Act 5, scene 5. Ask students to examine Brutus's words that follow:

> *Brutus:*   O, that a man might know
> The end of the day's business ere it come!
> But it sufficeth that the day will end,
> And then the end is known. (5.1.133–136)

How does the fatalism in these lines compare with Caesar's fatalism prior to his assassination? Are Cassius and Brutus inviting the worst to happen by imagining the possibility of it happening? Finally, if Shakespeare wishes us to see Brutus and Cassius as the villains in this story, why does he give them this moving final exchange in the script?

Act 5, Scenes 2 and 3

These two scenes have a total of five sections, as follows.
1. Scene 2, Brutus orders an attack.
2. Scene 3 opening, Cassius, Titinius, and Pindarus.
3. Pindarus gives mistaken report and kills Cassius.
4. Titinius returns with good news but finds Cassius dead and kills himself.
5. Brutus and others find Cassius and Titinius; Brutus eulogizes Cassius.

Scene 2 contains a total of 6 lines, one speech spoken by Brutus commanding Messala to send his legions on the attack. We may wonder why Shakespeare would include such a short scene as a stand-alone, but we must remember that the armies of Cassius and Brutus have split to fight against Octavius and Antony respectively. Therefore, in stage action, a director would give the illusion of different parts of the battlefield. Also, we will find out later that Brutus's command works, as his army defeats Octavius, but for Cassius and Titinius, from a distance, Brutus "gave the word too early" (5.3.5) and thus cannot help prevent them from being overcome by Antony. When Cassius perceives a fire in his tents from a distance, ironically, it is a physical defect in Cassius, his poor eyesight (5.3.22), which makes him dependent on Pindarus to report what is happening there. Cassius, who has hated Caesar for his physical defects, now will die following a mistaken report, but notice how Cassius is already resolved to die before Pindarus gives him the seemingly bad news (5.3.24–26). Cassius wastes no time asking Pindarus to kill him, giving him a command and the promise of freedom. Have students note that Cassius considers himself a coward not for contemplating suicide, but for living as long as he has. Cassius's last words are not for Rome, not for Brutus, not even for himself. Instead, he addresses the man he assassinated: "Caesar, thou art revenged / Even with the sword that killed thee" (5.3.50–51). After Pindarus runs off, this section of the scene ends. Why does Pindarus run off, and how is it a reminder of Roman class society?

Titinius, returning with Messala to give good news to Cassius, finds him dead. Have students read this and the final section of this scene paying attention to the way others speak about Cassius. Is he reviled as a villain? Is he honored as a hero? What do the words of Titinius, Messala, and Brutus tell us about Cassius that we didn't already know? Titinius calls him "the sun of Rome" (5.3.70) and shows despair. Messala philosophizes on Cassius's poor perception:

> O hateful error, melancholy's child,
> Why dost thou show to the apt thoughts of men
> The things that are not? O error, soon conceived,

Thou never com'st unto a happy birth
But kill'st the mother that engendered thee! (5.3. 75–79)

The allusion to a killed mother is not without significance in a tragedy that is filled with error in masculine judgment in the absence of feminine wisdom.

After Messala exits to give Brutus the bad news, we see a classic Shakespearean device of a minor character speaking poetically of a major character who has fallen. Titinius's suicide speech marks one of the most tender moments in the script. He shows almost feminine care in placing the wreath on Cassius's brow and then taking his own life. In a play where men are "lovers," Titinius shows the greatest measure of devotion to his fallen leader. Ask students how this scene parallels the scene with Antony offering a crown to Caesar as described by Casca in Act 1, scene 2.

The final section of Act 5, scene 3 brings Brutus on stage to find his dead friend and eulogize him while still keeping the focus on the battle at hand. He references the spirit of Julius Caesar and calls Cassius "the last of all the Romans" (5.3.111). What Brutus means by this is unclear—ask your students what they think.

DISCUSSION/JOURNAL TOPIC: CASSIUS, "THE LAST OF ALL THE ROMANS"?

Using the words used to describe him during his life and after his death, have students evaluate Cassius as they interpret him. Is he a tragic hero? An evil villain? A sidekick?

Act 5, Scene 4

By this point in Act 5, your students may notice that the action stays more with Brutus and Cassius's side than with Antony and Octavius. We meet in this scene young Cato, son of Marcus Cato, challenging the other army and boasting his name, only to be killed within the space of two lines. Students can imagine that this part of the production involves a good deal of stage combat, which would excite a crowd that's been listening to speeches and arguments for more than 2 hours. Cato's role and the deception of Lucilius, posing as Brutus and being taken to Antony, are both documented in Plutarch. Also noted in Plutarch (2003) is Antony's treatment of Lucilius, taking him in as a "friend" (p. 205). Historically, Lucilius then served Antony until his death, according to Plutarch. Here is an example of how the lines between friend and enemy start to blur. Unlike other commonly taught Shakespeare tragedies, such as *Hamlet* and *Macbeth*, the lines between good and evil are never clear in this text and are certainly blurred in the resolution.

Act 5, Scene 5

The final scene in the script is short and has two sections:
1. The death of Brutus.
2. The discovery of Brutus by Antony and Octavius.

The scene brings to an end the battle, the story, the life of Brutus, and the revenge of Caesar. Students may benefit from reading this scene as actors spread over a stage, as there is a great deal of shifting between Brutus and each of his men as he asks them, one by one, to kill him. We meet four new characters in this scene: Dardanus, Clitus, Volumnius, and Strato. Students will notice in the Folger edition a number of bracketed stage directions aimed at helping us visualize the action of Brutus whispering to his men. With just the dialogue, it is difficult to visualize the stage action, but students can do so with a cleared stage area in the classroom. We do not hear Brutus's first two requests to be killed (Clitus and Dardanus), but we hear his third and fourth requests, amidst the panic and turmoil of being attacked. Brutus delivers his famous last speech to his men, claiming,

> Countrymen,
> My heart doth joy that yet in all my life
> I found no man but he was true to me.
> I shall have glory by this losing day
> More than Octavius and Mark Antony
> By this vile conquest shall attain unto. (5.5.37–42).

Brutus is thinking of his own legacy, yet he says nothing of Rome. Is the future of his beloved republic implicit in his speech, or is he simply thinking about himself? Ask your students what they think. Also worth noticing in this scene are the tears of the stoic Brutus, as described by Clitus (5.5.15–16).

Three of Brutus's men disobey his order by refusing to kill him. When Strato agrees to hold his sword while Brutus runs on it, he fulfills Brutus's claim to Cassius that he would not slay himself, yet, of course, students will see that he effectively does kill himself, even if he doesn't hold the sword. Ask students to compare Brutus's final words to the final words of Caesar and Cassius. What do those words reveal about Brutus? Again, he makes no mention of Rome, only mentioning the friend he has betrayed, Caesar, and the desire that Caesar's spirit rest.

The final segment of the final scene, the eulogizing of Brutus by Antony and Octavius, further complicates our vision of these characters. The kind treatment of Messala, Lucilius, and Strato by their conquerors sets us up for the praise Antony and Octavius heap on Brutus. Have students discuss whether they believe Antony when he calls Brutus "the noblest Roman of them all" (5.5.74). How does his speech change or affect our interpretation of the other things he has said about Brutus? We are left with the two avengers of Caesar's death parting "the glories of this happy day" (5.5.87) and carrying off Brutus's body to be honored in Octavius's tent.

This chapter has taken us scene by scene through the script as a guide to reading in class with students. Chapter 6 will further explore opportunities the text presents for class discussions and debates, Chapter 7 will discuss interpretation through performance, and Chapter 8 will present ideas for writing about *Julius Caesar*.

Chapter Materials

Name: _____ Date: _____

Student Activity Sheet #8:
Is It Real or Is It Supernatural?

Applicable Portion of Play: Act 1, scene 3.

Objectives: 1. Students will interpret descriptions of the storm in Act 1, scene 3 as rational or supernatural.
2. Students will be able to support their categories with logical explanations.

Common Core Standard(s): 11-12.R.L.1, 11-12.R.L.4

Directions: Examine Casca's description of the storm and the things he has seen in Act 1, scene 3, which he interprets as unnatural. Then, construct possible rational explanations for the occurrences, and divide the sights described into two columns: those descriptions that may have natural causes, and those for which there are no rational explanations. For example, when Casca claims that this is the first time he's been through a tempest "dropping fire," could he be describing lightning? Discuss what those signs say about the time.

Natural	Supernatural

Advanced Placement Classroom: Julius Caesar © Prufrock Press • This page may be photocopied or reproduced with permission for single classroom use.

Student Activity Sheet #9:
The Women: Similarities and Differences in Their Tactics

Applicable Portion of Play: Act 2, scenes 1 and 2.

Objectives: 1. Students will compare and contrast the characters of Portia and Calphurnia.
2. Students will analyze rhetorical strategies of the wives.

Common Core Standard(s): 11-12.R.L.1, 11-12.R.I.6, 11-12.R.L.3

Directions: Read the scene between Portia and Brutus (Act 2, scene 1, lines 253–333) and the scene between Caesar and Calphurnia (Act 2, scene 2, lines 8–110). Construct a Venn diagram to compare and contrast the tactics that the two women use to persuade their husbands. Share your findings with your fellow students and the teacher, and discuss them as a class. Then summarize your findings in a paragraph.

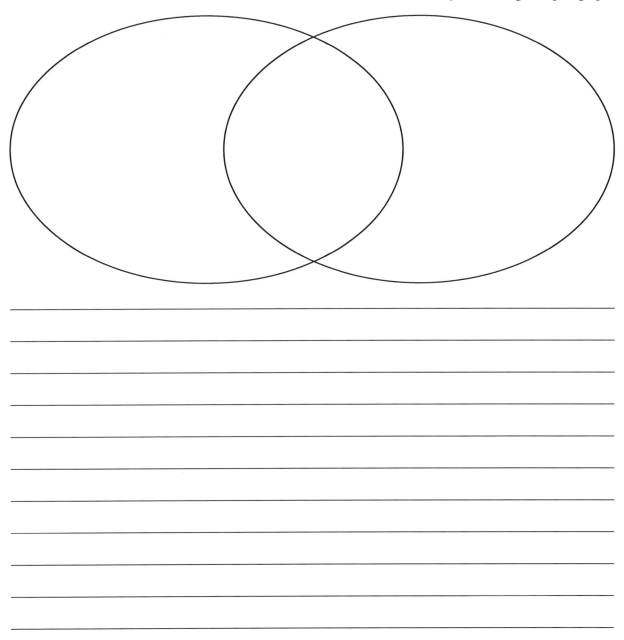

_____

_____

_____

_____

_____

_____

_____

_____

_____

_____

Student Activity Sheet #10:
Caesar Walking Into Death

Applicable Portion of Play: Act 2, scene 2 through Act 3, scene 1.

Objectives:
1. Students will draw inferences regarding Caesar the character by studying his reactions to arguments and signs contrary to his stated intention of going to the Capitol.
2. Students will construct a well-reasoned argument using textual evidence.
3. Students will use discussion to disagree appropriately regarding interpretations of Caesar's character.

Common Core Standard(s): 11-12.R.L.1, 11-12.R.L.2, 11-12.W.1.b

Directions: In Act 2, scene 2, Decius arrives at Caesar's house before Mark Antony and persuades Caesar to ignore the advice of his wife and the augurers. From Act 2, scene 2 through the assassination of Caesar in Act 3, scene 1, track how many times Caesar has a chance to save his life by listening to warnings. Analyze statements Caesar makes about death in Act 2, scene 2, and compare those statements to his behavior in the beginning of Act 3. Does Caesar knowingly step into his own assassination, or is he simply unwilling to be superstitious? Does Caesar have a death wish? Choose a side and make an argument in class discussion, using the debate form below.

❏ Caesar believes he is not in danger.
Evidence:

_____

_____

_____

_____

❏ Caesar knows he is in danger and walks into death.
Evidence:

_____

_____

_____

_____

Conclusion:

_____

_____

_____

_____

Name: _____   Date: _____

Student Activity Sheet #11:
Comparing Accounts of Caesar's Assassination in Shakespeare and Plutarch

Applicable Portion of Play: Act 3, scene 1.

Objectives: 1.   Students will compare and contrast accounts of Caesar's assassination in Plutarch and Shakespeare.
2.   Students will be able to describe how Shakespeare adapted Plutarch into his script.

Common Core Standard(s): 11-12.R.L.1, 11-12.R.L.7

Directions: Access the text of Plutarch's "The Life of Julius Caesar" online at http://penelope.uchicago. edu/Thayer/E/Roman/Texts/Plutarch/Lives/Caesar*.html. Chart the progression of events related to Caesar's assassination in Plutarch, then compare those to the dialogue in Act 3, scene 1 of *Julius Caesar*. Chart similarities and differences between the two in your journals or in the boxes below.

Plutarch	Shakespeare

Student Activity Sheet #12:
Prophesies and Portents

Applicable Portion of Play: Acts 1 and 2, and Act 3, scene 1, lines 280–301.

Objective: 1.   Students will compare Mark Antony's "prophesy" with the supernatural events that precede it.

Common Core Standard(s): 11-12.R.L.1, 11-12.R.L.7, 11-12.W.1

Directions: Think about the role of the supernatural to this point in the play. Antony is neither a sooth-sayer nor an augurer, but in Act 3, scene 1, lines 280–301, Antony delivers a soliloquy that prophesies civil war of such bloodiness "That mothers shall but smile when they behold / Their infants quartered with the hands of war." Compare Antony's prediction to the portents described in Act 2, prior to Caesar's assassination. List any similarities between the sights seen in the storm (or in Calphurnia's dream) and the sights Antony conjures.

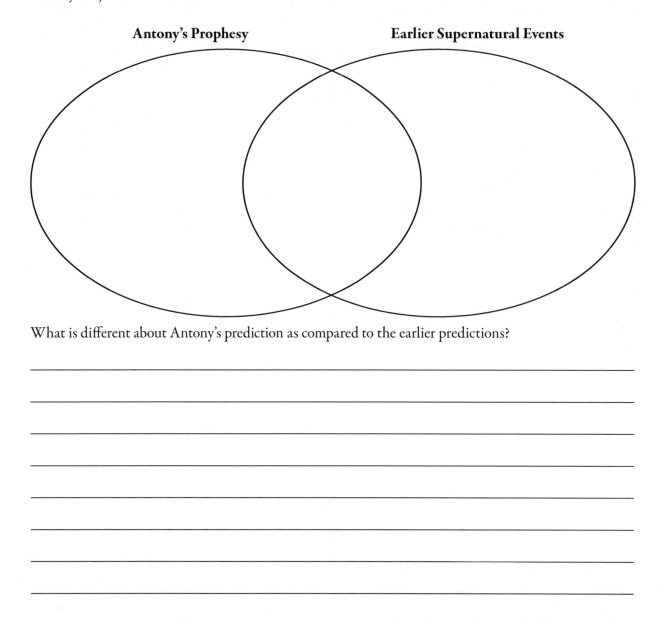

Antony's Prophesy   **Earlier Supernatural Events**

What is different about Antony's prediction as compared to the earlier predictions?

_____

_____

_____

_____

_____

_____

_____

_____

Name: _____   Date: _____

Student Activity Sheet #13A:
Copying Brutus's Rhetoric

Applicable Portion of Play: Act 3, scene 2, lines 14-49.

Objectives: 1. Students will analyze the rhetorical qualities of parallel structure in Brutus's funeral speech.
2. Students will imitate the style of Brutus in an argument of their own.

Common Core Standard(s): 11-12.R.L.1, 11-12.R.I.6, 11-12.W.1

Directions: Brutus uses what we call *parallelism* in his argument. Study Brutus's funeral oration in Act 3, scene 2, lines 14–49, identifying how he structures his sentences. Model Brutus's parallelism in an argument of your own. For example, "As I was busy, I forgot about the assignment, as I was confused, I left some questions blank, as I was hurried, I wrote sloppily, but as I was worried about my grade, I cheated."

_____

_____

_____

_____

_____

_____

_____

_____

_____

_____

_____

_____

_____

_____

_____

_____

_____

_____

_____

_____

Student Activity Sheet #13B:
Ethos, Pathos, Logos

Applicable Portion of Play: Act 3, scene 2

Objectives: 1. Students will analyze the rhetorical strategies of Brutus and Mark Antony in their funeral orations, using the classic strategies of ethos, pathos, and logos.
2. Students will describe how the strategies used in the speeches connect or do not connect with the plebeian crowd.

Common Core Standard(s): 11-12.R.L.1, 11-12.R.I.6, 11-12.W.1

Directions: Compare the funeral speeches of Brutus and Antony in Act 3, scene 2 using the classical strategies of ethos, pathos, and logos. In other words, chart when and how each speaker appeals to the crowd's sense of the speaker's integrity, the crowd's emotions, and the crowd's sense of logic. You may consult the University of Kentucky's rhetorical strategies web page at http://www.uky.edu/AS/Classics/rhetoric.html for help with this and other persuasive speeches in the script.

Brutus	Antony
Ethos	Ethos
Pathos	Pathos
Logos	Logos

Student Activity Sheet #14:
Staging the Quarrel Scene

Applicable Portion of Play: Act 4, scene 3, lines 1–119.

Objectives:
1. Students will examine the script of *Julius Caesar* for performance signals
2. Students will describe possible stage action based on performance signals.

Common Core Standard(s): 11-12.R.L.1, 11-12.R.L.3, 11-12.R.L.5

Directions: Read on your own Act 4, scene 3, lines 1–119 and make notes for performance based on suggestions for action (signals) in the dialogue. Use the chart below to help you. Bring your staging ideas to class, and the class can share in groups, taking the most interesting ideas and combining them to create an effective description of stage action.

Line Number(s)	Signal/Suggested Stage Action

Student Activity Sheet #15:
"There is my dagger, and here my naked breast"

Applicable Portion of Play: All

Objectives: 1. Students will find examples of leading characters offering themselves for sacrifice.
2. Students will explain and compare the effects of the four different "sacrificial offers" made by Caesar, Brutus, Mark Antony, and Cassius.

Common Core Standard(s): 11-12.R.L.1, 11-12.R.L.2

Directions: Each of the four leading characters in this play offers himself up to be killed. Find and compare the situations and the effects of the "offers" of self-sacrifice made by Caesar, Brutus, Antony, and Cassius. Explain how the situations have similar or differing effects on the other characters. When you read Act 5 and see the manner in which both Cassius and Brutus die, you will see the culmination of this pattern.

Chart the act, scene, and situation wherein each character offers his life. Then describe the effect the offer has.

Caesar:

   Act, scene: _____

   Situation: _____

   Effect: _____

Brutus:

   Act, scene: _____

   Situation: _____

   Effect: _____

Antony:

   Act, scene: _____

   Situation: _____

   Effect: _____

Cassius:

   Act, scene: _____

   Situation: _____

   Effect: _____

Student Activity Sheet #16:
Brutus vs. Cassius

Applicable Portion of Play: All

Objectives: 1.   Students will trace situations wherein Brutus overrules the advice of Cassius.
2.   Students will explain the outcomes of Brutus's decisions.
3.   Students will discuss whether bad means can lead to good ends in politics.

Common Core Standard(s): 11-12.R.L.1, 11-12.R.L.2, 11-12.R.L.3

Directions: In the chart below or on a separate page, list each disagreement Brutus and Cassius have about the right action to take, beginning with Act 2, scene 1, line 124 and continuing through the end of Act 4. Place Cassius's advice and Brutus's decision side by side, then list the outcome of each situation. Finally, consider who ends up being right. Share your information in class and discuss the following topic: Based on the decisions of Brutus and Cassius, can good ends come from bad means in politics?

Act and Scene	Cassius's Advice	Brutus's Decision	Outcome

Who is right?

_____

_____

_____

"Friends, Romans, country-men, lend me your ears": Talking About *Julius Caesar*

Many of the best discussions of *Julius Caesar* will grow directly out of the experience of reading that work. The ideal discussion occurs when students are engaged enough with the text that they generate their own questions, leaving the teacher with a list of prepared discussion topics that the class either examines on its own or touches upon through the student-generated discussion, without the teacher having to provide prompts. Chapter 5 presented several discussion/journal prompts growing out of close reading, but those prompts are just the tip of the iceberg for what is possible for discussion of *Julius Caesar*. Certainly, as Jim Burke (1999) asserted, the best English classrooms are built around conversations, and it is through meaningful conversation that we discover what texts have to offer us and what we may bring to the illumination of texts. Eliot Eisner (2001) said that the crisis in our educational system is the lack of meaningful, challenging conversation. Talking about Shakespeare, and particularly *Julius Caesar,* provides the opportunity for challenging, meaningful discussion in a mutually respectful environment.

Although *Julius Caesar* provides us with fruitful classroom discussion opportunities, we need to think about what our goals are related to discussion and how we approach conversation in our classrooms, including how democratic we are in our methods. Granted, discussion in the classroom is rarely an end in itself, as usually our discussions lead to more formal assessment activities, such as writing essays, performing scenes, and answering test questions. We do well, however, to consider broadening our purposes for having discussions around *Julius Caesar*. Any classroom discussion provides an opportunity to develop listening and speaking skills in students, both of which are called for in the Common Core standards.

In this sense, the discussion itself can become the desired outcome, assuming we get broad participation from students. Not every discussion you have around *Julius Caesar* needs to translate into test questions or essay topics. That being said, discussion is a great mode of prewriting, and AP students need frequent chances to practice their writing skills.

Regardless of whether student conversation is the end goal or a means to other ends, how we approach discussion in the classroom often determines how successful we will be. Maureen Neal (2008) demonstrated how a pattern of discourse marked by teacher dominance has deluded many teachers into thinking they are having democratic, mutually beneficial conversation when what they are creating in reality is nothing more than recitation. Neal used Mehan's (1985) identified pattern of initiation, response, and evaluation (IRE) in classroom settings to show how teachers limit student discussion. In such discussions, teachers initiate student response with a prompt (I), and when a student responds (R), the teacher evaluates the response (E), either with approval or disapproval, then initiates a further prompt either to the same student or to another student. Such teacher-dominated exchanges hardly amount to the kinds of investigative, probing discussions envisioned by thoughtful teachers. In order to develop student participation and a more democratic feel to literary discussion, I suggest you take an approach that starts with student response to the reading, through journaling on their own or in connection to your prompts, followed by small-group sharing, and then whole-class discussion. When students have the opportunity to sort out their thoughts in response to their reading and your discussion prompts, then share them with peers in small groups, they are not only more prepared to enter a wider discussion with the teacher and the class, but they will display greater confidence.

A teacher who is prepared to discuss a work of literature from the standpoint of the students is less likely to lapse into IRE patterns that stifle student participation and, in the worst cases, lead to the teacher having a conversation with herself. I suggest that you have an arsenal of topics such as those provided in this chapter, but that you distribute them to students with some lead time, whether it be 5 minutes or a couple of days, before they actually discuss in class. An ideal scenario, if your school's technology permits, is to have students engage in online discussion as they read, then use the online discussion as a primer for in-class, face-to-face discussions. When we design discussion only to force students to the interpretive conclusions we want them to reach, classroom conversation becomes coercive, nothing more than the game of "guess what's in the teacher's head."

The discussion topics suggested in this chapter are divided into several categories, with short explanations of each and possible class activities to enhance them. Because Chapter 4 introduced several prereading strategies, all of which involved discussion, this chapter will not address additional prereading discussion. The first set of topics centers around reading the script, and thus augments the topics suggested in Chapter 5. One of these sets of topics will focus on the theatrical process and use theatre workshop as the basis for generating discussion. This approach also reflects back on activities described in Chapter 5 that involve student acting and prepares us for Chapter 7. Following the reading and performance discussion topics are potential class debate topics from the play. Finally, an additional set of multilevel discussion questions from each scene in the play will provide ideas that should augment what has been presented earlier.

We must remember before we approach any work of literature that discussing the work is never just about the work, but about ourselves. Reader response theory (Rosenblatt, 1983) has taught us that students will always be a part of the text that they encounter, whether they see themselves in the conflict, identify with one or another of the characters, or have a strong visceral reaction to events in the story. The best class discussions respect those connections to self that will inevitably come up when we ask students to discuss Caesar, Brutus, Cassius, Antony, or any of the other characters. Students' life experience becomes part of the realm of discussion, and we can both respect the literary work and stay diligent in our study of the text, yet still honor the interior lives of our students as they encounter these larger-than-life figures from the Roman past.

Reading Discussion Topics

Orientation Topics (Acts 1 and 2)

Topic 1: Setting. Describe the world of Rome as we find it in Act 1. Entering a Shakespeare script can be disorienting to say the least. But like Doctor Who, who time travels to distant planets in the universe, we must take our students to the distant world of Ancient Rome through Shakespeare's Renaissance representation of it. After students have read the first two scenes in the script, have them chat about what they have learned thus far about Rome just from what they've seen in the script. What do they see as the rules operating in the society there? What is the structure of the society? How would they see themselves fitting into Roman society? As plebeians? As patricians? What are the apparent attitudes of the two classes toward each other? Have students refer to the information provided through the "When in Rome . . ." activity described in Chapter 4.

Topic 2: How do these people speak? Have students read passages aloud from the first two scenes and discuss the language used by the characters, including the poetic meter, the imagery, and the apparent tone. Reading aloud will help to generate ideas regarding the speech of the Romans, which Humphreys (1984) described as "rational lyricism" (p. 43). What do students notice about differences in the speech of the plebeians and the tribunes or the major characters?

Topic 3: What is Caesar's situation at the opening of the play? Referring to the prereading activities described in Chapter 4, ask students to summarize what they know or believe to be true of Julius Caesar, the character, prior to reading. Then, taking everything that is said about Caesar in the opening scene and what we actually see and hear of him in Act 1, scene 2, have students describe Caesar and his situation. Ask them to describe his personality and his manner of speaking.

Topic 4: The Stakes Game, Act 1, scene 2. Play the Stakes Game with Act 1, scene 2. Although Chapter 5 presented a number of ideas for examining this scene, another approach is to think of the scene in terms of what is at stake for each character. The Stakes Game is a good discussion tool to use throughout the play, and students can learn it early on, then refer back to it in later scenes. Assign students (or groups of students) to represent each character. For this scene, you would have Caesar, the soothsayer, Cassius, Brutus, and Casca. You can also include Antony and Calphurnia, although neither contributes much to the scene. You, as the teacher, will act as the bank. Imagine that each speaking character in the scene has a certain amount of money that represents that character's "stakes" in the scene. Their stakes refer to what motivates them and how much they have to gain or to lose. Give students a certain amount of money to represent their stakes at the beginning of the scene. (Suggestions: Give Caesar and Cassius each $5,000, give Brutus $3,000, give the soothsayer and Casca each $2,000, and give Antony and Calphurnia each $1,000.)

"Stakes" refer to the importance to the character of what is happening in the scene. For example, in the beginning of Act 1, scene 2, the stakes are high for Caesar because he is in public and must act in a way that becomes a ruler home fresh from conquest. He must sway public opinion in his favor. The stakes are also high for Cassius, who seeks to win Brutus to his cause.

Whenever the stakes change for a character, based upon something that is said or done, the students representing that character either deposit money in the bank when the stakes go down (such as for Cassius when Brutus hints at his dissatisfaction with Caesar) or withdraw money when their stakes go up (such as for Cassius when he is described by Caesar). Discuss the progression of the scene, and every time something is said or done that affects a character's stakes, students can request a transaction.

This discussion game is a good way to get students thinking of characters as operating in a dynamic environment, where things change over time depending upon events. Students can apply the Stakes Game to their own lives, and the discussion can be extended into contemporary situations outside of the text, such as social interactions or school pressures. As their study of the *Julius Caesar* progresses, students may want to play the Stakes Game again, or they may interject comments in later discussions along the lines of "Brutus's stakes just went up." "How much, and why?" you might reply.

Topic 5: What does Cassius want? What does Brutus want? Related to the Stakes Game, but less involved, is a consideration of Cassius and Brutus. In Act 1, Cassius dominates the action and speaks the most lines. He is driven by a need to put together a conspiracy against Caesar, and he needs Brutus to join. Ask students the question, "What does Cassius want?" Have them consider the question beyond just his desire to persuade Brutus to the cause. Have them construct Cassius's version of what Rome stands for, and what gaps he sees between the Rome he imagines and the Rome he sees with Caesar in power. In Act 2, as the focus turns to Brutus and his concerns, have students ask the same questions regarding Brutus in this act as were asked regarding Cassius in Act 1. What does Brutus want? What is his vision for Rome, and how does Caesar threaten that vision?

Discussions of Conflict

Julius Caesar presents conflict from the opening line of the play, and the orientation topics above all address fundamental conflicts in the script. The central conflicts in the early part of the play center around the conspiracy to kill Caesar. Rather than employing the traditional (and sexist) "man vs. man," "man vs. self," and "man vs. nature" designations, it will be more productive for your discussions of conflict to focus instead on specific identification of conflicts such as "Cassius vs. Caesar" or "Brutus vs. his own sense of honor" or "Caesar vs. the omens" or "Antony vs. the conspirators." The best way to approach conflict in discussion is to have students generate a list of conflicts they perceive in the script, share them with each other in small groups, and then collate the list for whole-group discussion. Every conflict will have development points, turning points, and outcomes, so an early conversation of conflicts, many of which are well established by the end of Act 2, can provide material for later discussions. Students can generate visual representations of conflict and post them on the classroom wall. As new conflicts emerge following the assassination of Caesar, students can add those conflicts to the list.

ACTIVITY (SAS #17): CONFLICT.

Have students choose a conflict in *Julius Caesar* that interests them. Have them generate a visual representation of the conflict, tracing events in the script that develop the conflict. For example, students can trace the conflict between Brutus and Cassius by tracing pivotal events in their encounters. As a class, gather the list of conflicts students have generated. Have students discuss the conflict list and determine which conflicts have the most importance in the story.

Using your laptop or tablet technology, you can record the lists generated and make notes on the discussion of conflict, then return to the list for reference in later discussions or projects. Identifying conflicts can give students a sense of purpose when reading subsequent scenes. They can take an inquiry stance toward those conflicts, asking how the conflicts will be resolved. They will be focusing on interactions in the script that have bearing on those conflicts.

Discussions of Character

Students naturally gravitate toward characters in literature, as we need to establish characters we care about before any story involving them makes any difference to us. In this work, we are introduced to some of the most famous characters in human history, and Shakespeare's special talent is to humanize them for us in all of their nobility and imperfection. One aspect of the characters that stands out in *Julius Caesar* is that characters often refer to themselves in the third person. Caesar does it in public and in private, but Brutus, Cassius, and even Portia also refer to themselves in the third person. Humphreys (1984) pointed out that the third person reference could be related to their sense of "romanitas" (p. 40), a code of honor that makes the name a symbol for the person and what the person represents.

Julius Caesar: What is he like in person? Following from the orientation discussion related to the personality of Caesar, have students describe Caesar as he sees himself through his speeches in the script. Have students describe Caesar as other characters see him, including Cassius, Brutus, Portia, Decius, and Antony. What portrait of Caesar emerges from the perceptions of these different characters?

Brutus and Cassius: A study in contrasts. Compare and contrast the two main conspirators, Brutus and Cassius, in terms of their personalities, their philosophies, and their goals. Pay special attention to the reasons each man gives for opposing Caesar and then compare their behavior in their famous argument scene (Act 4, scene 3) and their respective suicides. Have students discuss how the men complement each other successfully and how their differences lead to disharmony and disaster.

Mark Antony: The avenging reveler. Discuss Antony as Caesar playfully describes him in the first two acts of the play, then examine how he emerges from Caesar's shadow in Act 3. How does Antony change in the final two acts, and what is our composite picture of him following his final speech over the body of Brutus?

Octavius Caesar: Young and powerful. Octavius enters the play in Act 4, but he plays a major role in the outcome of events and delivers the final speech in the play. Have students give their impressions of Octavius based on what he does and says to Antony, Brutus, and Cassius. For a great extension activity, or

ACTIVITY: THE THIRD PERSON REFERENCE.

Have students create a conversation for themselves wherein they and other characters speak of themselves in the third person. Have them engage in 5 minutes of classroom conversation, about any topic, using only the third person as opposed to using the first person pronouns "I" and "me," and furthermore referring to their classmates by their names as opposed to using the second person pronoun "you." For example, imagine the following conversation between students:

Shonique: Shonique believes that reading is the key to success in school.
Arthur: Arthur honors Shonique's beliefs, but he admits that he hates to read.
Marieke: Arthur makes Marieke laugh, as she always reads in her spare time.
Curt: Curt has seen Marieke reading, but agrees with both Arthur and Shonique.

Ask students to reflect on how the third person reference changes the tone and intimacy of their conversation, then apply that perception to their reading of *Julius Caesar*. Have students explain why the characters in different situations use the third person. Following the activity, have students discuss the following quotes from the script.

Caesar: Caesar should be a beast without a heart
             If he should stay at home today for fear.
             No, Caesar shall not. Danger knows full well
             That Caesar is more dangerous than he.
             We are two lions littered in one day,
             And I the elder and more terrible.
             And Caesar shall go forth. (2.2.45–51)

Cassius: Cassius from bondage will deliver Cassius. (1.3.93)

Portia: Dwell I but in the suburbs
             Of your good pleasure? If it be no more,
             Portia is Brutus' harlot, not his wife. (2.1.307–310)

Brutus: No, Cassius, no. Think not, thou noble Roman,
             That ever Brutus will go bound to Rome.
             He bears too great a mind. (5.1.121–123).

a differentiation activity for advanced students, have students read *Antony and Cleopatra* to see a fuller, more complex picture of Octavius, who will become Caesar Augustus.

Portia and Calphurnia: The feminine force. The two wives, and possibly the only women in the script (unless certain plebeians are played by female actors), provide a contrast not only with each other, but also against the men who dominate the action and the outcome of the story. Portia, in particular, suffers perhaps the most tragic fate in the story, killing herself in a violent fashion (swallowing coal). Each of these two characters appears in two scenes. Portia is referred to (through her death) in a third scene. What do these women contribute to the story, and how does Shakespeare contrast them? What do both of them offer to the men that the men need, yet refuse to take?

Casca: The first to raise his hand. Casca is first introduced in Act 1, scene 2 as Caesar's strongman, silencing the crowd when Caesar speaks. He reappears later in the same scene, and a different picture emerges. Have students examine Casca's prose description of Caesar's refusal of the crown (1.2.225–299) and develop character traits based not only on what he says, but also on what Cassius and Brutus say about him after he exits. Then have students discuss how their image of Casca changes in Act 1, scene 3, when he is out in the storm. Discussion of his personality will inevitably lead to the question of why Casca is the first to strike against Caesar.

Other conspirators: Decius, Ligarius, Metellus Cimber, Cinna, Trebonius. Each of these characters brings some individual quality or stamp to the conspiracy. They are more fully developed in Plutarch's description of the events portrayed in *Julius Caesar*, but Shakespeare gives each a role and speaking lines in his script, which actors may use to develop interpretations. Students can draw character maps for the conspirators or construct a larger graphic organizer with the names of each conspirator, listing details of their roles for discussion.

The Roman citizens (plebeians): From celebration to violence. Have students examine the scenes involving the Roman citizens and discuss their opinions of the people Caesar sought to rule. Three times the citizens appear on stage with speaking lines: in the opening scene, in the funeral scene (3.1), and in the last scene in Act 3, when they tear the poet Cinna to pieces. They are also described by Casca in Act 1, scene 2, and mentioned to by the major characters throughout the play. It may be beneficial for your students to discuss the crowd as a major character and to talk about how they are swayed by the arguments and actions of the other major characters.

> ### DISCUSSION/JOURNAL TOPIC: MOB RULE.
>
> Have students examine the role of the plebeians in *Julius Caesar* and compare them to the American public or the public of other countries today. What parallels in crowd behavior can we find between the ancient Romans as portrayed by Shakespeare and public opinion today?

Discussions of Plot

Discussion of plot can quickly become nothing more than a recitation quiz on reading. What happened next? Then what happened? This is not to say that students can't stumble in their reading or disagree on what happens, and as we will see with discussions around stage action and film adaptations, plot development can differ in interpretation. *Julius Caesar* has a plot that is linear and straightforward, without much subplot. The events leading up to the assassination are presented in a balance between public and private space, but always, the script is a set of directions for actors, and stage action becomes part of the plot. For example, if Portia stabs herself on stage in front of Brutus and the audience in Act 2, scene 2, that action becomes a part of the plot in a different way than it would if she enters with the wound already there. If the soothsayer is shoved out of the way after warning Caesar for the third time in Act 3, scene 1, that action becomes part of the plot.

ACTIVITY (SAS #18): PLOTLINE.

A good way to keep students on track with plot is to assign them to develop a plotline, like a timeline of the story, with all events we know of added as they occur in the reading. You can make a big plotline and post it on the wall of your classroom, having students add to it as they progress through their unit on *Julius Caesar*, or you can have students construct their own plotline and include the events they see as most important. Of course, the plotline itself will lead to a discussion of how time passes in the script. For example, we don't know how much time has passed between the end of Act 3 and the beginning of Act 4, but it must be some time, as the new rulers have already taken command in Rome, and Brutus and Cassius are "levying powers" (4.1.46) to oppose the triumvirate. Such questions will not affect the plotline, which is linear and should also extend backward to include events that happened before Act 1 opens and that are referred to in the dialogue. Good discussion can grow from having students summarize action and rank plot events in terms of their importance to the different characters or conflicts. They can also match the plotline with their conflict maps.

Discussions of Language

Pick a few memorable speeches from the script and have students discuss the language. Inevitably, the script provides lots of opportunities for reading speeches aloud, giving the students the chance to describe the language used and the tone conveyed by the characters. The language of this play has been described as "lucid and vigorous . . . clear and disciplined . . . passionate and picturesque, strong and direct . . . but also emotive, richly suggestive, and insistent in its drive" (Humphreys, 1984, p. 42). The language in *Julius Caesar* moves past the overly embellished imagery and excess of *Romeo and Juliet* and *A Midsummer Night's Dream* and is deeply influenced by the rhetorical structures employed by the characters (McMurtry, 1998). The best discussions of language in this play will revolve around the imagery used by the speakers, the predominance of unrhymed iambic pentameter, and the occasional changes to prose speech.

Activity: Side-by-Side Comparison, *Romeo and Juliet* and *Julius Caesar*.

Examine the following two passages, one from *Romeo and Juliet* and the other from *Julius Caesar*. Have students describe the differences between the two passages in terms of their difficulty and the language used.

From *Romeo and Juliet*:

Friar: Now ere the sun advance his burning eye
The day to cheer and night's dank dew to dry,
I must upfill this osier cage of ours
With baleful weeds and precious-juiced flowers.
The Earth that's Nature's mother is her tomb,
What is her burying grave, that is her womb,
And from her womb children of divers kind
We sucking on her natural bosom find,
Many for many virtues excellent,
None but for some and yet all different. (Shakespeare, 1597/1992d, 2.2.1–10)

From *Julius Caesar*:

Cassius: Well, honor is the subject of my story.
I cannot tell what you and other men
Think of this life; but, for my single self,
I had as lief not be as live to be
In awe of such a thing as I myself.
I was born free as Caesar; so were you;
We both have fed as well, and we can both
Endure the winter's cold as well as he. (1.2.99–107)

As an extension of this activity, have students imitate the style of writing in these two passages or others from the two scripts.

Ultimately, discussion of language in *Julius Caesar* must address the nature of argument and trace the rhetorical strategies used by characters to advance their arguments, as several topics from Chapter 5 suggest.

Discussions of Theme

Addressing theme in discussion can be one of the most difficult tasks for a teacher, especially with Shakespeare, because theme often leaves us nowhere to go. Students will naturally want to shift to moralizing or coming to conclusions regarding theme, as it is in our nature to define an interpretation in order to fit what we encounter, whether in reading or other arts, into our own worldview. I have a sort of rule regarding discussions and activities related to any text being studied. It runs something like this: Any activity that sends students back into the text is good, and any activity that excuses lack of attention to the text is bad. For example, an examination of the different times that various characters mention what it means to be a Roman will send students into the text to catalogue expressions of "a true Roman" or "such a Roman" to develop a sense of how the different characters agree or disagree on what being a Roman means. On the other hand, an activity which asks students to write sympathy cards to Calphurnia or discuss what would have happened if Brutus hadn't killed himself provide no motivation for students to do anything other than guess and tell.

DISCUSSION/JOURNAL TOPIC: THIS IS A ROMAN.

Have students trace all references to Romans or what it means to be a Roman, then define "Roman" as the characters define it. Do all of the characters agree on what it means to be a Roman?

With this premise in mind, discussion of theme tends to be more productive when it surfaces during discussion of certain points in text, rather than as a result of introducing theme and then expecting students to find examples of thematic development in the text. Pointing students to moments in the text, small passages that reflect theme, can generate discussion far better than starting with a broad theme. For example, let's say we want to address honor as a theme in *Julius Caesar*. Rather than mentioning honor and having students hunt for occurrences of the word or its relatives, find one such scene and have students read it. For example, prior to the passage quoted above as an example of the language of the script, Brutus says the following to Cassius:

> What is it that you would impart to me?
> If it be aught toward the general good,

Set honor in one eye and death i' th' other
And I will look on both indifferently (1.2.91–94)

You may ask students how Brutus is defining honor in this speech, and then alert them to look for references to the word as their reading of the script continues. Thus, the thematic thread is spun, and may be woven into the fabric of other discussions that emerge from the reading of specific scenes. As we will see in Chapter 7, student response journals can generate many ideas regarding theme that are worthy of class discussion, based on responses to individual scenes. One technique I have used to great effect regarding theme is to have students share their response journals with each other, then ask as a group, "What is this story about?" Answers will inevitably focus on theme, making the group aware for further investigation. Also, when we apply various critical lenses to our study of *Julius Caesar* (see Chapter 8), different themes emerge and already-identified themes are seen in a new light.

These biases of mine excepted, Advanced Placement exams (discussed in Chapter 8) often introduce themes and then ask student writers to apply those themes to a certain work, so eventually, when your students are nearing the end of their experience with the script, and perhaps have performed individual scenes (Chapter 7), opportunities to start with theme and work back to the text may be most appropriate. Another way into theme is through theatre games or short performances of scenes (see Tableau in Chapter 7). Looking at a specific moment from the script as a set of instructions for actors, then developing different performance versions of the moment can spark thematic discussion in a fresh way.

You may want to let your students determine discussion of theme. If your students want to examine a specific theme (which grows naturally out of conflict), let them drive the discussion and become willing and equal participants. In other words, let students facilitate the discussion. Have student volunteers lead the discussion based upon topics and questions they have developed themselves. You may find that they cover ground you had intended to cover yourself, and they do it with more enthusiasm because they determined the course of discussion inquiry.

One other caution on general reading discussion: Avoid getting students into the habit of telling what they liked and didn't like about the story or script. This caution refers back to my contention in Chapter 2 about suspending judgment. Students ultimately can evaluate their experience with Shakespeare and whether they would like to seek another experience, but they shouldn't be put in the position of making that evaluation as they are working through the script. Reader response theory, again, tells us that we cannot separate our emotional reactions (both good and bad) to a reading experience from our interpretation of the reading material, and students can keep a log of their struggles with *Julius Caesar* or their frustrations with the process (see Chapter 8), but again, overexposure to those judgments in the middle of the process can grind otherwise productive study to a halt and lead to hard feelings between erstwhile enthusiastic teachers and negative students.

To add one more point, discussion of theme can center on the many different social worlds (Beach & Myers, 2001) that Shakespeare's text examines: the political world and political order, the supernatural world, the world of revenge, the world of friendships and loyalty, and the world of combat. In your own preparation for teaching *Julius Caesar*, consider any or all of these worlds and then introduce your students to the script by pointing out the different worlds that they will encounter. You can either direct discussions around these worlds or split students into groups, giving each group one of the worlds to trace in its reading, which students can then present to the class. I caution you to avoid overwhelming or disengaging your students by expecting them to draw conclusions regarding themes attached to the different worlds presented in *Julius Caesar*. But don't avoid those discussions forever—go to them when your students are ready. Ultimately, they will write about themes in literary works, as that is what is most interesting to write about and what the AP examination requires. *Julius Caesar* presents many thematic topics that will bear fruitful discussion, such as time, constancy (or loyalty), the supernatural world and the human world, Roman-ness, blood, ambition, political rule, and many others.

Discussion Around Script Signals

Another major mode of discussion when studying *Julius Caesar* is in treating the script as a set of instructions for directors and actors. You may notice that thus far I have tried to avoid referring to *Julius Caesar* as a play. I define a play as a theatrical experience and the text of a play as a script. Any scene in the text of *Julius Caesar* can be examined as a dramatic script. The key is to teach students how to talk about the script in terms of what clues Shakespeare left behind to help bring the play to life. For example, let's examine an excerpt from the crucial murder scene:

Caesar:	Are we all ready? What is now amiss
	That Caesar and his Senate must redress?
Metellus:	Most high, most mighty, and must puissant Caesar,
	Metellus Cimber throws before thy seat
	An humble heart.
Caesar:	I must prevent thee, Cimber.
	These couchings and these lowly courtesies
	Might fire the blood of ordinary men
	And turn preordinance and first decree

Into the law of children. Be not fond
To think that Caesar bears such rebel blood
That will be thawed from the true quality
With that which melteth fools—I mean sweet words,
Low-crookèd curtsies, and base spaniel fawning.
Thy brother by decree is banishèd
If thou dost bend and pray and fawn for him,
I spurn thee like a cur out of my way.
Know: Caesar doth not wrong, nor without cause
Will he be satisfied.

Metellus: Is there no voice more worthy than my own
To sound more sweetly in great Caesar's ear
For the repealing of my banished brother?

Brutus: I kiss thy hand, but not in flattery, Caesar
Desiring thee that Publius Cimber may
Have an immediate freedom of repeal.

Caesar: What, Brutus?

Cassius: Pardon, Caesar; Caesar, pardon!
As low as to thy foot doth Cassius fall
to beg enfranchisement for Publius Cimber. (3.1.34–63)

Students may start with stage directions explicit in the dialogue of the characters. For example, when Brutus says, "I kiss thy hand" (3.1.57) to Caesar, we can assume that the actor will follow through on the action suggested by his comment. Another example is, "As low as to thy foot doth Cassius fall" (3.1.62). Although these words paint a clear picture of stage action, other phrases in the scene, particularly those of Metellus and of Caesar, provide examination for implied stage action that can render different interpretations of the scene. When Metellus "throws before [Caesar's] seat an humble heart" (3.1.37–38), what does the actor playing Metellus do? Have students discuss the options and look at Caesar's lengthy description, perhaps of what he sees Metellus doing (e.g. "couchings" [3.1.40] and "base spaniel fawning" [3.1.48]).

And what does the actor playing Caesar do when he says, "I spurn thee like a cur out of my way" (3.1.51)? Does the actor kick Metellus? Does he lean over and shove him, or does he merely walk away? What possible stage actions make sense? Discussion of these choices will lead to the more compelling decision in Caesar's reaction to Brutus kissing his hand (and perhaps kneeling, too). When Caesar says, "What, Brutus?" (3.1.60), what are the options for the actor at this point? Disbelief? Disgust? Does he also physically "spurn" Brutus away? How we decide to translate the language of the script into action will determine the story we tell. Students best discuss stage action when their classmates are willing to get up in front of the class and try out the directorial suggestions made by the class (see Chapters 2 and 7), but even from their seats during discussion, they can imagine the options available to them in the speeches, realizing that there are many different plays inside the script.

The list of what can be considered signals to actors is long and varied, but here are some of the major ones:

- stage directions (printed but not bracketed),
- explicit stage directions in dialogue (e.g., "You pulled me by the cloak"),
- implicit stage directions in dialogue,
- line length and structure,
- punctuation,
- poetry,
- diction,
- syntax,
- rhythm and pauses,
- rhyme,
- tone,
- imagery,
- sequence of speakers,
- length of speech,
- action in dialogue,
- song,
- prose,
- character,
- placement of scene,
- preceding action,
- subsequent action,
- soliloquy, and
- many more.

When students perform scenes from *Julius Caesar* (Chapter 7), they will need to examine all of these aspects of the script for clues to help them know what to do and how to speak in their scene.

When students are discussing dramatic choices, they do so on the basis of what makes sense given the words on the page. They also feel less inhibited by the need to answer a teacher's discussion questions because stage action is not right or wrong, only effective or ineffective. And students won't really know what is effective or makes sense to them until they see what it looks like in action. The laboratory feel that such discussions will establish can then easily lead to discussion of themes, such as Caesar's ambition or the treachery of the conspirators.

Having students choreograph the scene above and discuss emphasis in the speaking of the lines gets them right to the heart of script analysis. They should be taught to score (mark) their text with performance ideas throughout their reading. A good follow-up to this discussion would be to show two different stagings of the scene from the movie versions (Houseman & Mankiewicz, 1953; Snell & Burge, 1970). They can compare the choices the film directors made in comparison or contrast to each other and to what the students envisioned themselves.

Debate Topics

Any of the topics below could serve as a prompt for class debate, thus sending students back into the text and to outside sources as well for support to bolster their arguments. In their debate responses, students may employ some of the same rhetorical strategies used by the characters in the script.

- *Debate topic 1: Julius Caesar: An ambitious tyrant or a benevolent leader?*: Divide students into opposing groups and have them develop arguments portraying Caesar either as a danger to Rome or an asset to Rome. They may consult any speeches made by Caesar or about Caesar by other characters, as well as Plutarch's portrait of Caesar in North's translation of Plutarch's *Lives of the Noble Greeks and Romans*. Have small groups present their cases and let the rest of the class decide which case is more convincing.

- *Debate topic 2: Does Caesar deserve to be assassinated?*: This topic is simply another way to frame the debate above, but adding the twist of Caesar's deserved fate. In other words, students in Debate 1 may decide that Caesar is a dangerous tyrant and yet still feel that he should not be assassinated. But a group can also present the arguments in favor of Brutus and Cassius in convincing language.

- *Debate topic 3: Is Brutus an honorable man?*: Have students trace the actions and speeches of Brutus throughout the play, including his argument with Cassius in Act 4, scene 3. At different points in the script, Brutus is described as both honorable and treacherous. Despite the fact that Antony gives him a positive eulogy at the end of the story, Antony and Octavius also call Brutus a traitor and a murderer. Have groups decide, based on what Brutus says and does, to argue for his honor or his treachery.

 Debate topic 4: Mark Antony: Righteous avenger or ruthless opportunist?: Antony presents one of the most compelling contradictions in literature. Have students debate whether Antony is a sympathetic or nonsympathetic character based on references to him in the first two acts, his funeral speech, and his behavior in Acts 4 and 5. Have one group focus on his role as Caesar's righteous avenger and another focus on his role as an opportunist who manipulates the public and takes command following Caesar's death. Evidence for both interpretations may be found in abundance in the script.

Debate topic 5: Is it in our stars or in our selves? Fate vs. human will in Julius Caesar: This may be one of the most fun topics for your students to debate, as it allows them to argue cosmological ideas within the context of the literature rather than simply arguing their own spiritual beliefs. Some characters in *Julius Caesar*, including Caesar himself, imply that human actions and destinies are preordained by "the gods." Others, such as Cassius, believe that humans carve their own destinies (even though he wavers in his belief in Act 5). Have students examine the supernatural events in the story and debate whether those events shape the outcome of the plot or whether it is the conscious will of the characters that shapes the outcomes.

Debate topic 6: What kind of leadership do the Romans deserve?: Based on the behavior of the citizens in this play, have two groups debate whether Rome deserves a representative republican government or the rule of a dictator. It may be helpful for students to see the citizens as a major character in the play.

Debate topic 7: Who is the protagonist of this play?: Arguments have been advanced in favor of Caesar, Brutus, and Antony as the protagonist. Most scholars reject Cassius, though I believe he deserves an argument as the protagonist as much as any of the others. Split students into four groups and assign each group one of the four men. Have them make their case for their chosen character as the protagonist of the play. Included in their argument should be some rationale for excluding the other three characters. Have students reflect on the arguments made following the debate, and take votes on whose argument is most convincing.

Debate topic 8: Julius Caesar *in the 21st century—does the play still have relevance?*: This debate, which may be done either in groups or simply as a reflective discussion, should come at the very end of students' experience with the text, once they have read, discussed, performed, and written about it. Have students share their personal connections with the story, and whether elements of the script resonate with them or leave them cold. Be prepared to respect student views that discount the story as outdated and irrelevant, even as you construct or listen to reasons why it is relevant.

Debate topic 9: A cowardly death or an honorable death? Suicides in Julius Caesar: Several characters in *Julius Caesar*, including Brutus and Cassius, take their own lives. Attitudes toward suicide are expressed at various points in the script. Have students debate whether the suicides of Brutus and Cassius are cowardly or honorable. The discussion may move to the problem of teen suicide in contemporary culture.

The fishbowl approach may be appropriate for these debates. In the fishbowl, students are put in a seating arrangement that has two concentric circles. The students in the inner circle engage in the debate as students in the outer circle listen and take notes. Following the debate, students in the outer circle can either take the place of the inner circle and continue the debate, or comment on the arguments made by the inner circle and add to those arguments or detract from them.

Additional Multilevel Discussion/Writing Topics

The categories of these discussion topics are modeled on Raphael's (1986) Question/Answer Relationships with important changes. Rather than the categories of increasing intellectual demand inherent in typical QAR strategies, the categories of comprehend, connect, extend, and imagine cover various levels of thinking from Bloom's taxonomy and combine interpretation with creativity.

Act 1, Scene 1

Comprehend
1. Describe the setting for the opening scene. What is happening?
2. Why are the tribunes, Marullus and Flavius, upset with the plebeians?
3. What verbal jokes does the cobbler make regarding his profession?
4. What reasons does Marullus give as to why the plebeians should not celebrate Caesar's victory?
5. What do the tribunes resolve to do after dispersing the crowd?

Connect
1. What words are used to describe the plebeians in this scene, and how do these descriptions match or contradict descriptions of the crowd in other scenes?
2. Is the change in public opinion based on Marullus's speech believable? Why or why not?

3. What difficulties did you experience with the language or imagery in this scene?

Extend
1. How do people argue politics today? How do representatives get their views out to the public?
2. Do you tend to respond more to appeals to your logic or to your emotions?

Imagine
1. Write an argument explaining why a current politician of your choosing should be supported or not supported, then deliver it to your classmates.

Act 1, Scene 2

Comprehend
1. Describe Caesar as he appears in this scene, giving details.
2. How does Caesar respond to the soothsayer? Why?
3. What is Cassius's argument against Caesar?
4. How does Brutus respond to Cassius in this scene?
5. What does Casca's story reveal about his attitude toward the plebeians and what does it reveal about Caesar?

Connect
1. What parallels do you find between this scene and the opening scene?
2. What do we learn of in this scene that will need to be resolved in later scenes?

Extend
1. Cassius's story told to Brutus is about "honor." Does his definition of honor match your own?
2. Does Caesar appear to be a good leader? Why or why not?
3. Are our lives governed by forces beyond ourselves or by our own decisions?

Imagine
1. Think of someone you know, then create an argument explaining why that person should think more highly of him or herself than he or she does.

Act 1, Scene 3

Comprehend
1. What effect does the storm have on Casca? Cicero? Cassius?

2. In Cassius's interpretation, what does the storm signify?
3. What do we learn about the state of the conspiracy in this scene?

Connect

1. How does Cassius's description of the Romans compare with his idea of what Romans should be like?
2. Compare Cassius's argument to Casca in this scene with his argument to Brutus in the previous scene. How are his reasons for opposing Caesar similar and different?

Extend

1. Which sights seen by Casca have evident explanations in nature and which do not?

Imagine

1. Write a journal entry by Cassius detailing his desires and his plans for Brutus and the other conspirators.
2. Describe the most powerful storm in your memory. How did it affect you?

Act 2, Scene 1

Comprehend

1. What argument does Brutus make for killing Caesar?
2. Describe the letters that are thrown in at Brutus's window.
3. What is the meaning of the argument between Decius, Casca, and Cinna about where the sun rises?
4. Why does Brutus reject Cassius's call for an oath between the conspirators?
5. Why does Brutus reject Cassius's argument that Antony should be killed?
6. Why is Decius confident that Caesar will come to the Capitol?
7. What is Portia's complaint against Brutus? How does she make her argument?
8. What is the meaning of Caius Ligarius's scene with Brutus?

Connect

1. How does the dynamic between Cassius and Brutus in this scene differ from Act 1, scene 2?
2. When Cassius tells the conspirators to show themselves "true Romans" (2.1.241), how does that compare to his description of Romans in Act 1, scenes 2 and 3?

Extend

    1. What are some examples of political conspiracy in contemporary society or literature?

    2. Are there situations under which murder is justified?

    3. Should married people always share their secrets?

Imagine

    1. Pick one of the other conspirators besides Brutus and Cassius, find out what you can about his history, then write a soliloquy for him that explains his reasons for joining the conspiracy.

Act 2, Scene 2

Comprehend

    1. What is Calphurnia worried about in this scene? Why?

    2. Describe Caesar's attitude in this scene. Does it change?

    3. What signs indicate that Caesar should take the day off and not go to the Capitol?

    4. How convincing is Decius's interpretation of Calphurnia's dream? Why is Caesar persuaded?

Connect

    1. Compare and contrast the relationship between Caesar and Calphurnia with the relationship between Brutus and Portia.

    2. How does Calphurnia's dream corroborate what Casca had seen in Act 1, scene 3?

Extend

    1. Do you believe in superstitions or omens? Have you ever avoided going somewhere or doing something because you were afraid?

    2. What do you think of Caesar's question, "What can be avoided / Whose end is purposed by the mighty gods?" (2.2.27–28)?

Imagine

    1. Do you remember any dreams you've had that were particularly scary or symbolic? Can you describe them?

Act 2, Scene 3

Comprehend

    1. What is the message Artemidorus wants to give to Caesar?

Extend

    1. Have you ever tried to warn someone of something but were unable to do so?

Act 2, Scene 4

Comprehend

    1. What is Portia's problem in this scene? How can Lucius help her?

    2. Why does Portia question the soothsayer?

    3. What does Portia say about women in this scene?

Connect

    1. Compare Portia's thoughts on the nature of women with what she says about herself in Act 2, scene 2. Is she consistent or not?

    2. Compare the soothsayer in this scene with the way you imagined him in Act 1, scene 2. Do his words in this scene fit your image of him? How will you revise your image?

Extend

    1. How is Lucius's behavior typical of a youth who doesn't know what an adult wants?

    2. How do you act when you are nervous?

Imagine

    1. Write the story of Lucius going to the Capitol and witnessing the murder of Caesar.

    2. Imagine the soothsayer's thoughts as he goes to meet Caesar and what he thinks he will say to Caesar.

Act 3, Scene 1

Comprehend

    1. What prevents Artemidorus from successfully delivering his warning to Caesar?

    2. What are the conspirators worried about before the assassination of Caesar?

    3. What is Metellus Cimber's role in the assassination?

    4. How does Caesar compare himself to the others in his final speech?

    5. Describe what happens immediately after the death of Caesar.

    6. How does Antony behave toward Caesar's assassins in this scene? How does he behave when they leave?

Connect

1. What is the significance of the assassins' ritual of bathing in Caesar's blood? Why do Brutus and Cassius make reference to the acting of the scene in future societies?
2. How does the murder of Caesar fit with the events that precede it in the play?

Extend

1. Does Caesar deserve to die? Why or why not?
2. Who in your mind is most to blame, if anyone, for Caesar's death?
3. Does might make right?

Imagine

1. Draw a picture or compose a photograph of the death of Caesar.
2. Write a poem about the death of Caesar, including references to the characters.

Act 3, Scene 2

Comprehend

1. What is the mood of the plebeians in this scene? How does it change throughout the scene?
2. What reasons does Brutus give for killing Caesar? How convincing is he?
3. Do the plebeians accept Brutus's rationale for killing Caesar? Do they understand it?
4. How does Antony persuade the crowd that Caesar was not ambitious?
5. Describe the comments of the plebeians in this scene.

Connect

1. How does this scene develop the relationship between Caesar and Antony, based on what we saw in earlier scenes?
2. How has Antony fulfilled Brutus's conditions for letting him speak on Caesar's behalf? How has Antony violated those conditions?

Extend

1. What does it mean that "The evil that men do lives after them; / The good is oft interrèd with their bones" (3.2.84–85)? Do you agree?
2. How easily are you persuaded to change your mind about people?

Imagine
   1. Write a speech that praises a friend and convinces others of that friend's worthiness.
   2. Write a speech that uses irony to make its point.

Act 3, Scene 3

Comprehend
   1. Why is Cinna the poet murdered?
   2. How is the crowd's behavior consistent with its behavior in the previous scene?

Connect
   1. How does this scene fit with the rest of the play? Is it a turning point?
   2. How is Cinna the Poet's dream reminiscent of other dreams in the play?

Extend
   1. Do you see the repeated line "tear him for his bad verses" (3.3.3132) as ironic, humorous, or tragic? Why?
   2. What other literature have you read that contains innocent characters victimized by mob violence?

Imagine
   1. Imagine being in a place where your identity is mistaken for someone else, and your explanation of the mistake is not accepted. What would you do?

Act 4, Scene 1

Comprehend
   1. What are Antony, Octavius, and Lepidus doing in the first part of this scene?
   2. What is Antony's opinion of Lepidus?
   3. How does Octavius respond to what Antony says about Lepidus?

Connect
   1. How has Mark Antony changed since the last time we saw him in Act 3, scene 2? What is he saying about Caesar's will?
   2. What do references to Brutus and Cassius indicate about their fortunes following the assassination?

Extend

1. When Saddam Hussein took power in Iraq in July of 1979, he read a list of alleged co-conspirators against his government, most of them ranking officials, and had them arrested and subsequently executed. Research this event and compare it to what the triumvirs do to the senators in *Julius Caesar*.

Imagine

1. Antony compares the qualities of an ass (and a horse) to the role of Lepidus. Make a list of qualities of several animals that would be admirable or not admirable in humans.

Act 4, Scene 2

Comprehend

1. Describe this scene as you imagine it looking on stage.
2. What does Brutus mean by the phrase "hollow men" (4.2.26) in this scene?
3. What is the tone of conversation between Brutus and Cassius in this scene?

Connect

1. This is the first time we have seen Brutus and Cassius together since the assassination scene. How has their relationship changed?

Extend

1. Is it better to argue in public or in private? What are the advantages of each venue?

Imagine

1. Write a possible conversation between Pindarus and Lucilius as they travel between Cassius's army and Brutus's tent.

Act 4, Scene 3

Comprehend

1. What are Brutus and Cassius arguing about in this scene? Who has the better argument?
2. At what point or points does the argument appear to come close to violence? How is violence avoided?
3. How does Brutus speak of Portia's death?

4. What are Cassius's reasons for wanting to let the enemies come to them, and what are Brutus's reasons for wanting to attack at Philippi?

5. How does Brutus respond to the visitation of the ghost?

Connect

1. Why does Brutus allow Messala to tell him of Portia's death even though we know that Brutus has already received the news?

2. Knowing what has happened between Brutus and Cassius earlier in the script, what subtexts are present in their argument?

3. What if Brutus and Cassius were actual lovers? How would that change the way you read this scene?

4. Based on this scene and earlier scenes, explain Brutus's relationship with Lucius.

Extend

1. Brutus is identified as a "stoic" and Cassius as an "epicurean" in philosophy. Research these two philosophies and discuss how they fit (or don't fit) the behavior of these two men as you perceive it.

2. How do you approach arguing with people you love?

3. Do you believe in the wisdom of Brutus's speech, "There is a tide in the affairs of men . . ." (4.3.249–252)?

Imagine

1. Pick two historic figures who are linked together, and imagine an argument between them. Write the argument as dialogue.

2. Write a scene featuring a current politician who is visited by the ghost of a famous politician from the past.

Act 5, Scene 1

Comprehend

1. What two things do Octavius and Antony disagree on in the first part of this scene?

2. Describe the conversation between the rival generals. What do they think of each other?

3. What is Cassius's attitude about the coming battle as presented in his speech to Messala?

4. On what terms do Brutus and Cassius part company?

Connect

1. Based on this scene and earlier scenes, what are Brutus and Cassius's attitudes toward suicide?
2. How has Cassius changed from Act 1?
3. How do you feel about Brutus and Cassius at the end of this scene? Are you on their side or against them?

Extend

1. Under what circumstances is war justified? Does the war depicted in *Julius Caesar* fit those circumstances?

Imagine

1. Think of a situation in the world today that involves conflict that could lead to war. Imagine a dialogue between rival leaders in the conflict and write what they would say to avoid war.

Act 5, Scene 2

Comprehend

1. What is Brutus's message to Messala?

Connect

1. Based on what you know of Brutus's strategies in the play, do you think his attack will work? Why or why not?

Act 5, Scene 3

Comprehend

1. Describe the tone of this scene.

Connect

1. What do we learn about Cassius in this scene?
2. What does Pindarus misinterpret in the scene?
3. Describe Titinius's feelings for Cassius as shown in this scene.
4. Why does Brutus call Cassius "the last of all the Romans" (5.3.111)?

Extend

1. What do you think of the Roman attitude toward suicide as an act of bravery? Do you agree? Do you see suicide as an act of cowardice?

Imagine

    1. Imagine Cassius appearing to Brutus in a dream following his death. What would Cassius say to Brutus?

Act 5, Scene 4

Comprehend

    1. Summarize the events in this scene.
    2. What role does young Cato play in this scene, and how is his role important to the play?
    3. Why does Antony show mercy to Lucilius when he is captured?

Connect

    1. Why does Lucilius call Brutus "my country's friend" (5.4.8)? Is Brutus a friend to Rome?
    2. What does this scene reveal about Lucilius? About Antony?

Extend

    1. Would you sacrifice yourself to save a friend? Under what circumstances?

Imagine

    1. Write a diary as though you are the young Marcus Cato, readying for battle. In the diary, explain how you see the situation, and why you are fighting for Brutus and Cassius, instead of for Antony and Octavius.

Act 5, Scene 5

Comprehend

    1. What do we learn about Brutus based on the descriptions given of him by the other characters in this scene?
    2. What is the significance of Brutus's claim, "My heart doth joy that yet in all my life / I found no man but he was true to me" (5.5.38–39)?
    3. How do Antony and Octavius speak of the dead Brutus?

Connect

    1. How is Brutus's behavior in this scene consistent or inconsistent with his character?
    2. Does this scene provide a fit ending to the play? What alternative endings could there be?

Extend

    1. Whose death is the most tragic in this play? Caesar's? Brutus's? Cassius's? Cinna's? Portia's? Titinius's? Young Cato's? Explain.

Imagine

    1. Construct a dream cast of actors and actresses to play in a movie version of *Julius Caesar*, with reasons why you would pick each character. Who would you like to see play Brutus? Cassius? Caesar? Mark Antony? Portia? The others?

Chapter Materials

Name: _____ Date: _____

Student Activity Sheet #17:
Conflict

Applicable Portion of Play: All

Objectives: 1. Students will identify conflicts in the script that interest them.
                   2. Students will be able to trace conflict development through the script.
                   3. Students will be able to represent conflict visually or in flow charts.

Common Core Standard(s): 11-12.R.L.1, 11-12.R.L.2, 11-12.R.L.5

Directions: Choose a conflict in the play that interests you. Generate a visual representation of the conflict, tracing events in the play that develop the conflict. You can make a timeline, a flowchart, or a conflict map. For example, you can trace the conflict between Brutus and Cassius by tracing pivotal events in their encounters. As a class, gather the list of conflicts students have generated. Discuss the conflict list and determine which conflicts have the most importance in the play.

Reflection: How can you best represent the conflict you chose? A map, a flowchart, a timeline, or some other way? How does your conflict affect the outcome of the play?

_____

_____

_____

_____

_____

_____

_____

_____

_____

_____

_____

_____

_____

_____

_____

_____

_____

Student Activity Sheet #18:
Plotline: What happens?

Applicable Portion of Play: All

Objectives:
1. Students will trace events in the play as they interpret the script of *Julius Caesar*.
2. Students will be able to argue for the significance of different plot events.

Common Core Standard(s): 11-12.R.L.1, 11-12.R.L.2, 11-12.R.L.5

Directions: Develop a plotline, like a timeline of the play, with all events we know of added as they occur in the reading. Create your own plotline, and compare it to the large class plotline displayed on the wall. On your own plotline, include the events you see as most important. In class discussion, argue for inclusion of plot events that you see as important, and seek class approval to add your event to the class plotline. Continue to develop your individual plotline with events your classmates convince you to add. You may use your plotline as a reference when you write about the play.

Reflection: How do you decide which events in the plot have greater importance, and which have lesser importance?

_____

_____

_____

_____

_____

_____

_____

_____

_____

_____

_____

_____

_____

_____

_____

"Speak, hands, for me!": Performing *Julius Caesar*

The purpose of this chapter is not to share a design for a theatrical production of *Julius Caesar*, but to examine to a greater degree than has already been suggested in previous chapters how performance can inform classroom study of Shakespeare's text. From quick, in-class workshop activities that extend discussion to more sustained, time-consuming scene work, using the theatrical process will open *Julius Caesar* to diverse interpretations and will also teach your students reading skills that are transferable to other reading tasks.

At the heart of this book and this chapter in particular is the well-accepted notion that Shakespeare wrote scripts. Inside the script for *Julius Caesar* are many potential plays, and it is through the process of getting up, putting the words in our mouths, making the motions that create stage action, and adding visual and auditory elements that we understand the full power of the literary work. What play will we find inside our script of *Julius Caesar*?

Most of us don't have the luxury of 8 weeks to mount a full production, nor can we justify turning our English classes into theatre classes. What we do have is the ability to use performance as a learning tool through which we develop talent, engage all of the senses, and make studying *Julius Caesar* a memorable experience for our students. In this chapter, we will start with easy exercises that can be done within one class period and progress through serious scene work, then talk about culminating performances.

Reader's Theatre

An easy way to incorporate performance into your classroom study of *Julius Caesar* is to have students engage in reader's theatre, an activity that involves students in small groups standing in front of the class and reading the script in character, emphasizing vocal variations to fit meaning without actually moving around on a stage. Reader's theatre allows students to hear the words spoken with dramatic effect, and thus introduces the auditory modality. The differences between reader's theatre and simple in-class reading aloud are subtle, but important.

Students should be given short (5–10 minute) scenes and be given enough time to practice their parts, so that they can learn pronunciations and definitions for words they don't know. Have students also practice the rhythms of the lines, paying attention to situations where one character finishes another's line, indicating quick response, or when an unfinished line is left unfinished, indicating a pause. A 10-minute reading will typically create at least 10 minutes worth of discussion, and you can ask questions of the readers about the choices they made regarding vocal emphasis or what they think the character would be doing on stage if they were allowed to add action to the scene.

The main purpose of reader's theatre is to get the words of Shakespeare coming out of your students' mouths in a way that is nonthreatening. Because the emphasis is not on stage projection or acting skill, it is perfectly fine (and sometimes beneficial) to provide microphones for your readers, and with available technology, record the readings. Students will step up their involvement when they know they will get to hear their recorded scene. One student from each of the groups can be in charge of sound effects to accompany the scene, including noises, music, and weather factors like wind. If time permits, you may even have your students work at laptops to practice their scenes with the aid of a laptop audio recording program (like Garage Band™ or ProTools™) before the live reading in front of the class. You can even combine the recorded reader's theatre performances into a radio show format and podcast them, making them available to the rest of the student body through your school's website.

Because the script of *Julius Caesar* moves quickly into action, virtually every scene is a good candidate for reader's theatre. Let your students decide which scenes they would like to read for the class, and then work with them if they need to trim the scene. Be careful with your pruning, so that you do not cut the heart of the scene. I generally recommend against cutting lines in readers' theatre, but in scene performance, especially with younger students, cutting may be necessary. (See Chapter 8 for a scene-cutting activity.) Creating a 30–40 minute reader's theatre version of the *Julius Caesar* script, cut from the larger script, somehow including most or all scenes, would make a great project for the class or for a student who has strong inclinations toward editing.

Theatre Games

Playing theatre games in your class can build community and break down inhibitions to discussion and acting. There are a number of resources for fun and productive theatre games in the classroom, including a recent volume in the Cambridge School Shakespeare series dedicated to theatre games and activities related to Shakespeare (Stredder, 2009). One activity that Marilyn Halperin and the staff at the Chicago Shakespeare Theater do with their Bard Core participants every summer is the "name game," wherein the participants develop alliterative tags for their names and add a motion that exemplifies the dynamics of the tag. For example, instead of just Tim, I might be "Ten-foot-tall Tim!" I would add a huge stretch with my arms rising far above my head when I announced my name loudly. Participants stand in a circle and announce their names. Each of their peers then repeats the name and motion in rapid succession, all the way around the circle. Then the next person gives his or her name, gesture, and tag. In a short time, everyone knows everyone else's names, tags, and motions.

Another activity that I use frequently because it is easily applicable to Shakespeare is a game called Protector-Aggressor. I learned this game from Doug Paterson of the University of Nebraska-Omaha, and it is adapted from Augusto Boal's (2002) *Games for Actors and Non-Actors*. To play Protector-Aggressor with your students, you will need to move all of the desks to the periphery of your room or find another space that is large enough for all of the students to have room to walk around freely. Have students walk in random paths, silently, imagining that they are part of a community. You can give students various prompts to express (only through gestures, movement, and facial expression) communal sentiments such as "tragedy," "springtime," and "prosperity." Then, as they continue to walk around the "town" which is defined by the space you have created in your class, say to them, "One of the other people in this town is your protector. That person cannot know that you have chosen him or her to be your protector. Just silently choose someone and keep them in your mind as you move about the town." Give students a few seconds to silently choose their protectors. Then say, "Okay, I assume that everyone has chosen a protector. Now, you must identify, silently, and only to yourself, another person in this group who is your aggressor. That person cannot know he or she is your aggressor—just keep it in your mind. So now you have a protector in the crowd and an aggressor, someone who is out to get you." Give students a few seconds to make sure they have chosen aggressors. Continue with, "Now, your goal, without talking or grabbing, is to keep your protector between you and your aggressor. Go."

What typically ensues is a little like mayhem, as some students will have picked for their aggressor the very person who chose them for protector. The playing space becomes twisted as people chase one another and rotate and spin to try to get away from their aggressors. Call "stop" or "freeze" whenever appropriate and debrief with students regarding what is happening in the scene. The activity can be connected to the script, wherein relationships are complicated, and those who may believe they know their allies and enemies fail to see reality from the other person's perspective. The other benefit of this game, besides the fact that it is fun to play, is that you can demonstrate to students that they are acting. They were "playing" the roles of protector, aggressor, and helpless person caught in the middle. When students are reading the script of *Julius Caesar*, they may refer to the game in terms of defining relationships, such as, "Brutus is Caesar's aggressor, but Caesar believes he's a protector."

Tableau

This activity has many variations and applications across the curriculum. The French word for "picture" indicates that we need to give our students something they can visually observe, and a 3-dimensional "tableau vivant" allows students to study what is communicated by positions and expressions of characters relative to one another, as though studying museum pieces. If we find that we have much to say about the still, silent tableau, think about the options for what we experience when we add motion, voices, and other effects.

Directions for Tableau

Bring to the front of the class five or six student volunteers, mixed male and female, and tell them to bunch up in a huddle. Tell them you are going to give them a word prompt, and they will have 5 seconds to strike a pose and then freeze. Before they freeze, they must be in physical contact with at least one other member of the group. The goal is for the group to communicate the prompt word through the positions the members of the group take. Ask them to keep in mind that they can make use of different levels, as in lying down, kneeling, or climbing on one another. After the group freezes, the rest of the students will study their tableau and comment on what is communicated. Possible prompt words for *Julius Caesar* tableaus include:

- Warm-up Tableau: Celebration,
- Tableau 1: Conquest,
- Tableau 2: Oppression,
- Tableau 3: Treachery,
- Tableau 4: Civil war, and
- Tableau 5: Love.

Add On-Stage Auditors

Following one of the tableaux, ask the actors to remain on stage and frozen, then add two students as observers. Have the class study the extra figures studying the sculpture created by the tableau. Discuss with students what is added when we observe the observers of the artwork. This dimension of tableau can lead to a good discussion of the role of the audience in creating art and can add commentary on how we perceive art. The same can be done by staging short scenes from *Julius Caesar* and then adding observers (see below).

Tableau Option Two

This simple activity asks students to create a picture of a stage scene from a certain moment in the script using themselves as the characters. Students can choose their own moments to portray and can add everything from costumes to background, props, and furniture. They need only present the tableau to their peers and allow their peers to study it and talk about it. Students should be able to defend their choices. You can stop classroom reading or discussion of a scene at any time and construct the picture with the students, as a sort of laboratory activity. A simple "What does this look like on stage?" can initiate a 5–10 minute tableau vivant activity that allows students to argue for what they see in their mind's eye as they work through the script.

20-Second Speech

An easy way to help your students develop confidence in their ability to speak in front of their peers (and to sneak in discussion of the play's themes) is to do impromptu speaking in 20- to 30-second bursts. Take index cards and write a number of themes or topics that surface in *Julius Caesar* on them. Examples might be, "power," "loyalty," "superstition," "murder," or even less abstract ideas, such as "heeding warnings," "talking someone into doing something," "injuring yourself," or "being tired." Choose topics that you think will resonate with the particular group of students you have. Make three or four copies of each topic, depending upon class size. Divide your class into groups of five or six students and distribute the cards facedown with the instructions that no one turn their card over until his or her name is called. With you serving as the timekeeper for the class, have each student turn over his or her card and speak to the group, nonstop, for 20–30 seconds on the topic written there. The only rule is that the student must keep talking for the entire time allowed.

Students will surprise themselves and you with what they have to say because there's no pressure of preparation. Once everyone has had the opportunity to speak in each group, groups can nominate group members to share their impromptu speeches with the entire class. Let the discussion go where it may, with the dual objective of building confidence in speaking and familiarizing students with the themes of the play.

Scene Workshop Activities

Understanding that the words in the script contain clues for actors, engage your students in the following variations on scene work that range from short, easy-to-implement, single-line exchanges to longer, more sustained scene work.

Single-Line/Short Exchanges

Willing volunteers can help you to create simple, high-impact dramatic moments in your study of *Julius Caesar* by experimenting with the physical position, delivery, and impact of single exchanges between characters. These performances are low-pressure for the actors and can lead to great discussions. You can assign them as small-group activities or you can do them as impromptu, whole-class activities while reading the script. In Chapter 2, we examined one such exchange from the script:

> *Soothsayer:* Beware the Ides of March.
> *Caesar:* He is a dreamer. Let us leave him. Pass. (1.2.28–29)

As noted before, students may consider various options for the positioning of the characters for this exchange, their tones of voice, and the pace and volume of their voices. In each case, have students discuss how the tone and meaning of the exchange—what is communicated—changes with the alteration of performance elements.

ACTIVITY: SHORT EXCHANGES.

Have students find one exchange of dialogue between two or three characters and play with different options for performing it. Have them experiment with loud versions, whispered versions, versions with a lot of movement, or versions that involve technology, sound effects, or music. When they have decided upon a performance option, have them do their mini-scene for the class, then discuss the performances as a class.

Even with no preparation time, single-line exchanges can produce good classroom discussion. Below are several examples of short exchanges from throughout the script of *Julius Caesar* that offer a variety of possible performance interpretations, leading us to discussion of intent, character, theme, and relationships. If these examples are not satisfactory, you may pick single-line exchanges that you think would make better candidates to workshop in class.

From Act 1, scene 2:

Casca:	He fell down in the marketplace and foamed at mouth and was speechless.
Brutus:	'Tis very like; he hath the falling sickness.
Cassius:	No, Caesar hath it not; but you and I
	And honest Casca, we have the falling sickness. (1.2.263–267)

This scene takes place on a public street, and Casca has been derisively telling the story of Caesar being offered a crown by Antony. He is describing Caesar's epileptic fit, which Cassius uses to imply something about himself and his companions. Have students explore different degrees of animation or emotion that accompany Casca's description and the reactions of Brutus and Cassius. Then have students decide which interpretations work best, given what they know about the characters.

From Act 1, scene 3:

Casca:	Who ever knew the heavens menace so?
Cassius:	Those that have known the world so full of faults. (1.3.47–48)

This exchange, I'll admit, is a little chilling, given some of the preposterous statements made following the devastating earthquake in Japan in 2011, and the specious claims of some politicians and commentators that the disaster was somehow divinely instigated. But in Rome, such belief was common, and Cassius is playing upon Casca's fear of the storm to win him to the conspiracy.

From Act 2, scene 1:

Cassius:	Good morrow, Brutus. Do we trouble you?
Brutus:	I have been up this hour, awake all night. (2.1.95–96)

This exchange provides another opportunity to examine the physical dynamic between Cassius and Brutus. Cassius still is the aggressor, hoping to win Brutus to the cause against Caesar, and Brutus has just been rationalizing the idea of killing Caesar in his soliloquy. Have students play with attitudes (or subtexts) underneath these lines. As Dakin (2009) showed, students can be given one line of dialogue with different subtexts that would alter their performance and delivery of the line. As an example, you could give your student playing Brutus directions to deliver his line with different characteristics based on the following subtexts: I'm very confused, I'm prepared to lead, I'm very angry, I'm giving in. How would those different "subtexts" affect this exchange? What subtexts might lie beneath Cassius's line?

From Act 2, scene 1:

Brutus:	Give me your hands all over, one by one.
Cassius:	And let us swear our resolution.
Brutus:	No, not an oath. (2.1.123–125)

This is the first exchange indicating that Brutus has joined the conspiracy officially, and his handshake to the others indicates it. But notice that in the very next line, he contradicts Cassius. Have volunteers examine through their stage actions what his immediate censure of Cassius's suggestion might indicate about their relationship, now that Brutus has joined the cause. Another exchange in the same scene may also work:

Cassius:	Let Antony and Caesar fall together.
Brutus:	Our course will seem too bloody, Caius Cassius
	To cut the head off and then hack the limbs (2.1.174–176)

Two groups of students may perform the two exchanges to see whether there is a progression in the sentiments expressed in the first exchange that is amplified in the second.

From Act 2, scene 1:

Brutus:	Kneel not, gentle Portia.
Portia:	I should not need, if you were gentle Brutus. (2.1.300–301)

Students may want to examine the lines that surround this exchange for information that would aid performance. The obvious stage direction in the dialogue is that Portia is kneeling. Does Brutus pull her up? Does she resist? Why is the word "gentle" repeated, and how is it used?

From Act 2, scene 2:

Calphurnia:	What mean you, Caesar? Think you to walk forth?
	You shall not stir out of your house today.
Caesar:	Caesar shall forth. (2.2.8–10)

Again, students may want to look at the context of these lines, but this single exchange can establish physical dynamics between Caesar and his wife. Have students notice that she gives the command for him to stay at home, which puts him in the position of asserting his will to leave. Examine the range of emotions possible in each character's lines, plus the possible physical movements (grabbing? restraining? hand-holding?) that may accompany the lines. Later in the same scene is another great exchange for workshop, this time with another character, Decius, on stage:

Calphurnia:	Say he is sick.
Caesar:	Shall Caesar send a lie? (2.2.69–70)

Here are some other exchanges pulled from the text.
From Act 3, scene 1:

Popilius:	I wish your enterprise today may thrive.
Cassius:	What enterprise, Popilius?
Popilius:	Fare you well. (3.1.14–16)

From Act 3, scene 1:

Brutus:	But here comes Antony.—Welcome, Mark Antony!
Antony:	O mighty Caesar, dost thou lie so low? (3.1.163–164)

From Act 3, scene 3:

Cinna:	I am Cinna the poet, I am Cinna the poet!
Fourth Pleb.:	Tear him for his bad verses, tear him for his bad verses! (3.3.30–32)

From Act 4, scenes 2 and 3 (the argument scene or the "tent scene" offers any number of exchanges to workshop in class.):

Cassius:	Most noble brother, you have done me wrong.
Brutus:	Judge me, you gods! (4.2.41–42)

Cassius:	Do not presume too much upon my love.
	I may do that I shall be sorry for.
Brutus:	You have done that you should be sorry for. (4.3.72–74)

Cassius:	Of your philosophy you make no use
	If you give place to accidental evils.
Brutus:	No man bears sorrow better. Portia is dead. (4.3.166–168)

The benefits of using single-line exchange as a performance activity in the classroom are that it doesn't take a great deal of time, it provides actors and their classmates the opportunity to wrestle with interpretation, and it usually leads to rigorous discussion of the characters and their situations. You can assign the exchanges above to different groups and have them present their interpretations one by one, or you can choose one or two of these exchanges and have the entire class "workshop" the exchange. You may also find exchanges that you would like to see students workshop that aren't listed here. Although only 14 exchanges are listed here, there are many, many one-line exchanges in this text that bear further study.

Historical Interpretations

Stephen Buhler (1999) explained how students or teachers can find explanations of historical productions of Shakespeare and then try to recreate the descriptions of those interpretations in short scenes. One can find what was written about earlier productions of *Julius Caesar*, going back hundreds of years, and ask students to play certain scenes or speeches in those styles.

For example, let's say we want to take a scene featuring Brutus, or a speech made by Brutus. Two historical descriptions may help. First, the late 17th and early 18th century actor Thomas Betterton portrayed Brutus as follows:

When the Betterton Brutus was provoked in his dispute with Cassius, his spirit flew only to his eye; his steady look alone supplied that terror which he disdained an intemperance in his voice should rise to. Thus with a settled dignity of contempt, like an unheeding rock he repelled upon himself the foam of Cassius. (Cibber cited in McMurtry, 1998, p. 105)

A nice collection of critical comments on historical stagings can be found on the Internet Shakespeare Editions website at http://internetshakespeare.uvic.ca/Foyer/plays.html.

Shared Readings, Choral Readings

Shared readings, such as the reader's theatre and the shared jump-in and pointing activities demonstrated in Chapter 5, build community in the classroom and allow students to hear the words in new ways. Several speeches in *Julius Caesar* offer wonderful opportunities for choral readings. Choral readings involve students in shared reading of the same lines, as would be sung in choruses. You can assign small portions of a speech to pairs or groups of three and have them read those lines in succession when their turn comes. As they read their lines, they can create a tableau or mimed enactment of what is suggested by those lines. A great speech for this activity is Brutus's soliloquy in Act 2, scene 1. In the following activity, it is presented with logical breaks in sense and/or imagery denoted by a forward slash (/), which would designate changes of groups.

possible meanings and what it tells us about Brutus. For extension, you can then have individual students or small groups of students read the entire speech out loud with the benefit of new comprehension. (*Reminder:* A forward slash indicates change in choral speakers.)

Brutus: It must be by his death. / And for my part
I know no personal cause to spurn at him, /
But for the general. / He would be crowned: /
How that might change his nature, / there's the
question. /
It is the bright day that brings forth the adder, /
And that craves wary walking. / Crown him that,
And then I grant we put a sting in him /
That at his will he may do danger with. /
Th' abuse of greatness is when it disjoins
Remorse from power. / And, to speak truth of Caesar, /
I have not known when his affections swayed
More than his reason. / But 'tis a common proof
That lowliness is young ambition's ladder, /
Whereto the climber-upward turns his face; /
But, when he once attains the upmost round, /
He then unto the ladder turns his back, /
Looks in the clouds, scorning the base degrees
By which he did ascend. / So Caesar may. /
Then, lest he may, prevent. / And since the quarrel
Will bear no color for the thing he is, /
Fashion it thus: / that what he is, augmented,
Would run to these and these extremities. /
And therefore think him as a serpent's egg, /
Which, hatched, would, as his kind, grow
mischievous /
And kill him in the shell. (2.1.10–36)

Many variations on group or choral readings can be developed in the classroom or with time for rehearsal, and the process of sharing the reading of one character's speech or an exchange between characters (read by groups rather than individuals) invites your students to explore the sound of the words and the rhythm of the dialogue. All of these explorations can increase comprehension and appreciation.

Translations Into Modern English

Many teachers ask students to paraphrase scenes from Shakespeare into contemporary language in the form of a parallel script to *Julius Caesar*, then perform their modernized versions. I favor this activity over finding preexisting modernizations (and they are out there) because paraphrasing, as a form of summary writing, is a scientifically proven strategy for reading comprehension (Graham & Perin, 2007; Marzano, Pickering, & Pollock, 2001). Paraphrasing is more exacting than summary writing, in the sense that everything in the original script must be accounted for.

If students are able to take the words of Shakespeare and translate them with reasonable accuracy, retaining the sense, tone, and rhythm of the Shakespearean original, opportunities for talking about staging and class discussion will present themselves. The best way to approach this work of paraphrasing for translated performance is in small chunks.

Another variation on the translation theme is to do echo-performances, where students pair up, translate a speech or section of a scene, then perform as doubles, with one student speaking the lines in Shakespearean verse and the other student, standing behind the first student, repeating the line in modern English. The visual and verbal effect can be entertaining and enlightening.

ACTIVITY (SAS #19): IN YOUR OWN WORDS.

Ask students to start with a small speech by any character and put it in their own words, retaining the length and leaving nothing out. Each phrase and reference should be represented. Then have them try again in a passage involving more than one character. Have students share their individual work. Next, have groups translate complete subsections of scenes for performance (see Chapter 5 for subdivisions of scenes). Students work together to develop the scenes and check each other's comprehension in the process.

A few details to consider for advanced learners or for those who demonstrate verbal agility: Have students try to maintain some aspect of the Shakespearean script, such as staying with iambic pentameter or constructing original imagery to convey the ideas of the text. Have students create action based on their scripts in order to bring them to life. Students can use film, photography, or animation to augment their scenes. Students can come up with original costumes, set designs, and properties. Most importantly, a return to the original text following the performance, or a parallel performance with the same stage action, will allow for deeper analysis of Shakespeare. Students can even write original narratives or scripts that embed stage directions in the dialogue.

Multimedia Representations

Students have access to a wide array of media tools that can aid them in producing multimedia representations of scenes from *Julius Caesar*. These possibilities run from audio podcasts, to short films, to animation, to collages of images, text, and voiceover. Theatre has always been about producing a complete sensory experience, and students who may not be interested in standing in front of their peers acting live theatre may discover directorial or studio skills by presenting a scene from *Julius Caesar* in Windows Media, Flash animation, or any number of other programs.

It helps if you have a rudimentary knowledge of and access to equipment and software students will use to produce their films, podcasts, music videos, and image collages, but students who have those skills can work independently with your guidance as the expert in Shakespeare, allowing them to be the experts in the media. For examples of this type of project, you can find many amateur and student-produced Shakespeare adaptations on YouTube.

Possible multimedia adaptations of *Julius Caesar* include:

- videotaped performance of scenes from *Julius Caesar*;

- videotaped performance with music and sound effects added;

- audio podcast of script reading (with or without sound effects);

- podcast of commentary on the script with discussions;

- live news report sharing events in the script (see Chapter 8);

- musical collage of images representative of events and/or themes in the play;

- recorded musical adaptation of themes, events, and characters in the script;

- animated sequence of dialogue and storytelling from *Julius Caesar* using Flash, Alice, or another animation program;

- videotaped interpretive dance representing a theme, scene, or character from the play; or

- voiceover for mimed actions from the play.

A beneficial element of these media-based performances and projects is that they can be posted in a web environment that allows for students and visitors to comment on what they have seen and heard, much like readers comment on electronic news stories through blogs and list postings. The postings themselves can constitute a kind of performance around the media performance and stimulate discussion through the web, which you can continue in class.

Scene Lab in Class

As demonstrated, you may choose a scene cutting of a few exchanges of dialogue and turn it into a classroom laboratory tool that enhances student comprehension of the text. Any set of lines from the script may be examined for performance signals, but if you pick an early scene with multiple speakers, you will have broader participation. A great scene from *Julius Caesar* for such a laboratory exercise is the opening of Act 1, scene 2. Here is the cutting:

Enter Caesar, Antony for the course, Calphurnia, Portia, Decius, Cicero, Brutus, Cassius, Casca, a Soothsayer; after them Marullus and Flavius [and Citizens.]

Caesar:	Calphurnia.
Casca:	Peace, ho! Caesar speaks.
Caesar:	Calphurnia.
Calphurnia:	Here, my lord.
Caesar:	Stand you directly in Antonius' way
	When he doth run his course.—Antonius.
Antony:	Caesar, my lord.
Caesar:	Forget not, in your speed, Antonius,
	To touch Calphurnia, for our elders say
	The barren, touchèd in this holy chase,
	Shake off their sterile curse.
Antony:	I shall remember.
	When Caesar says "Do this," it is performed.
Caesar:	Set on, and leave no ceremony out.
Soothsayer:	Caesar.
Caesar:	Ha! Who calls?
Casca:	Bid every noise be still. Peace, yet again!
Caesar:	Who is it in the press that calls on me?
	I hear a tongue shriller than all music
	Cry "Caesar." Speak. Caesar is turned to hear.
Soothsayer:	Beware the ides of March.
Caesar:	What man is that?
Brutus:	A soothsayer bids you beware the ides of March.
Caesar:	Set him before me. Let me see his face.

Cassius:	Fellow, come from the throng. Look upon Caesar.
Caesar:	What sayst thou to me now? Speak once again.
Soothsayer:	Beware the ides of March
Caesar:	He is a dreamer. Let us leave him. Pass. (1.2.1–29)

When you have assigned roles for each of the parts listed, you will have at least 12 students up in front of the class. Have the class create, with your help, a starting tableau, or an original position for the players. We know from the previous scene that Caesar is returning in triumph to Rome and that he is celebrating the feast of the Lupercal. You can give your students background on Lupercal, or you can assign a student or students to investigate the holiday, perhaps assigning the role of "Google guru" to one of the more tech-savvy students. Once the players are in position, have them start to speak the lines, with the understanding that you will stop them and consult with your directors (the other students) frequently, so they should expect to be speaking the lines more than once. Let's break down the scene and discuss it in sections, as we would once the action begins.

Caesar:	Calphurnia.
Casca:	Peace, ho! Caesar speaks.
Caesar:	Calphurnia.
Calphurnia:	Here, my lord. (1.2.1–4)

As soon as the first line is spoken, we have a signal. Caesar calls his wife's name. The next person to speak, however, is not his wife, but Casca, who commands quiet from the crowd. These five first words of the scene, "Calphurnia" and "Peace ho, Caesar speaks" tell us a number of things about staging. First, Calphurnia must not be standing right next to Caesar, or he wouldn't have to call for her in order to speak to her. If your class has placed Calphurnia next to Caesar previous to the start of the action, they now have to figure out where would be a better place for her to stand. Should she be behind Caesar? Off to the side? Why? When she says, "Here, my lord," is it a signal that he can't find her in the crowd or something else, perhaps that she is ceremoniously announcing her presence? Also, what does Casca's call for quiet indicate? First, it is a signal that the scene is noisy. If an actor on stage calls for quiet, and it's already quiet, the actor's line doesn't make sense. But could Casca's line signify more than just an attempt to help Caesar locate his wife?

Caesar:	Stand you directly in Antonius' way
	When he doth run his course.—Antonius.
Antony:	Caesar, my lord.
Caesar:	Forget not, in your speed, Antonius,

To touch Calphurnia, for our elders say
The barren, touchèd in this holy chase,
Shake off their sterile curse. (1.2.5–11)

Is Caesar's conversation with Calphurnia, which is about the very personal topic of her sterility, intended to be heard by everyone present, or is it a private exchange between the two? Within the first few lines of the text, therefore, we have directorial decisions to make that will affect our audience's perception of the scene and of Caesar. What do we think of a Caesar who plays out his superstition regarding his wife's "sterile curse" in front of the public? It is here that you have students read the lines with both actions that represent intentions, first having Caesar pull Calphurnia and Antonius aside, and then having Caesar speak for all to hear. Students will see immediately that the script, the words on the page, can come to indicate a variety of meanings based on the accompanying actions.

And what is Caesar's tone of voice as he discusses his wife's "sterile curse"? Is he amused, hopeful, disgusted? What nonverbal communication, if any, is shared between Calphurnia and Antony? See what your students think. Also, how would the other players on stage react? In order to develop possibilities for scene interpretation, we must consider the notion of character intent or objective. In essence, similar to the "stakes game" from Chapter 6, thinking in terms of character objective or what the character wants in the scene helps students to discuss what the character *does* on stage. As Rocklin (2005) so clearly described it, "The objective of action is the character's intended outcome, and it *must be stated as a desire or wish*, with an active verb in the infinitive form" (p. 133–134). An example might be, "Caesar wants his wife to bear a child" or "Antony wants to please Caesar." Related to objective, then, we must consider action. Does Caesar touch Calphurnia? Pull her by the arm? Keep her at a distance? What about Antony? Does Caesar touch him? Does the fact that Antony answers immediately (unlike Calphurnia) indicate where he is standing relative to Caesar? Let's look at the further progression of the scene.

Antony:	I shall remember.
	When Caesar says "Do this," it is performed.
Caesar:	Set on, and leave no ceremony out.
Soothsayer:	Caesar.
Caesar:	Ha! Who calls? (1.2.12–16)

Students can consider Antony's response to Caesar as a statement of fact, brown nosing, or a warning to those around him. How should Antony deliver his line? Does he address it to Caesar, to Calphurnia, or to others? When Caesar gives the command to "set on and leave no ceremony out" (1.2.14), what is he talking about? What if the crowd were to cheer between "set on" and "leave no ceremony out"? How would that affect the scene? As students discuss these options, you can "rewind" the scene and have your students play it in the fashion the class directors have decided makes the most sense to them. Other than modeling the process of considering the relationship between the words of the script and the actual play, this process will be a good tutorial for the independent scene work you assign to students after they have read the script in its entirety.

What happens next, involving the soothsayer, also demands treatment of script signals. Notice that Caesar stops immediately with "Ha! Who calls?" (1.2.16). Is it odd that a man who we will soon learn is deaf in one ear, and who is working his way through a crowd, should so quickly hear and acknowledge someone saying his name, theoretically mixed with many others who could be calling his name as well? A clue comes in the next few lines.

Casca:	Bid every noise be still. Peace, yet again!
Caesar:	Who is it in the press that calls on me?
	I hear a tongue shriller than all music
	Cry "Caesar." Speak. Caesar is turned to hear.
Soothsayer:	Beware the ides of March. (1.2.17-21)

Clearly, it is the fact that the voice is "shriller than all music" (1.2.19) that draws Caesar's attention. Have the student playing the soothsayer experiment (to his or her peers' delight) with such voices as will catch Caesar's attention. Ask students to consider why Caesar would stop suddenly to acknowledge this voice. Is Caesar annoyed? Pleased? Worried? Have your student playing Caesar apply each of those subtexts to the line "Speak. Caesar is turned to hear" (1.2.20) and have student directors choose what they would like to hear. Also, what does it mean that "Caesar is turned to hear"? We will see in the lines that follow that Caesar has Brutus pull the fellow from the crowd, so we can't have the soothsayer right in front of Caesar initially.

Caesar:	What man is that?
Brutus:	A soothsayer bids you beware the ides of March.
Caesar:	Set him before me. Let me see his face.
Cassius:	Fellow, come from the throng. Look upon Caesar.
Caesar:	What sayst thou to me now? Speak once again.
Soothsayer:	Beware the ides of March
Caesar:	He is a dreamer. Let us leave him. Pass. (1.2.22–29)

At this point, your students will already have the opportunity to see the text as a set of instructions, and they will have ideas for how to stage the scene. They may wonder how Brutus knows that the man is a soothsayer. Is the man dressed in a way that signifies his profession, or does Brutus know him? Or does Brutus have a quiet conversation with the man between Caesar asking "What man is that?" (1.2.22) and Brutus's response? In the final lines of the exchange, we have the soothsayer pulled from the crowd and "set" before Caesar. Students can experiment with the handling of the soothsayer and his confrontation with Caesar. Is he ominous in his delivery of the warning? Pitying? Pleading? Does Caesar flinch? What about Calphurnia, Antony, and the others? How do they react? Gasps? Laughter? By making these decisions regarding this small section of an early scene, students start to articulate a vision and a process for reading that is informed by consideration of staging. Using theatrical processes, they create, discuss, and communicate meaning.

Extended Scene Work

Having created a scene through this in-class scene lab, students will be ready to work independently in groups to develop their own scenes. Below is a description of the several steps you can take to create a patchwork production of scenes with your students, followed by further discussion of signals as a reading/directing strategy.

ACTIVITY (SAS #21): SCENE PERFORMANCE.

Dramatizing the script can lead us to a deeper interaction with *Julius Caesar* and understanding of it, which is also the best practice for students in the classroom. If you and your students can invest a week or more in the process, the results can be very satisfying. Here's how it works:

1. Complete initial reading of the script with classroom activities and discussion (see Chapters 4, 5, and 6).
2. Having read the script, have students as a large group select scenes or sections to perform. Select cuttings of 30–50 lines (just a guideline, not a rule). You can involve individual students in this step or make the cuttings yourself. Be sure to include cuttings from each act of the play so that most major events are represented.
3. Assign groups and assign scenes (see SAS #21). You can decide, based upon your knowledge of your students, whether to allow them to choose their own partners and scenes, or whether to assign groups yourself. Hand out scene cuttings to the students and have them begin reading.
4. Review the difference between a script and a play. Show them how Shakespeare left clues (signals) for actors in the scripts (see list of signals on SAS #21). Have them explore possible clues for the actors in their individual scenes.

---

5. Conduct your class in a large space, like the auditorium or gym, to allow students the time to rehearse and develop their scenes. Give guidance according to their level of engagement.

6. Have the entire group generate ideas for set and backdrop painting. Have students submit designs, then have the group vote on how to incorporate designs into the set. Have students interested in painting the backdrop begin with that, and have students interested in building a set do that, if time and budget allow.

7. Encourage students who play musical instruments to bring them to class. Demonstrate how only a few notes are necessary, when combining instruments, to create an overture and musical scene transitions. Have students acting in early scenes perform musical transitions for late scenes, and visa versa. Give students time to create their own musical interludes.

8. Create a storytelling element to link the scenes in the performance. Students can generate the narrative transitions between scenes as a creative writing exercise. Choose interested students to perform these links between scenes either by reading or reciting the storytelling transitions.

9. Encourage students to create their own costumes and props. Rehearse the entire performance and give students the opportunity to make changes. Invite students to share any additional ideas for set, backdrop, music, special effects, acting, storytelling, or any other aspect of the production.

10. Invite parents, relatives, other classes, and others to watch the performance. Celebrate your achievement, and then ask students to write reflectively on what the experience meant to them. Discuss those reflections with students.

For in-class scene work, it is better to give students short cuttings typed on separate pages rather than photocopied out of the text. A scene with three to five actors, with 30–50 lines of text, is more than sufficient for students to develop an interpretation by using the signals presented in the script. The scene excerpted on pages 187–188 from Act 1, scene 2 is of an appropriate length. All editorial stage directions, commonly bracketed, may be removed, as they are often arbitrary, and sometimes just wrong.

Once you have chosen chunks of the text to perform, address the notion of signals and how the text holds the clues the students need to bring the scene to life. Every line, every word, every exchange of dialogue implies its own action, movement, and impact. The student rehearsals are collaborative. Together they discover a meaning that makes sense to them that they can present dramatically to their peers. As the teacher, you may help in the process, make suggestions to prompt struggling groups, and lend an extra set of eyes to the scene, but be careful not to prescribe action because at that moment the scene becomes your constructed reality and not the students'.

Students' ability to memorize lines will be variable, not only due to talent levels but due to commitment levels to the process. What will help them memorize their lines more than any process will be their understanding of what they are saying, which will come through study of performance clues in the dialogue. Listening for the rhythm of their lines will also help with memorization. The collective performance, with each group having a different cutting and presenting them in the order they appear in the play, gives the class the opportunity to see a production that shows different interpretations of character and action. Scenes will be linked together through the storytelling, done by the teacher or by the students themselves, and the added elements of set, props, costumes, and music immerse them in the play.

As students reach advanced levels of study, or for those students showing giftedness in acting, teachers can involve them in lengthened, serious textual analysis for work on monologues or extended scene dramatizations. The issues of subtext can emerge in character portrayals. Character motives can drive scene action, and ultimately, teachers may want to take the next, most gratifying step, which is the production of an entire play.

The dramatic process also involves multiple intelligences, from the analytical, verbal, and interpersonal, to the musical, spatial, and bodily-kinesthetic. Students analyze the text critically; they take on a language that is new and challenging, and then work together to create meaning. They design sound to accompany their scenes, they negotiate space in order to communicate, and they challenge themselves physically to portray character and action. No other educational process involves a more comprehensive utilization of children's capacities, and few educational processes are nearly as much fun for them as acting Shakespeare.

Whether you decide to take one day from your classroom study of *Julius Caesar* to create a dramatic laboratory or to take 2–3 weeks to have students develop their own scenes for dramatic performance, you will find that thrusting students into the roles of actors and directors and teaching them to read Shakespeare while making decisions based upon the text will be one of your most rewarding classroom experiments.

Scene Painting/Set Design/Visual Art

Studying *Julius Caesar*, students can create visual art to represent their understanding of the conspiracy, the ideals of Rome, or the war. Virtually all aspects of the story, from the themes of revenge and honor, to the characters and the events, can become the subject matter for paintings, drawings, and sculptures. Eisner

(1979) and Gardner (1999) have both explained how representations of knowledge can take many forms, and students, especially gifted students, benefit from opportunities to develop artistic representations of what they know (Duggan, 2007). Students can match their visual elements with written or spoken explanations of the effects they were hoping to achieve, or they can team with classmates to perform scenes that make use of the visual representations they have developed.

ACTIVITY (SAS #22): SCENIC PAINTING.

As previously mentioned, students can easily add scenic backdrops of Rome or other stage design elements to their performances, including properties such as furniture, walls, and natural elements. The visual elements of the scene, such as a backdrop and stage furniture, can become valuable artistic endeavors for the students.

Music

Beyond the uses of music discussed above in connection with multimedia presentations, students can adapt or create musical responses to *Julius Caesar* that provoke thought and discussion and that force students back into the text, mining for details about characters and events that they can transform into music. Students can find existing music that represents their notions of Rome or Caesar, but brain research (Jensen, 1998) has shown that students are intellectually more engaged when they are involved in actual music composition as opposed to simply listening to music. Musical representation of literature is as old as literature itself, and Shakespeare made extensive use of music in his plays. Students can compose theme music for *Julius Caesar* or for individual scenes or lines from *Julius Caesar*, or they can write songs with lyrics that explain the story.

ACTIVITY (SAS #23): THE CHARACTER'S THEME.

Challenge students who are musical to pick characters from the play and write short riffs (melodic progressions) that represent the characters. Have students who play different instruments combine their riffs to create musical dialogue. Then put those characters (riffs) together and start a musical conversation to represent a scene that involves multiple characters. This process is exactly how thematic music can start, and students can be given the option to create an entire overture for the play, a character, or an individual scene. As always, the students should be willing to explain either in writing or verbally to you and to the class the decisions they made in composing the music. Another option is to have students write their own lyrics to tell the story of *Julius Caesar*.

Stage Production of *Julius Caesar*

The commitment to mount a full production of *Julius Caesar* is an enterprise that will require a considerable time commitment, much more than what you can accomplish in a conventional 3–6 week unit in an AP or regular English class. As we have seen throughout this text, integrating performance into your classroom study is not only a must, but it is the very key to unlocking the play. Producing the play as a full production, on the other hand, will involve collaboration with your theatre department, and you will need to make decisions regarding set design, rehearsal schedules, casting, costume design, lighting, sound, and all of the normal conventions required by theatre production. You will need to decide whether you as the teacher will direct the play, or whether the students will direct themselves (or whether you will hire an outside director). You will need to decide what kind of budget you have before making decisions about set, costume, and work schedules. You may want to have someone direct who can lead the production toward some sense of unity, but who also allows the student actors to make discoveries as they develop their characters. If you can meet these contingencies, a full production of *Julius Caesar* will be possible.

The purpose of this chapter has been to show how performance can unlock the themes of *Julius Caesar* and help your students to create their own interpretations of the script. The next chapter will culminate our consideration of *Julius Caesar* by examining how we understand and write about the text.

Chapter Materials

Student Activity Sheet #19:
In Your Own Words

Applicable Portion of Play: Students' choice

Objectives: 1.   Students will be able to put Shakespeare's characters' speeches into modern English.

              2.   Students will be able to represent scenes from *Julius Caesar* in their own words.

Common Core Standard(s): 11-12.R.L.1, 11-12.W.2

Directions: Pick a short speech by any character in *Julius Caesar* and put it in your own words, retaining the length and leaving nothing out. Each phrase and reference should be represented. When you have finished and are happy with your work, try again using a passage involving more than one character. Share your translation with your class, recruiting fellow students to speak the lines. Ask your teacher to allow you to perform your translated speeches and scenes.

Example: From Act 2, scene 2:
Original:
    Decius: This dream is all amiss interpreted.
             It was a vision fair and fortunate.
             Your statue spouting blood in many pipes,
             In which so many smiling Romans bathed,
             Signifies that from you great Rome shall suck
             Reviving blood, and that great men shall press
             For tinctures, stains, relics, and cognizance.
             This by Calphurnia's dream is signified.

Translation:
    Decius: This dream has not been interpreted correctly.
             It was a good dream, meaning that good things will
             happen. Your statue spouting blood from many
             places on your body means that Rome will be
             greater because of your leadership, and great men
             shall seek favors from you, as though you are a saint. This
             is what Calphurnia's dream really means.

Reflection: What is difficult about translating Shakespeare? What is easy? How does this activity affect your ability to understand what Shakespeare wrote?

_____

_____

_____

_____

_____

Student Activity Sheet #20:
Multimedia Shakespeare

Applicable Portion of Play: Students' choice

Objectives:
1. Students will be able to incorporate media into understanding Shakespeare.
2. Students will be able to present some aspect of *Julius Caesar* using media tools.

Common Core Standard(s): 11-12.R.L.1, 11-12.R.L., 11-12.R.L.7, 11-12.SL.5

Directions: Working in groups of three or four, develop a multimedia representation of a scene, theme, or conflict in *Julius Caesar*. You have a great deal of freedom with this assignment, but the list below may provide some guidance. Use technology available to you or available in the school. Possible multimedia adaptations of *Julius Caesar* are listed below:

- videotaped performance of scenes from *Julius Caesar*;
- videotaped performance with music and sound effects added;
- audio podcast of script reading (with or without sound effects);
- podcast of commentary on the script with discussions;
- live news report sharing events in the script;
- musical collage of images representative of events and/or themes in the play;
- recorded musical adaptation of themes, events, and characters in the script;
- animated sequence of dialogue and storytelling from *Julius Caesar* using Flash, Alice, or another animation program;
- videotaped interpretive dance representing a theme, scene, or character from the play;
- voiceover for mimed actions from the play; or
- a project of your own choosing that incorporates multimedia elements.

Reflection: How did technology choices affect your presentation of your topic?

_____

_____

_____

_____

_____

_____

_____

_____

Student Activity Sheet #21:
Scene Performance

Applicable Portion of Play: Student-selected scenes

Objectives:
1. Students will be able to memorize, rehearse, and perform a short scene from *Julius Caesar*.
2. Students will apply knowledge of script signals to the rehearsal process.

Common Core Standard(s): 11-12.R.L.1, 11-12.R.L.2, 11-12.SL.1.b

Directions: This assignment will take a week to complete. Working with a group of classmates, choose a short scene from *Julius Caesar* to develop for performance. Assign roles, memorize your lines, and rehearse the scene, using signals in the script to give clues for performance. Try different options in performance until you discover what makes sense to you and your scene-mates. Fill in your scene with any special effects you wish to add, costumes, etc., and perform for your classmates.

This list of signals should be helpful for you:

- stage directions (printed but not bracketed),
- explicit stage directions in dialogue (e.g., "Then fall, Caesar"),
- implicit stage directions in dialogue,
- line length and structure,
- punctuation,
- poetry,
- diction,
- syntax,
- rhythm and pauses,
- rhyme,
- tone,
- imagery,

- sequence of speakers,
- length of speech,
- action in dialogue,
- question and answer,
- song,
- prose,
- character,
- placement of scene,
- preceding action,
- subsequent action,
- soliloquy, and
- many more.

Reflection: How did the process of rehearsing this scene increase your understanding of the scene and the play? What signals did you find most important to your character?

_____

_____

_____

_____

_____

_____

_____

Name: _____ Date: _____

Student Activity Sheet #22:
Scenic Painting

Applicable Portion of Play: All

Objectives: 1.   Students will be able to sketch scenic backdrops for the various scenes in *Julius Caesar.*
                2.   Students will be able to connect their scenic painting designs to the themes and elements of the story.

Common Core Standard(s): 11-12.R.L.7, 11-12.R.L.2, 11-12.SL.5

Directions: Using a computer program or freehand drawing, design a scenic backdrop or backdrops for *Julius Caesar.* You may create one large design that incorporates all of the scenes, or create a series of backdrops that represent the Roman Capitol, the residence of Caesar or Brutus, or the battlefields. As a class, display the different designs.

If time permits, you can translate your sketches into full-size backdrops.

Reflection: How does a scenic backdrop affect our perception of the action of the play?

_____

_____

_____

_____

_____

_____

_____

_____

_____

_____

_____

_____

_____

_____

_____

_____

Name: _____   Date: _____

Student Activity Sheet #23:
The Character's Theme

Applicable Portion of Play: All

Objectives:
1. Students will be able to create melodic representations of major characters in *Julius Caesar*.
2. Students will write original lyrics to tell the story of a character, a scene, or any aspect of *Julius Caesar*.

Common Core Standard(s): 11-12.SL.5, 11-12.R.L.1

Directions: Choose a character or set of characters from *Julius Caesar* and create original musical riffs to represent them. You may work individually or with classmates. Have different instruments to represent the different characters, and try to match the musical representation with the character's personality. Put your musical characters together and create a musical conversation that you can then share with your classmates. Explain the sounds you chose and how they represent that character. Another option is to play your music while your fellow students act out or read the scene. A third option is to make a melody and write lyrics to represent a character, a scene, or any other aspect of the story. Sing and play your song for the class.

Reflection: How did you arrive at the choices you made for developing your musical response to the play?

_____

_____

_____

_____

_____

_____

_____

_____

_____

_____

_____

_____

_____

_____

_____

Advanced Placement Classroom: Julius Caesar © Prufrock Press • This page may be photocopied or reproduced with permission for single classroom use.

"What meanst thou by that?": Understanding and Writing About *Julius Caesar*

In English classes everywhere, analytical or critical writing completes the cycle of inquiry that begins with introduction to a piece of literature, reading and concurrent discussion, informal writing, and performance. In assessment plans constructed by thoughtful teachers, students demonstrate their achievement of unit and course objectives by arguing an interpretation and perhaps an evaluation of the literary work they are tasked with examining. Such writing, typically structured around a thesis and support organized via textual progression or thematic strain, dominates literature classes in high schools and colleges (see Pirie [1997], and Blau [2003], for thoughtful critique of the "hegemony" of the thesis essay). Such writing is also the stuff of the AP examination in English Literature and Composition. Highly structured analytical essays are typically a summative expression of learning and, as such, constitute only a portion of the writing students may do while studying challenging works, such as *Julius Caesar*.

This chapter will present ideas for using writing to learn (Murray, 2004) throughout the process of studying Shakespeare's text. I will showcase innovative ways to introduce research-based writing strategies to help students articulate their struggles and their breakthroughs in constructing meaning out of the text. Furthermore, we will consider the structure and nature of Advanced Placement examination topics, engage critical perspectives, and entertain the notion of creative responses to the text.

Students studying *Julius Caesar* benefit from frequent writing that spans the range from informal, immediate response to highly structured, revised, critical analysis. Students can use writing as a means of developing their thinking about the text and clarifying their understanding of specific passages. Students in

Advanced Placement classes will ultimately be called upon to demonstrate their ability to clearly express compelling and well-reasoned interpretations of specific passages of literature and broad themes in a timed setting, through the essays on the Advanced Placement exam. As stated in the course description for AP English Literature and Composition (College Board, 2011a):

> Writing to understand a literary work may involve writing response and reaction papers along with annotation, freewriting, and keeping some form of a reading journal. Writing to explain a literary work involves analysis and interpretation, and may include writing brief, focused analyses on aspects of language and structure. Writing to evaluate a literary work involves making and explaining judgments about its artistry and exploring its underlying social and cultural values through analysis, interpretation, and argument. (p. 50)

These writing tasks spring from the basic premise of literary study, which centers on reading experience, interpretation, and evaluation. One kind of topic students address in writing their AP essays, examples of which appear later in this chapter, calls upon students to produce an interpretation of a work in relation to a specific theme or literary element. The other kind of topic involves reading a passage from a work that may be unfamiliar (one poetry and one prose) and demonstrating the ability to arrive at an interpretation by activating good reading strategies, ranging from context clues to examination of imagery, structure, tone, or rhetorical devices (e.g., repetition, antithesis, reasoning models). Teaching literature at this level also means teaching students to construct written arguments that use specific evidence from the text and that stand up to close scrutiny.

Effective study of challenging texts includes giving students opportunities to write informal responses to their reading, responses that typically are not graded and that are used to further understanding or jumpstart discussion. These informal written responses occur throughout the unit. Chapters 5 and 6 include several discussion/journal topics that call for the kind of ungraded, informal response writing that becomes part of students' formative process. These writings can then provide raw material for more focused analytical writing. Informal response writing acknowledges that engagement with literature may involve emotional responses as well as intellectual ones (Rosenblatt, 1983). Whether using dialectical journals or learning logs (Gillespie, 2010), students can address global or local aspects of their reading in a nonthreatening way. Following are some typical prompts for informal responses.

Informal Response Writing

As mentioned in Chapter 4, students can begin informal writing about *Julius Caesar* before they begin reading it. Prereading prompts such as the following can get students thinking about the experience they are entering:

1. Reflect on your experiences reading or watching Shakespeare prior to this class.
2. What do you know or what have you heard about *Julius Caesar*?
3. Describe how you feel about Shakespeare's works at this point.
4. What are your greatest concerns about reading *Julius Caesar*?
5. What do you expect this experience reading *Julius Caesar* to be like? What do you expect of yourself, and what do you expect from your teacher?

Before beginning their study of the text, students can also write in response to topics that relate to themes they will encounter in the play such as:

1. Have you ever worried that a friend of yours was too full of himself?
2. How do you respond when someone you love is clearly troubled?
3. How do you feel about the notion of revenge? Is revenge ever justified, and if so, under what circumstances?
4. Is killing another human being ever justified? If so, under what circumstances?
5. Is our greatest responsibility to ourselves, our families, our friends, or our country? Would you sacrifice your family relationships or your friendships in order to serve your country?
6. Do you believe in the supernatural? How easy is it for you to suspend disbelief when you see supernatural elements in TV shows or movies?

You can certainly generate your own prereading topics, but any of these can get students thinking about the imaginative world they are about to enter as they read *Julius Caesar*.

Once they have started their writing-as-thinking relationship with the text, you will want to have them continue writing informally as they work through the script, act by act, and sometimes scene by scene. I would caution you against just giving them a list of 50 journal questions/topics (like the list of study questions at the end of Chapter 5), then expecting them to do periodic writing, as that method will become tedious for them and you. What you want is genuine response writing that asks your students to engage with the text, think about what they are encountering, and then write as a means of developing an individual experience. You may even find yourself making use of "quick-writes" in the classroom either before, during, or after discussions.

Although students will benefit from writing after reading a substantial portion of the script, they should also be encouraged to have a writing journal or computer screen available *as* they read, so that they can write down questions, concerns, or insights they have while reading. If students have their own scripts that they can write on, all the better, as you can teach them to make marginal notes and "score" their text.

There's a good deal of freedom in response-based writing, and you can learn about what your students notice in their reading that spurs their writing. One student may write about the characters almost exclusively, whereas another may focus primarily on his frustration with the difficulty of the language, and another may compare Brutus's situation with her own. Personal reactions, feelings, and progressions of feelings are valid as well.

ACTIVITY (SAS #24): ONGOING JOURNAL.

Here are some ideas that may help students generate writing as they work through the text from the beginning to the end:

1. Have students keep track of *how* they read the script. For example, how much they read alone, how much they read in class with classmates, and how much they read aloud. Have them log how much time they spend reading during each sitting and gauge (from 1–10) how difficult the reading is. They may note whether they get tired before they stop or whether they feel they could go on further than what was assigned.

2. Have students write how they feel while reading, what their involvement with the various characters is, and what they think the story is about. If their thoughts change as they progress through the script, have them note it in their journals.

3. Have students try to make connections between what is happening in the script and experiences they have heard of or experienced themselves. They can also write about examples from popular culture that the story reminds them of, or if they see the story as wholly extraordinary, they can write about what makes the story extraordinary.

4. Have students write a journal of one of the characters, like Cassius, Brutus, or Portia, writing as that character, reflecting on that character's feelings and thoughts about Caesar or Rome.

5. Have students write about themselves and specifically their own sense of self, as reflected in the story. What qualities of different characters do they see in themselves? What qualities do they lack but admire? What qualities are they glad they do not possess? These inquiries into self can increase students' interest in the plot of the story.

I would strongly encourage pre- and postdiscussion writing as a way to help students prepare for conversation and retain what they heard and said during discussion and as a form of metacognition. Students can use these informal writings as a way to track their own understanding of the text and identify personal breakthroughs during their process of reading and interpreting.

One additional benefit of informal response-based writing, especially if students are allowed the freedom to write whatever comes to mind as they work through the script, is that student responses may lean toward a particular kind of critical inquiry (Gillespie, 2010). If a student writes primarily about Rome and the political situation, political theory may be a good set of ideas to introduce for the student. If the student writes mainly about characters and their relationships or their motivations, psychological or sociological lenses may work for them.

In *The Digital Writing Workshop*, Troy Hicks (2009) demonstrated how students can build online learning communities related to their reading with blogs, wikis, or other social networking software. Students can start homepages for characters, share their thoughts as they read in a reviewable version of their reading journals, or collaborate in building commentary on the action.

Writing About Character: Intervention

Although the topics for informal writing considered thus far have been somewhat global in focus, students can also use informal writing to address character development and features of individual scenes. Character analysis is always a good place to start in attempting to come to an understanding of a text, and *Julius Caesar* offers us a number of larger-than-life characters to examine. Each of the leading characters demonstrates strengths and weaknesses as they act in the story and negotiate relationships with the other characters.

ACTIVITY (SAS #25): CHARACTER INTERVENTION.

One activity that focuses on character and can introduce elements of psychological theory is what I call Character Intervention. As students read the script, have them develop profiles of different characters using terms that translate easily to character analysis. For example, students can make categories as follows: positive traits/demonstrated by, negative traits/demonstrated by, motivations/demonstrated by, fears/demonstrated by. You will notice that the designations of traits, motivations, and fears are judgments on the character, and the "demonstrated by" column requires specific reference to character words or actions. You can add categories in a visual diagnosis sheet such as biggest mistake, next likely move, potential protector(s), and potential aggressor(s).

Anticipating problems on the horizon for that character, students then write a summary, framed as a speech to be delivered at an intervention for that character. Have students identify the point in the script where they would have the intervention for the character in order to prevent disaster. For example, an intervention with Caesar himself may happen right before Act 3, scene 1, and an intervention with Brutus might come earlier or later, depending upon the focus of the intervention. With the character intervention script, your students will engage in the kind of character analysis we would typically expect in analytical writing, but the context of the intervention will frame the task in a way that motivates students. Students can even act out their intervention scripts or read them to the class.

Sample excerpt from Character Intervention with Cassius, to happen during Act 1, scene 3:

Cassius,

I'm worried that you are on the wrong path in your life. I can see by the story you told Brutus about your swimming match with Caesar that you are very competitive, which can be a good thing. But I also sensed a lot of jealousy on your part toward Caesar, and I'm concerned that you are trying to turn others against him just to feed your own envy. I appreciate your talent in persuasion, especially your use of analogies. Calling Caesar a wolf and the Romans sheep was brilliant. But you are engaging in reckless behavior, walking around in the storm with your shirt wide open, daring the gods to strike you with lightning. . . .

As a follow-up to the character intervention activity, have students identify spots in the script where characters attempt to do interventions with other characters, and discuss how successful those interventions are. Examples include Portia with Brutus (2, 1), Calphurnia with Caesar (2, 2), and Cassius with Brutus (3, 1).

Teenagers demonstrate wonderful candor about characters, and they will form opinions of the characters in *Julius Caesar* that are both positive and negative. We only have what people say and what they do upon which to base our judgments of character, and with scripts, we have to create some of the "do" part ourselves, based on how we interpret action in the script. Students can take advantage of several tools, such as visual representations (character maps) that can build their thinking. The joint IRA/NCTE website http://www.readwritethink.org offers many visual thinking tools that can help students keep track of their growing understanding, and character maps are just one option (see http://www.readwritethink.org/materials/dramamap).

Another approach to character is to look at visual interpretations of *Julius Caesar*. For example, have students examine the movie poster for the 1953

(Houseman & Mankiewicz) version of *Julius Caesar* shown on the Internet Movie Database (http://www.imdb.com). Students should notice that Antony (Marlon Brando) has by far the largest image on the poster. They may also notice that Brutus (James Mason) is depicted in the arms of Portia (Deborah Kerr), and Cassius (John Gielgud) is shown at an awkward angle. What vision of the characters is presented in the poster? Have students journal their responses.

As discussed in Chapter 5, students can also trace their interpretations of character, then gather to form "character committees" (Thisted & Mertens, 1994) to share observations of characters. What will be important in choosing to write about character is to trace changes in the character during the action of the play. We are interested in people, I believe, not just because of who they are, but also for who they may become.

Analytical Writing

Referring back to the paragraph from the AP course description, we find the second type of writing recommended is analytical writing: "Writing to explain a literary work involves analysis and interpretation, and may include writing brief, focused analyses on aspects of language and structure" (College Board, 2011a, p. 50). Such thinking and writing form the heart of any rigorous literature course, and *Julius Caesar* offers us limitless topics for analysis. As evidenced by two volumes of *Julius Caesar* criticism published in the past 10 years alone (Wilson, 2002c; Zander, 2005b), scholars continue to examine several of the play's major elements, often applying specific critical lenses to the text.

What your students will hope to achieve through active reading are footholds into the text from which they can develop rational thesis statements and well-supported arguments. Suggestions for analytical writing here fall into these categories: summary writing, writing about stage signals, cutting the script, using literary elements, writing in response to model Advanced Placement examination topics, critical analysis, and using critical sources.

Summary Writing: News Report

According to Graham and Perin (2007), summarization is the second-most effective type of writing instruction for improving writing among middle and high school students, and that assertion echoes an earlier meta-analysis by Marzano, Pickering, and Pollock (2001) that ranked summary writing and note-taking second among teaching strategies that had the most impact on student learning across disciplines. Assuming you and your students are willing to take on the heavy work of summary writing, decisions must be made about how many summaries to write and how detailed they must be. Will you have them summarize scene by scene or act by act? Will you have them summarize arguments made by individual characters? You may also give students the opportunity to collaborate to produce summaries, which is another research-based strategy (Graham & Perin, 2007). Students can produce visual summaries with maps and timelines to visually enhance their writing. The program Inspiration allows for a variety of visual representations of outline summaries. An even better summary exercise that can be collaborative and technology driven is the interactive news report.

ACTIVITY (SAS #26): INTERACTIVE NEWS REPORT.

One way to have students write summaries that get them to delve deeper than mere plot summary is to have students write news reports of the events of the play, together with associated "feature stories." Using the journalistic questions of what, who, when, where, how, and why, students can generate leads and stories that they present to their classmates in an online format. If your school does not have access to a web-based format, you can use Google Groups, Blogspot or any other freely available online format. Just as readers can respond to news stories in the *New York Times*, MSNBC, or other major news organizations, your students can add blog-like comments in response to the news stories posted, making the experience of writing about *Julius Caesar* akin to witnessing an ongoing news event. The comments on the news stories serve to extend the consideration of the events described into analysis and criticism. Notice in the example below from Act 1, scene 2 how the comments posted in response to the story represent a number of readings, from the silly to the serious.

News Headline: Caesar Refuses Crown; Faints

In a stunning act of selflessness, Julius Caesar today refused to be crowned king during the Lupercal celebration. He was offered the symbol of monarchy by local celebrity Mark Antony, and his refusal of the crown set off deafening cheers from the plebeian crowd. The crown was offered to him three times, and according to one eyewitness who wished to remain anonymous, "each time he put it by more gently than before." According to the witness, the cheering and bad breath of the crowd led Caesar to have an epileptic seizure, and he was observed falling down and foaming at the mouth. Details are unconfirmed, but rumors are that before he fainted, he offered to have the crowd cut his throat. We will keep our audience updated as more details of this wild holiday come to us.

In celebrity news, Marcus Brutus and Caius Cassius were seen talking together on a nearby street of Rome, and our reporters say they were whispering.

Post comments on this story:

1. bk: I wasn't there, but I think it was an act. Caesar is too smart to do anything stupid in front of the people.
2. tf: Woo, hoo, Lupercal! Pagan fertility festival!
3. gg: If I were Caesar, I would keep an eye on Cassius and Brutus. Especially Cassius because he has a "lean and hungry look."
4. gl: I was there. Cicero spoke Greek. I didn't understand him. It was Greek to me. Ha ha.
5. dd: This is a great news report. I also heard that Casca was talking to Brutus and Cassius, and that he was putting Caesar down. Are these men really Caesar's friends?

Casting summary writing in the format of a news story allows students to take on a voice that may not be their own, which takes pressure off of them to write in a stiff academic voice that is unconvincing. Students can videotape their news reports and post them for their classmates to see. Sharing responsibility for "reporting," students can track stories as they work through the play, and you can assign different students or groups of students to produce the story/summaries.

Writing About Stage Signals

As developed throughout this book, reading *Julius Caesar* as a script containing a set of instructions for actors and directors is a fruitful method, and can lead to increased comprehension, as well as clear and persuasive student writing. Students sometimes see what choices would make sense for a performance based upon their reading, but they don't see themselves in the roles of actors, and would prefer to sit on the sidelines while more gregarious students take on the roles. But even these shy students can use writing as a means of expressing their analysis of stage signals in the script.

ACTIVITY: REVISIT SAS #21 FROM CHAPTER 7.

Rather than performing your scene (or following the performance), write what stage directions you find in the words spoken by the characters that indicate actions. Describe how you would direct your chosen scene using the clues Shakespeare leaves in the script. Here are some sample scenes that work well (based on Folger edition numeration of lines):

- Act 1, scene 2, lines 1–29
- Act 1, scene 2, lines 188–208
- Act 1, scene 3, lines 136–169
- Act 2, scene 1, lines 94–123

- Act 2, scene 1, lines 335–363
- Act 2, scene 4, lines 1–23
- Act 2, scene 4, lines 24–54
- Act 3, scene 3, lines 1–30
- Act 4, scene 3, lines 1–29
- Act 4, scene 3, lines 30–59
- Act 4, scene 3, lines 60–87
- Act 4, scene 3, lines 88–121

Such written analysis of stage signals, and even a broader look to consider what actions happen around these scenes, can lead to interpretations that are supported by very specific elements of specific lines, which is the essence of close reading and interpretation. Remembering that words in scripts only provide half the evidence for interpretation of a dramatic work, our struggle to provide intelligent choices for staging constitutes the heart of the discipline because we are using the visual and auditory portals to construct meaning that is only suggested in the written source. Even if students do not wish to act, they can write about what they think actors should do in the scenes.

Other literary elements come into play in this dramatic process as well, such as figures of speech and rhetorical devices that provide material for any poetic analysis. We cannot forget that Shakespeare's scripts are also poetic texts, and that Shakespeare is a master of many poetic devices, from personification and metaphor (see Chapter 2) to elements of sound, like alliteration and euphony, and rhetorical tools such as repetition, antithesis, and parallelism. All of these literary elements may be used to interpret stage action and to write analytical prose in response to the play. One pitfall to watch for is that students, having seen a filmed version of the play, may write as though the version they saw on film is the script itself. When students write about a scene, they should be able to distinguish their own thinking from the thinking of the director of the movie. Although the scene suggestions above can work as they are, any section of the script will work for this activity if you are willing to cut lines from some of the longer speeches.

Cuttings

Speaking of cutting lines, theatre directors very seldom use the entire script of *Julius Caesar* (or any other Shakespeare script) when mounting a production of the play. One great analytical reading tool that mimics an authentic, real-world practice is scene cutting. Marilyn Halperin at Chicago Shakespeare Theater suggested this activity to me. The strategy requires students to take a segment of a scene and cut it for performance. You may frame this activity by using the following guidelines.

ACTIVITY (SAS #27): SCENE CUTTING.

Give these instructions to your students. "Today we are going to assume we are a theatre company mounting a production of *Julius Caesar*, and we need to make a tough decision. These scenes (identify the scene or scenes you want to use) must be trimmed in order to stage them, because we just don't have time to stage them in their entirety. Your job is to decide which lines may be cut without ruining the scene or lessening its potential impact. For each segment you cut, you must write a rationale that includes (1) why you chose that segment to cut and (2) what is lost by removing the segment. Then write similar rationales for the segments of the scene that you decided to keep. You must cut at least 25% of the scene and not more than 50%."

Model the activity with your students before asking them to write their analysis. This writing assignment will present a challenge to even your most talented readers. It may be done as an informal journal activity or a more formal, revised analysis. You may want to consider using this activity as a test item. Here is an example from Act 1, scene 3. I have crossed out lines for this sample, but other options, from shading on paper to using editing features in an electronic document, will work just as well.

From Act 1, scene 3:

Cassius:	Who's there?	
Casca:	A Roman.	
Cassius:	Casca, by your voice.	
Casca:	Your ear is good. Cassius, what a night is this!	45
Cassius:	A very pleasing night to honest men.	
Casca:	Who ever knew the heavens menace so?	
Cassius:	Those that have known the earth so full of faults.	
	For my part, I have walked about the streets,	
	Submitting me unto the perilous night,	50
	And thus unbracèd, Casca, as you see,	
	Have bared my bosom to the thunder-stone.	
	~~And when the cross blue lightning seemed to open~~	
	~~The breast of heaven, I did present myself~~	
	~~Even in the aim and very flash of it.~~	55
Casca:	But wherefore did you so much tempt the heavens?	
	~~It is the part of men to fear and tremble~~	
	~~When the most mighty gods by tokens send~~	
	~~Such dreadful heralds to astonish us.~~	
Cassius:	You are dull, Casca, ~~and those sparks of life~~	60

~~That should be in a Roman you do want,~~
~~Or else you use not.~~ You look pale, and gaze,
~~And put on fear, and cast yourself in wonder,~~
To see the strange impatience of the heavens.
But if you would consider the true cause   65
Why all these fires, why all these gliding ghosts,
Why birds and beasts from quality and kind,
~~Why old men, fools, and children calculate,~~
Why all these things change from their ordinance
~~Their natures, and preformèd faculties,~~   70
To monstrous quality—why, you shall find
That heaven hath infused them with these spirits
To make them instruments of fear and warning
Unto some monstrous state. (1.3.42–74)

Student Response:

In making my cuts to this segment of Act 1, scene 3, I decided to keep lines 42–52 because they move quickly and they establish the meeting of Cassius and Casca. In these lines, we also see the difference in their attitudes, as Casca is frightened by the storm (something established earlier in the scene through Casca's conversation with Cicero) and Cassius is not frightened, or at least he is not showing fear. I made my first cut of lines 53–55 because they simply repeat what Cassius said in lines 49–52. What we lose by cutting these lines is the image of "the breast of heaven" that parallels Cassius's naked breast. I kept line 56 because Casca has to ask his question to further the scene, but I cut lines 57–59 because, while Casca is trying to teach Cassius proper behavior toward the gods when they are angry, a good actor can portray that fear through voice and body language without speaking those lines. I kept the first part of the next line, "You are dull, Casca" because it's a great line and sets up the rest of Cassius's speech, but I cut the following two lines because they simply reiterate and define his "dullness." I kept the last three beats of line 62 because they fit with "You are dull, Casca" to complete the iambic pentameter. I cut line 63 because it simply adds detail to "You look pale and gaze," but I kept the next line to complete the logic of the sentence. I also kept lines 65–67. Line 65 starts a new sentence and a change in tactic by Cassius, as here he starts to connect the storm and the strange occurrences to Caesar. Lines 66–67 start the rhetorical repetition of "Why . . ." and we need at least two of those, but I cut line 68, losing three more examples. I kept 69 because it sets up line 71, but I cut 70 to save space, figuring that "ordinance" can stand for "natures and preformèd faculties" without losing the logic connected to the next phrase, "To monstrous quality." I kept the rest of the speech because there's no repetition, and Cassius is using those lines to instruct Casca on the meaning of the signs.

Other Literary Elements

All of the other traditional literary elements can be used as springboards for examination of *Julius Caesar* for interpretation. As I mentioned in the introductory chapter, we need to make literary elements and devices operational for our students, so that discussion and writing in connection with those elements and devices becomes second nature. Setting, for example, can be examined by looking at both the public spaces in Rome used in the story and the private residences. We can think of Rome and the time period in their physical and temporal senses or in the sense of what is happening socially and politically. Students can examine the setting in each scene, and also look at movie versions of the play to see how the setting is presented on film. Setting can best be interpreted through study of references to setting in the dialogue, as in the scene presented in Act 1, scene 3 (excerpted above). Beyond character and setting, conflict, dramatic structure (e.g., exposition, rising action, turning point, falling action, denouement), and symbolism all offer fruitful lines of inquiry for this play. By evoking specific analysis based upon such literary elements, students may take a week or two to develop papers, having identified a line of inquiry while initially reading the script. You can lead them through typical stages of the writing process (i.e., prewriting, drafting, and revising) and allow them forums for sharing their analyses with their peers. By encouraging analysis that engages literary elements, we will be closer to what AP examiners expect of students. The only difference, of course, is that students writing AP exams have only 40 minutes for each of three essays. With that in mind, we will examine some examples of free-response topics and consider what they require of the student.

Advanced Placement Essay Free-Response Topic Formats

On the Advanced Placement Exam, students complete a series of multiple-choice questions in connection with reading passages, followed by three 40-minute written responses, called free-response questions. These free-response questions on poetry, fiction, and drama come in two basic forms. The first two responses on the exam challenge students to analyze authorial technique based on a specific literary passage (one poetry and one prose), requiring on-the-spot close reading and interpretation. I will refer to these as "passage-based," conflating the poetry and prose topics into one discussion. The third topic on the exam, sometimes referred to as the "open" topic, poses a challenge of theme, literary device, or interpretation and then lets students choose which work they wish to write about in connection with the prompt. Some of these open topics identify a theme and then ask the students to address the theme as it is presented in the work they choose. Other open topics present an interpretation from a secondary source, either commenting on a single work or on a certain type of work, and then ask students to write about how that interpretation may be applied to a work of their choosing. Both variations of the open topic offer a list of works from which to choose, but allow students to use nonlisted works if they are defensible as worthy (canonical). Below are examples and discussions of both the passage-based free-response topics and the open topics.

Passage-based free-response topics. The passage-based topics require students to analyze a passage of poetry or prose and discuss it in relation to some type of literary technique. Authorial intent is implied in these topics, as the techniques that are mentioned are typically methods that authors would not arrive at haphazardly. For example, one topic from 2005 paired two poems and asked students to "compare and contrast the two poems (by William Blake), taking into consideration the poetic techniques Blake uses in each" (College Board, 2005a). Poetic techniques are not specified here, but in another topic related to a passage of narrative, "characterization" is used to reflect the narrator's attitude and writers are told to consider "diction, tone, detail, and syntax" (p. 2). Yet another topic asks the writers to "write an essay in which you show how the author uses literary devices to achieve her purpose" (College Board, 2005a, p. 3). Indeed, imagery, tone, syntax, structure, and other literary devices, all addressed throughout this book, commonly come up in these topics.

ACTIVITY (SAS #28): SAMPLE FREE-RESPONSE PROMPT 1.

One way you can help your students prepare for these passage-based AP examination questions is to use the sample questions provided by the College Board, then take a piece of dialogue from the script of *Julius Caesar* and substitute it for the passage that originally appeared. You may need to change the wording of the question to accommodate the substitution, but you will have something that your students can use for practice. Another option is to create your own original topics using passages from the script, modeling them on those that appear on the exams. Below is one example of a passage-based topic I created for *Julius Caesar*, which is reprinted on SAS #28.

In the following speech from *Julius Caesar*, Antony has begun to turn the Roman citizens against the conspirators who killed Caesar. Read the speech closely, then write a well-organized essay explaining how Shakespeare uses imagery, rhetorical structure, and tone in Antony's speech to persuade the Romans.

From Act 3, scene 2:

Antony: If you have tears, prepare to shed them now.
You all do know this mantle. I remember
The first time ever Caesar put it on.
'Twas on a summer's evening, in his tent,
That day he overcame the Nervii.
Look, in this place ran Cassius' dagger through.
See what a rent the envious Casca made.
Through this the well-belovèd Brutus stabbed,
And as he plucked his cursèd steel away,
Mark how the blood of Caesar followed it,
As rushing out of doors to be resolved
If Brutus so unkindly knocked or no;
For Brutus, as you know, was Caesar's angel.
Judge, O you gods, how dearly Caesar loved him!
This was the most unkindest cut of all.
For when the noble Caesar saw him stab,
Ingratitude, more strong than traitors' arms,
Quite vanquished him. Then burst his mighty heart,
And, in his mantle muffling up his face,
Even at the base of Pompey's statue,
(Which all the while ran blood) great Caesar fell.
O, what a fall was there, my countrymen!
Then I and you and all of us fell down,
Whilst bloody treason flourished over us.
O, now you weep, and I perceive you feel
The dint of pity. These are gracious drops.
Kind souls, what, weep you when you but behold
Our Caesar's vesture wounded? Look you here,
Here is himself, marred as you see with traitors. (3.2.181–209)

Open free-response topics. From 2005–2010, free-response questions released in the College Board study guides included the following open topics that included *Julius Caesar* in the list of suggested works.

From 2005: One of the strongest human drives seems to be a desire for power. Write an essay in which you discuss how a character in a novel or a drama struggles to free himself or herself from the power of others or seeks to gain power over others. Be sure to demonstrate in your essay how the author uses this power struggle to enhance the meaning of the work. (College Board, 2005b, p. 4)

From 2009: Many works of literature deal with political or social issues. Choose a novel or play that focuses on a political or social issue. Then write an essay in which you analyze how the author uses literary elements to explore this issue and explain how the issue contributes to the meaning of the work as a whole. Do not merely summarize the plot. (College Board, 2009, p. 4)

On their faces, both of these open free-response prompts offer students the opportunity to write lucidly about *Julius Caesar*. Students can address the first topic using Brutus and the other conspirators as the oppressed and Caesar as the oppressor, or they can write from the standpoint of the plebians pushing for "honorable" leadership. They can use their understandings developed through close reading, discussion, and performance (Chapters 5–7) to provide evidence for their essay. In response to the second topic, students may choose to write about tyranny, succession, appropriate celebration of holidays, the function of the senate, use of the military, or any of the other political and social themes discussed in this book. Most helpful in terms of building support for their written responses will be direct reference to the specific passages they have analyzed through performance.

Also of help will be an understanding of the logic behind the structure of the open free-response questions themselves. What is vital to our discussion of the first topic is the idea of using a theme or issue common to human society, in this case "power," and applying it to logical, supported written argument. What the topic tells us is that something is true: "One of the strongest human drives *seems to be* a desire for power" (College Board, 2005b, p. 4, itals. mine). What the examiners are asking students to do is accept the premise of the statement first, and then, having accepted the premise, apply it to a literary work. Students have the flexibility to either write about the will to escape the power of others (which is essentially to write about the theme of oppression from the point of view of the oppressed), or to write about the desire of one character or another to gain power, which is closer to the premise as laid out.

The essence of the final statement in the topic, however, which is common to both topics listed here and nearly all free-response topics, is the connection between either theme or authorial technique and the meaning of the entire work. The topic tells us to show "how the author uses this power struggle *to enhance the meaning of the work*" (College Board, 2005b, p. 4, itals. mine). Implied in that statement is another premise: that the literary work has a singularly definable meaning, and that the theme of power is "used" to "enhance" that meaning, rather than constituting meaning itself. Theme is connected to technique, which reveals meaning. Looking at the other open free-response topic above, we will see nearly the exact same wording: "explain how the issue contributes to the meaning of the work as a whole" (College Board, 2009, p. 4). If nothing else, be sure to tell your students to read all parts of the topic they are addressing.

What teachers can take out of this discussion of the open free-response topics is that the theme or element described will be a common characteristic of great literature, such as unconventional characters, power struggles, important events, or physical journeys, and that the writer will be required to connect the theme or element specifically to the meaning of the entire work. Detailed references to the work and an understanding of the way a work develops its meaning will be essential. In that regard, another useful tool will be to pull samples from the Wall of Notable Quotes (Chapter 2) from the script, then ask students to identify the speaker for each and explain how the quote functions within the context of the entire play.

> ## ACTIVITY (SAS #29):
> ## SAMPLE FREE-RESPONSE PROMPT 2.
>
> Give students the sample open free-response questions above and have them use *Julius Caesar* to address the questions. Giving students opportunities to write these types of analysis both in timed and untimed settings will be valuable. Topics are printed on SAS #29 at the back of this chapter.

More test advice. In its guide to preparing to write for AP topics, the College Board emphasized four key guidelines:

1. Take time to organize your ideas.
2. Make pertinent use of the text given to you to analyze.
3. Quote judiciously from it to support your observations.
4. Be logical in your exposition of ideas. (College Board, 2011b. p. 1)

Writers are encouraged to use the vocabulary of the field, which in their example list runs the gamut from specific rhetorical devices (e.g., allusion, syllogism) to broad concerns (e.g., ideology, persuasion). The formula is simple on its face: Form a logical thought about the work and lay it out so that a reader can understand it, supporting it with direct evidence from the work. The other key is to know your literary devices. Beyond practicing with model topics like those above, engage your students in operational discussion of literary elements while working through the script and journaling to aid comprehension, and you will have done well.

Once your students have an investment in taking the AP exam, have them develop their expertise by creating a poster of "advice" for taking the AP exam in English Literature and Composition. Students can also create/draft an oral or written defense of example AP exam essays they have written on *Julius Caesar* as deserving a certain score on the exam based upon its merits and the College Board 9-point rubric. These kinds of activities will make test prep less monotonous.

Critical Analysis and Making Connections

Judith Langer's (2000) study *Beating the Odds: Teaching Middle and High School Students to Read and Write Well* showed conclusively that teachers who achieve the best results in student reading and writing performance are those who are willing to go beyond reaching their simple comprehension goals and make connections between the literary works and students' lives, broader contexts, and other subjects. Such connection building fits the final realm of the AP course description that leads to critical writing on a work of literature. The College Board description of the writing required in college writing courses reads, "Writing to evaluate a literary work involves making and explaining judgments about its artistry and exploring its underlying social and cultural values through analysis, interpretation, and argument" (College Board, 2011a, p. 50). This type of critical analysis and writing represents the most complex and challenging task associated with studying literature, as it asks us to make value judgments on material that we may perceive as far beyond us. Who are we to discuss Shakespeare's artistic value or social significance? But we must, and engaging in that process leads students to enter conversations with the great thinkers of the past and present, as we compare Shakespeare's plays with Aristotle's thesis on the dramatic unities, or write about how *Julius Caesar* presents the archetype of political assassination plots. We can examine the lack of female characters and feminine influence in the play. We can also go back to Elizabethan society, study events and cultural norms of Shakespeare's time, and determine how Shakespeare embeds references to contemporary events and practices.

Although the topics for the free-response essays on the AP exam often ask students to relate specific authorial techniques to the meaning of the work as a whole, meaning is something arrived at referentially, through comparison between the world of the literary work and the frame of reference of the reader. In order to get students to reach this point of critical examination of text, we must give them opportunities to forge connections between the world of the play and social or political realities today.

Perhaps the best tools students will have to aid them in developing critical perspectives will be their informal journal writing in response to reading the script of *Julius Caesar* and any writing they have done in reference to stage signals. Through the processes of reading, responding, discussing, and listening, students may develop perspectives that they would be more likely to share with their peers outside of class than in class. Perhaps a student reader sees the text as representative of the power struggles typical in any hierarchical institution, such as families, schools, and communities. Perhaps another student sees the play as representing aggression caused by repressed male-to-male sexual attraction. These and hundreds of other thoughts about the script can be defended with "logical exposition of ideas" and "judicious" use of quotes (College Board, 2011b. p. 1). But beyond strict analysis, these perceptions take the work of literature beyond itself and into the broader world of ideas. If we think of the play as representative of power struggles in institutions, we must look to both the script and the world in order to explain our ideas. We start to make value judgments of the work as an expression of those ideas. We criticize.

ACTIVITY (SAS #30): NOTES, NOTES, NOTES.

Have students look at all of the notes they have taken in the process of reading and performing *Julius Caesar*, then ask them to draw some conclusions about the text. Have them consult their notes for thoughts and impressions that will lead to conclusions about the script. Have them write a short critical essay on some aspect of the text of their own choosing, evaluating its relevance or connection to contemporary culture.

Another way to approach critical perspectives as a tool for understanding and writing about *Julius Caesar* is to apply recognized critical lenses to the script and then to see how they shape our interpretation (Appleman, 2009; Gillespie, 2010). We can begin these forays into the world of critical theory by asking broad questions that encourage students to look at the text through the lenses we wish to employ. For example, we might ask one of these questions:

1. Are women's perspectives valued in the text of *Julius Caesar*?
2. How does social class operate as a liberating or limiting influence in *Julius Caesar*?
3. Where is the moral center of this text? Is it represented in one character or is moral norming shared?
4. How does Shakespeare's representation of Julius Caesar's story parallel the life of Jesus Christ?
5. What does this play teach us about history?

Such questions can be laid out for inquiry before students enter the text or after they have completed their own reading. You and your students can create questions of your own that reflect student interests. In his book *Doing Critical Theory*, Gillespie (2010) offered a companion CD with short explanations of different critical theories that can be handed out to students to inform their inquiry.

Other questions that relate to critical perspectives will require students to examine primary or secondary critical sources. For example, you may ask the question, "How does this play reflect Machiavellian political philosophy?" Such a question will require students to learn about Machiavelli and perhaps read *The Prince* in connection with their study of *Julius Caesar*. As Machiavelli wasn't writing specifically about Shakespeare's play (indeed, his work predates it by 86 years), we would consider it a primary source. Students can read Freud, Marx, Virginia Woolf, or any other major thinker and then look for parallels that illuminate the play. Although examining primary sources challenges students and broadens their perspectives, secondary sources in the form of historical or contemporary written criticism of *Julius Caesar* offer similar opportunities.

Introducing Critical Sources

When students have exhausted their own resources and energy in building their individual readings of the script, they will be ready to join the larger conversations about *Julius Caesar* by reading published commentary and criticism. I have mentioned earlier in this book that I encourage teachers to avoid frontloading students' experience with *Julius Caesar* by bogging them down in criticism prior to their first reading of the script. But by the time they have read, analyzed, discussed, written about, and criticized the text, they will be ready to see what the scholarly world has had to say about this play.

As their teacher and tour guide, you will have the responsibility of bringing your students into the discussion in a way that does not overwhelm them, yet challenges their thinking. Knowing something of what the conversation about *Julius Caesar* is and has been will be helpful to you in deciding how to introduce criticism into your unit on the play, given the time you have.

As mentioned in the section on the AP examination topics, some open free-response questions present an interpretation from a secondary source, either commenting on a single work or on a certain type of work, and then directing students to write about how that interpretation may be applied to a work of their choosing. You may prepare your students for this sort of topic by consulting a handful of critical essays on *Julius Caesar*, pulling short excepts that demonstrate a major point in the essay, and asking students to either accept the premise and defend it in writing or reject it, similarly defending the rejection. Below are a few examples, with the sources from which they came:

Example 1:

What is perhaps more precisely characteristic of Shakespearean tragedy, more striking and significant in *Julius Caesar* than in earlier tragedies, is the reversibility of public and private scenes. It is not so much that there are public and private scenes or that there is a conflict between a public and a private self as that the public scenes tend to develop private concerns as well as the public ones and that the private scenes are simultaneously public ones in intent and result. (Spevack, 2003, p. 17)

Example 2:

The central value that directs the behavior of all the aristocrats in *Julius Caesar* is emulation in the several, contradictory senses of that word. To focus on one of its aspects: the emulation they all feel appears in the form of their omnipresent rivalry with one another, in their competition for pre-eminence, in their factionalism that leads to assassination and civil strife. (Rebhorn, 2002, p. 32)

Example 3:

That the people want a Caesar is most graphically illustrated by their reaction to Brutus's funeral oration. "Let him be Caesar" shouts the Third Plebeian, and the Fourth continues in the same spirit: "Caesar's better parts / Shall be crowned in Brutus." The mob needs a Caesar, and now that Julius is dead, his assassin can easily supply the office. And he will be given the full imperial ceremony of a "triumph home unto his house" and "a statue with his ancestors." The mob is not concerned with Caesar the man, but only with Caesar as a public image. These exclamations also at once deny the whole political issue of the conspiracy. (Charney, 1968, pp. 74–75)

Students' encounters with written criticism shouldn't be limited to short excerpts like these. Have students, either with you, in small groups, or on their own, examine full texts of critical essays and then work that reading into their own writing in connection with the text. In identifying appropriate sources, the problem for you will not be finding examples of criticism, but rather deciding how to focus your students' access so that they and you do not get overwhelmed. In Chapter 9, I list resources that I have found useful for a variety of reasons, but that list is in no way exhaustive. Your students are attempting to construct their own authority, and the rationale for bringing in secondary texts is to further their frame of reference for constructing that authority.

The procedure I suggest you use for guiding your students into the world of *Julius Caesar* criticism is to get excerpts or full copies of a couple of the historical commentaries on *Julius Caesar* (virtually all of them can be found on the web through the usual search engines) and show them to your students, then give them contemporary critical sources that they can study independently or in groups. Students can find critical essays to review in nearly every edition of the script available, including the Folger Shakespeare Library edition (Mowat & Werstine, 1992), which includes a critical essay by Coppèlia Kahn. Likewise, the Signet Classic edition (1998) contains commentaries by Kahn, Maynard Mack, Roy Walker, Richard David, Ralph Berry, Peggy Goodman Endel, and Sylvan Barnet.

Most larger Shakespeare collected works also include scholarly introductions. Even looking at one or two of these sources will help your students develop the critical analysis skills that prepare them for AP writing and for college writing. If you have access to a good library database, you can use search terms to find what you are looking for. *Shakespeare Quarterly* is the leading Shakespeare scholarly journal, and while the articles will be challenging for high school students, they are not utterly inaccessible.

Another method I suggest, especially if you do not have access to a university library, is to make use of a few great websites. The first is the well-known "Mr. William Shakespeare and the Internet" (http://shakespeare.palomar.edu), a project of Palomar University professor Terry A. Gray. What Gray has given us is a collection of resources on everything from Elizabethan customs to articles on every play. If your students go to the "Criticism: Plays/Works" link on the lefthand menu, then click on "Julius Caesar," they will see a short list of articles on *Julius Caesar*. More importantly, each title is linked to a full-text version. The University of Victoria's Internet Shakespeare Editions website (http://internetshakespeare. uvic.ca) also provides useful material, and the Folger Shakespeare Library website (http://www.folger.edu) is another great resource.

ACTIVITY (SAS #31): CRITICAL SOURCES.

Have students find two critical essays related to *Julius Caesar* and read them carefully. Then, using the chart provided, they should write the main points from the essays, each in one column. Then in the third column, students can write their own thoughts on the ideas presented in the two essays. Students can identify points of overlap in the interpretations and points of possible difference or even disagreement, then summarize their discoveries in a short paper.

One principle you will want to follow in introducing *Julius Caesar* criticism is to present alternative or even competing views of the play. Students will feel more able to enter a conversation when they perceive that the conversation is not a lecture with one acknowledged authority. The articles on the Palomar site and in recently published critical collections (Wilson, 2002c; Zander, 2005b) offer a variety of viewpoints, not all of which are in agreement with one another.

An opportunity for a special project exists in the use of critical resources for studying *Julius Caesar*. If you have a student who engages in the activities and secondary readings in a way that outstrips the interest of his or her peers, that student may be able to make a semester project of examining selected documents of *Julius Caesar* scholarship as a way of developing expertise and identity. A long semester paper, project, or presentation on the research can prove valuable for the student and for his or her peers, and will give you a valuable resource to use the following year. Students who engage in extensive reading over a small aspect of the play will learn firsthand the kind of deep analysis that characterizes professional literary study. All of your students should engage in the process in some form, but given the constraints of a busy semester, they will not have the luxury to read *Julius Caesar* criticism for 4 months. But that one student who shows an extreme interest may be happily swept away, if you let it happen.

Student critical writing, ultimately, is the outgrowth of a rigorous process of examining Shakespeare's text, either for performance, classroom study, or the combination of the two. The value of historical perspectives is that they remind us that the play was conceived, written, and performed in a society very different from our own. If we wish to address the work on its own terms, we will need to take into account those differences. On the other hand, we experience *Julius Caesar* in our own world, which requires us to address its significance or relevance to our own lives. One role of literary criticism is to illuminate literary work. By virtue of the scholar's activity, we gain a deeper understanding and appreciation for a work, or we devalue the work as counter to contemporary pursuits, be they mental, emotional, political, or otherwise. Criticism at its best functions similarly to other kinds of scholarly activity, such as scientific research or spiritual and humanist philosophy, to help us understand ourselves through the literary expressions that are part of our cultural heritage. Some of the greatest critical writings on Shakespeare are considered valuable literary works themselves. Through greater understanding of difficult texts, and by arguing for what is true in literature and life, we engage in the long, slow process of making life better.

Your students gain important critical thinking skills by engaging in literary criticism, and they can also participate in a conversation that is greater than themselves, thus growing in inestimable ways. They may misfire when they attempt to place value on aspects of *Julius Caesar* that they only partially understand or use critical lenses that they don't understand, but the process itself is vital, and you can easily show them that even published essays on *Julius Caesar* reach sometimes questionable conclusions. I hope you will take the time to bring criticism into your unit on *Julius Caesar*.

A Note on Creative Writing

Students can write creatively in connection with their study of *Julius Caesar* to help them connect the play to their lives and further their understanding of the work. One way to get students engaged in creative writing is to have them study the play's memorable speeches, then write persuasive speeches of their own, not as the character, but as themselves or another character they invent. Or they can write an argument that uses the same rhetorical strategies as the character they are modeling. Have students watch for shifts in thinking and tone within the speech, and trace an arc of thought that leads from the character's state at the beginning of the speech to his or her state at the end of the speech. Students can create their own speeches, try to express their train of thought through a problem of their own, or go where their thinking leads them.

Creative writing can also grow out of student exploration of *Julius Caesar*'s place in popular culture. For example, you can have students write scripts that superimpose characters or situations from the play into television show plots and scenarios (e.g., a *CSI* investigation into Caesar's assassination). Once you acknowledge that students can learn to understand the play and its connection with our world through creative writing, the opportunities are manifold. Songs, stories, poems, and companion scripts all represent genres that allow students to dabble in interpretation and creativity.

Final Thoughts

Good luck incorporating writing into your study of *Julius Caesar*. Think about your objectives laid out in your unit plan, and construct writing activities that help your students to meet those objectives. My hope is that this volume has provided more than enough options from which to choose that will help you achieve your objectives. The chapter that follows presents a list of resources that may be helpful to supplement this volume. Many of them have already been cited often in this book.

Chapter Materials

Student Activity Sheet #24:
Ongoing Journal

Applicable Portion of Play: All

Objectives: 1. Students will be able to trace their habits in reading and studying *Julius Caesar*.
2. Students will be able to describe their feelings while reading *Julius Caesar*.
3. Students will be reflective readers of the script.

Common Core Standard(s): 11-12.R.L.1-7, 11-12.W.2

Directions: As you read the script of *Julius Caesar* and as we study the play more deeply, keep a reading journal that makes use of any or all of the following approaches:

1. Keep track of *how* you read the script. For example, how much you read alone, how much you read in class with classmates, and how much you read aloud. Log how much time you spend reading during each sitting and whether you get tired before you stop or whether you feel you could go on further.

2. Write how you feel while reading, what your involvement with the various characters is, and what you think the story is about. If your thoughts change as you progress through the script, note it in your journal.

3. Make connections between what is happening in the script and experiences you have heard of or experienced yourself. You can also write about examples from popular culture that the story reminds you of, or if you see the story as wholly extraordinary, you can write about what makes the story extraordinary.

4. Write a journal of one of the characters, like Cassius, Brutus, or Portia, writing as that character, reflecting on that character's feelings and thoughts about Caesar or Rome.

5. Write about yourself and specifically your own sense of self as reflected in the story. What qualities of different characters do you see in yourself? What qualities do you lack but admire? What qualities are you glad you do not possess?

Student Activity Sheet #25:
Character Intervention

Applicable Portion of Play: All

Objectives: 1. Students will analyze character traits and decisions for major figures in *Julius Caesar*.
2. Students will generate a script for a character intervention for a character of their choice.

Common Core Standard(s): 11-12.R.L.1, 11-12.R.L.3

Directions: As you read the script, develop profiles of different characters using terms that translate easily to character analysis. Using the chart below, you will notice that the designations of traits, motivations, and so forth are judgments on the character and the "demonstrated by" column requires specific reference to character words or actions. Anticipating problems on the horizon for that character, write a summary, framed as a speech to be delivered at an intervention for that character. Identify the point in the script where you would have the intervention for the character in order to prevent disaster. For example, an intervention with Caesar himself may happen right before Act 3, scene 1, and an intervention with Brutus might come earlier or later, depending upon the focus of your intervention.

Character Name:	
Positive Traits:	
Demonstrated by:	
Negative Traits:	
Demonstrated by:	
Motivations:	
Demonstrated by:	
Fears:	
Demonstrated by:	
Biggest Mistake:	
Next Likely Move:	
Potential Protector(s):	
Potential Aggressor(s):	

Name: _____ Date: _____

Student Activity Sheet #26:
Interactive News Report

Applicable Portion of Play: Specific scenes

Objectives:
1. Students will present events in the script of *Julius Caesar* in the form of news stories.
2. Students will be able to summarize their reading for comprehension.
3. Students will engage in discussion of action in the script.

Common Core Standard(s): 11-12.R.L.1, 11-12.R.L.2, 11-12.R.L.3, 11-12.SL.5

Directions: Pick a scene from *Julius Caesar* and present it as a news story, complete with a headline, a lead paragraph, and details to follow. You may use lines from the play as quotes, and you should focus on what is most important in the scene. Publish your story on the class website or discussion board, so that classmates can respond to the story. You may also want to present your news report as a TV report, perhaps on YouTube. Then, respond to stories posted by fellow students in response to other scenes in the play.

Reflection: How does writing a story about a scene help with the process of understanding the scene? What do you learn from reading your classmates' stories and responding to them?

_____

_____

_____

_____

_____

_____

_____

_____

_____

_____

_____

_____

_____

_____

_____

_____

Student Activity Sheet #27:
Scene Cutting

Applicable Portion of Play: Specific scenes

Objectives: 1. Students will remove lines from specific scenes in the script for performance.
2. Students will be able to defend cutting choices made based on interpretation of the script.
3. Students will analyze the function of specific lines in the script.

Common Core Standard(s): 11-12.R.L.1, 11-12.R.L.6, 11-12.W.1, 11-12.W.1.a

Directions: Select a short scene (50 lines or fewer) from *Julius Caesar* and decide which lines may be cut without ruining the scene or lessening its potential impact. For each segment you cut, you must write a rationale that includes (1) why you chose that segment to cut and (2) what is lost by removing the segment. Then write similar rationales for the segments of the scene that you decided to keep. You must cut at least 25% of the scene and not more than 50%.

Student Activity Sheet #28:
Sample Free-Response Prompt 1

Applicable Portion of Play: Act 3, scene 2, lines 181–208.

Objectives: 1. Students will be able to analyze structure, rhetorical strategies, and tone in a passage from *Julius Caesar*.
2. Students will be able to organize their analysis into a coherent written response.

Common Core Standard(s): 11-12.R.L.1-6, 11-12.W.1-1e

Directions: In the following speech from *Julius Caesar*, Mark Antony has begun to turn the Roman citizens against the conspirators who killed Caesar. Read the speech closely, then write a well-organized essay explaining how Shakespeare uses imagery, rhetorical structure, and tone in Mark Antony's speech to persuade the Romans.

Antony: If you have tears, prepare to shed them now.
You all do know this mantle. I remember
The first time ever Caesar put it on.
'Twas on a summer's evening, in his tent,
That day he overcame the Nervii.
Look, in this place ran Cassius' dagger through.
See what a rent the envious Casca made.
Through this the well-belovèd Brutus stabbed,
And as he plucked his cursèd steel away,
Mark how the blood of Caesar followed it,
As rushing out of doors to be resolved
If Brutus so unkindly knocked or no;
For Brutus, as you know, was Caesar's angel.
Judge, O you gods, how dearly Caesar loved him!
This was the most unkindest cut of all.
For when the noble Caesar saw him stab,
Ingratitude, more strong than traitors' arms,
Quite vanquished him. Then burst his mighty heart,
And, in his mantle muffling up his face,
Even at the base of Pompey's statue,
(Which all the while ran blood) great Caesar fell.
O, what a fall was there, my countrymen!
Then I and you and all of us fell down,
Whilst bloody treason flourished over us.
O, now you weep, and I perceive you feel
The dint of pity. These are gracious drops.
Kind souls, what, weep you when you but behold
Our Caesar's vesture wounded? Look you here,
Here is himself, marred as you see with traitors.

Student Activity Sheet #29:
Sample Free-Response Prompt 2

Applicable Portion of Play: All

Objectives:
1. Students will be able to apply a general theme to *Julius Caesar* and write in response to it.
2. Students will gain confidence in their ability to write in response to AP exam questions.

Common Core Standard(s): 11-12.R.L.1-6, 11-12.W.1-1e

Directions: Choose one of the topics below, taken from past AP exams, courtesy of the College Board (2005b, 2009), and write a well-developed and edited response. Be sure to:

- Take time to organize your ideas.
- Make pertinent use of the text given to you to analyze.
- Quote judiciously from it to support your observations.
- Be logical in your exposition of ideas.

Sample 1:
One of the strongest human drives seems to be a desire for power. Write an essay in which you discuss how a character in *Julius Caesar* struggles to free himself or herself from the power of others or seeks to gain power over others. Be sure to demonstrate in your essay how the author uses this power struggle to enhance the meaning of the work.

Sample 2:
Many works of literature deal with political or social issues. Choose a political or social issue that is prevalent in *Julius Caesar*, then write an essay in which you analyze how Shakespeare uses literary elements to explore this issue and explain how the issue contributes to the meaning of the work as a whole. Do not merely summarize the plot.

Name: _____ Date: _____

Student Activity Sheet #30:
Notes, Notes, Notes

Applicable Portion of Play: All

Objectives: 1. Students will be able to examine their reading notes to find critical perspectives and argue an interpretation of *Julius Caesar*.
2. Students will be able to write persuasively using support from the script.

Common Core Standard(s): 11-12.R.L.1-6, 11-12.W.1-1e

Directions: Review all of the notes you have taken in the process of reading and performing *Julius Caesar*. What conclusions can you draw about the play based upon what you have written? Write a short (2–3 page) critical essay on your interpretation of *Julius Caesar*. Use evidence from the script to support your assertions. If you wish, you may take just one specific aspect of the play, as reflected in your notes, and develop that into an essay. Once you have written your essay, we will look at published critical essays on *Julius Caesar*, which you may wish to support or argue, based upon your own interpretation.

Reflection: How did your interpretation of *Julius Caesar* grow out of the activities you've completed while studying the play?

_____

_____

_____

_____

_____

_____

_____

_____

_____

_____

_____

_____

_____

_____

_____

_____

Student Activity Sheet #31:
Critical Sources

Applicable Portion of Play: All

Objectives:　　1.　Students will be able to express their comprehension of published critical perspectives on *Julius Caesar*.
　　　　　　　　　2.　Students will be able to write persuasively to support or refute these critical essays.

Common Core Standard(s): 11-12.R.L.1-6, 11-12.W.1-1e

Directions: Find two critical essays related to *Julius Caesar* either in print or on the web and read them carefully. Then, using the chart below, write main points from the essays, each in one column. In the third column, write your own thoughts on the ideas presented in the two essays. Identify points of overlap in the interpretations and points of possible difference or even disagreement. Summarize your discoveries in a short paper.

First Source:	Second Source:	My Own Thoughts:
Main Points:	Main Points:	

"Is there no voice more worthy than my own?": Additional Resources

What follows is a list of resources that have been helpful to me in writing this book and that I can recommend to you as having value toward increasing your understanding of and appreciation for Shakespeare and for *Julius Caesar* and your ability to teach it well. Some of these works also appear in the reference list for this book, but they are highlighted here in several categories to help you decide which works most fit your own educational goals. That being said, you may also find materials of value to you listed in the references that are not listed here.

Books About Shakespeare's Life and Works

Bate, J. (2008). *The genius of Shakespeare* (10th anniversary ed.). New York, NY: Oxford University Press.

Bloom, H. (1998). *Shakespeare: The invention of the human.* New York, NY: Riverhead Books.

Greenblatt, S. (2004). *Will in the world: How Shakespeare became Shakespeare.* New York, NY: W. W. Norton and Company.

Shapiro, J. (2005). *A year in the life of William Shakespeare: 1599.* New York, NY: HarperCollins.

Guides to Teaching Shakespeare

Carnegie, D. (2009). *Julius Caesar: A guide to the text and the play in performance.* New York, NY: Palgrave Macmillan.

Cohen, R. A. (2006). *ShakesFear and how to cure it: A handbook for teaching Shakespeare.* Clayton, DE: Prestwick House.

Dakin, M. E. (2009). *Reading Shakespeare with young adults.* Urbana, IL: National Council of Teachers of English.

Metzger, M. J. (2004). *Shakespeare without fear: Teaching for understanding.* Portsmouth, NH: Heinemann.

Riggio, M. C. (Ed.). (1999). *Teaching Shakespeare through performance.* New York, NY: Modern Language Association of America.

Rocklin, E. L. (2005). *Performance approaches to teaching Shakespeare.* Urbana, IL: National Council of Teachers of English.

Shand, G. B. (Ed.). (2009). *Teaching Shakespeare: Passing it on.* Chichester, England: Wiley-Blackwell.

Stredder, J. (2009). *The north face of Shakespeare: Activities for teaching the plays.* Cambridge, England: Cambridge University Press.

Introductions to Editions of *Julius Caesar*

Humphreys, A. (2009). Introduction. In A. Humphreys (Ed.), *Julius Caesar* (pp. 1–83). Oxford, England: Clarendon Press.

Spevack, M. (2003). Introduction. In M. Spevack (Ed.), *Julius Caesar* (Updated ed., pp. 1–45). Cambridge, England: Cambridge University Press.

Collections of Essays on *Julius Caesar*

Dean, L. F. (Ed.). (1968). *Twentieth century interpretations of* Julius Caesar: *A collection of critical essays.* Englewood Cliffs, NJ: Prentice-Hall.

Knight, W. G. (1984). *The imperial theme: Further interpretations of Shakespeare's tragedies, including the Roman plays.* New York, NY: Routledge.

Wilson, R. (Ed.). (2002). *New Casebooks* Julius Caesar: *Contemporary critical essays.* New York, NY: Palgrave.

Zander, H. (Ed.). (2005). Julius Caesar: *New critical essays.* New York, NY: Routledge.

Julius Caesar Study Guides

McMurtry, J. (1998). Julius Caesar: *A guide to the play.* Westport, CT: Greenwood Press.

Thomas, V. (1992). *Twayne's new critical introductions to Shakespeare:* Julius Caesar. Boston, MA: Twayne.

Historical Works Related to *Julius Caesar*

Gelzer, M. (1968). *Caesar: Politician and statesman*. Cambridge, MA: Harvard University Press.

Plutarch. (2003). Excerpts from Plutarch. In M. Spevack (Ed.), *Julius Caesar* (pp. 178–207). Cambridge, England: Cambridge University Press.

Plutarch. (n.d.). *The life of Julius Caesar*. Retrieved from http://penelope.uchicago.edu/Thayer/E/Roman/Texts/Plutarch/Lives/Caesar*.html

Plutarchus. (1898). *Plutarch's lives, Englished by Sir Thomas North in ten volumes* (W. H. D. Rouse, Ed.). London, England: J. M. Dent.

Spencer, T. J. B. (1968). *Shakespeare's Plutarch: The lives of Julius Caesar, Brutus, Marcus Antonius, and Coriolanus in the translation of Sir Thomas North*. Harmondsworth, England: Penguin.

Online Resources

Folger Shakespeare Library—http://www.folger.edu

Internet Shakespeare Editions—http://internetshakespeare.uvic.ca

Mr. William Shakespeare and the Internet—http://shakespeare.palomar.edu.

The Shakespeare Book of Lists and Shakespeare 101—http://www.lomonico.com/bookindex.html.

Julius Caesar Movies

Houseman, J. (Producer), & Mankiewicz, J. L. (Director). (1953). *Julius Caesar* [Motion Picture]. USA: MGM.

Snell, P. (Producer), & Burge, S. (Director). (1970). *Julius Caesar* [Motion Picture]. UK: Commonwealth United Entertainment.

References

Appleman, D. (2009*). Critical encounters in high school English: Teaching literary theory to adolescents* (2nd ed.). New York, NY: Teachers College Press.

Baines, B. J. (2005). 'That every like is not the same': The vicissitudes of language in *Julius Caesar*. In H. Zander (Ed.), Julius Caesar: *New critical essays* (pp. 139–154). New York, NY: Routledge.

Barker, S. (2005). 'It's an actor, boss. Unarmed': The rhetoric of *Julius Caesar*. In H. Zander (Ed.), Julius Caesar: *New critical essays* (pp. 227–240). New York, NY: Routledge.

Bartlett, J. (1980). *Familiar quotations* (15th ed.). Boston: Little, Brown.

Bate, J. (2008). *The genius of Shakespeare* (10th anniversary ed.). New York, NY: Cambridge University Press.

Beach, R., & Myers, J. (2001). *Inquiry-based English instruction: Engaging students in life and literature.* New York, NY: Teachers College Press.

Blau, S. D. (2003). *The literature workshop: Teaching texts and their readers.* Portsmouth, NH: Heinemann.

Bloom, H. (1994). *The Western canon: The books and the school of the ages.* New York, NY: Harcourt.

Bloom, H. (1998). *Shakespeare: The invention of the human.* New York, NY: Riverhead Books.

Boal, A. (2002). *Games for actors and non-actors* (2nd ed.). New York, NY: Routledge.

Buhler, S. (1999). Introducing stage history to students. In M. C. Riggio (Ed.), *Teaching Shakespeare through performance* (pp. 220–231). New York, NY: Modern Language Association of America.

Burke, J. (1999). *The English teacher's companion.* Portsmouth, NH: Heinemann.

Candido, J. (2005). 'Time . . . come round': Plot construction in *Julius Caesar.* In H. Zander (Ed.), Julius Caesar: *New critical essays* (pp. 127–138). New York, NY: Routledge.

Charney, M. (1968). The images of Caesar. In L. F. Dean (Ed.), *Twentieth century interpretations of* Julius Caesar (pp. 73–75). Englewood Cliffs, NJ: Prentice Hall.

Cohen, R. A. (2006). *ShakesFear and how to cure it: A handbook for teaching Shakespeare.* Clayton, DE: Prestwick House.

College Board. (2005a). *2005 AP® English composition and literature free-response questions.* Retrieved from http://apcentral.collegeboard.com/apc/public/repository/_ap05_frq_englishlit_45549.pdf

College Board. (2005b). *2005 AP® English composition and literature free-response questions (Form B).* Retrieved from http://apcentral.collegeboard.com/apc/public/repository/_ap05_frq_englishlit__45550.pdf

College Board. (2009). *2009 AP® English composition and literature free-response questions (Form B).* Retrieved from http://apcentral.collegeboard.com/apc/public/repository/ap09_frq_english_literature_formb.pdf

College Board. (2011a). *AP® English literature.* Retrieved from http://www.collegeboard.com/student/testing/ap/sub_englit.html?englit

College Board. (2011b). *Study skills: Writing.* Retrieved from http://www.collegeboard.com/student/testing/ap/english_lit/writing.html?englit

Cross, T. (2001). *On the social and emotional lives of gifted children.* Waco, TX: Prufrock Press.

Dakin, M. E. (2009). *Reading Shakespeare with young adults.* Urbana, IL: NCTE.

Dewey, J. (1938). *Experience and education.* New York, NY: Simon & Schuster.

Duggan, T. J. (2007). Ways of knowing: Exploring artistic representations of concepts. *Gifted Child Today, 30*(4), 56–63.

Eisner, E. (1979). *The educational imagination.* Upper Saddle River, NJ: Merrill/Prentice Hall.

Eisner, E. (2001). What does it mean to say a school is doing well? *Phi Delta Kappan, 82,* 367–372.

Frye, N. (1968). The tragedy of order: *Julius Caesar.* In L. F. Dean (Ed.). *Twentieth century interpretations of* Julius Caesar (pp. 95–102). Englewood Cliffs, NJ: Prentice Hall.

Gardner, H. (1999). *Intelligence reframed: Multiple intelligences for the 21st century.* New York, NY: Basic Books.

Gelzer, M. (1968). *Caesar: Politician and statesman.* Cambridge, MA: Harvard University Press.

Gillespie, T. (2010). *Doing literary criticism: Helping students engage with challenging texts.* Portland, ME: Stenhouse.

Graham, S., & Perin, D. (2007). *Writing next: Effective strategies to improve writing of adolescents in middle and high schools.* New York, NY: Carnegie Corporation.

Greenblatt, S. (2004). *Will in the world: How Shakespeare became Shakespeare.* New York: W. W. Norton and Company.

Hawkes, D. (2005). Shakespeare's *Julius Caesar:* Marxist and post-Marxist approaches. In H. Zander (Ed.), Julius Caesar: *New critical essays* (pp. 199–212). New York, NY: Routledge.

Hicks, T. (2009). *The digital writing workshop.* Portsmouth, NH: Heinemann.

Hirsch, E. D., Jr. (1987). *Cultural literacy: What every American needs to know.* New York, NY: Houghton Mifflin.

Holderness, G., & Nevitt, M. (2005). Major among the minors: A cultural materialist reading of *Julius Caesar.* In H. Zander (Ed.), Julius Caesar: *New critical essays* (pp. 257–270). New York, NY: Routledge.

Holmes, C. (2001). *Time for the plebs in* Julius Caesar. *Early modern literary studies.* Retrieved from http://extra.shu.ac.uk/emls/07-2/holmjuli.htm

Houseman, J. (Producer), & Mankiewicz, J. L. (Director). (1953). *Julius Caesar* [Motion Picture]. USA: MGM.

Humphreys, A. (1984). Introduction. In A. Humphreys (Ed.), *Julius Caesar* (p. 1–83). Oxford, UK: Clarendon Press.

Jensen, E. (1998). *Teaching with the brain in mind.* Alexandria, VA: ASCD.

Kahn, C. (1992). *Julius Caesar*: A modern perspective. In B. A. Mowat & P. Werstine (Eds.), *Julius Caesar* (pp. 215–224). New York, NY: Washington Square Press.

Kahn, C. (2005). 'Passion of some difference': Friendship and emulation in *Julius Caesar.* In H. Zander (Ed.), Julius Caesar: *New critical essays* (pp. 271–283). New York, NY: Routledge.

Knight, W. G. (1931). *The imperial theme: Further interpretations of Shakespeare's tragedies, including the Roman plays.* London, England: Methuen.

Langer, J. A. (2000). *Beating the odds: Teaching middle and high school students to read and write well* (2nd ed.). Albany, NY: National Research Center on English Learning and Achievement.

Marzano, R. J., Pickering, D. J., & Pollock, J. E. (2001). *Classroom instruction that works: Research-based strategies for increasing student achievement.* Alexandria, VA: ASCD.

McMurtry, J. (1998). Julius Caesar: *A guide to the play.* Westport, CT: Greenwood Press.

Mehan, H. (1985). The structure of classroom discourse. In T. A. Van Djik (Ed.), *Discourse and dialogue: Handbook of discourse analysis* (Vol. 4, pp. 119–131). London, England: Academic Press.

Metzger, M. J. (2004). *Shakespeare without fear: Teaching for understanding.* Portsmouth, NH: Heinemann.

Mowat, B. A., & Werstine, P. (Eds.). (1992). *Julius Caesar*. New York, NY: Washington Square Press.

Murray, D. (2004). *Write to learn* (8th ed). Belmont, CA: Heinle.

National Council of Teachers of English, & International Reading Association. (1996). *Standards for the English language arts*. Retrieved from http://www.ncte.org/about/over/standards/110846.htm

Neal, M. (2008). Look who's talking: Discourse analysis, discussion, and initiation-response-evaluation patterns in the college classroom. *Teaching in the two-year college, 53*, 272–281.

Palmer, J. (1968). Decius. In L. F. Dean (Ed.). *Twentieth century interpretations of* Julius Caesar (pp. 17–20). Englewood Cliffs, NJ: Prentice Hall.

Parker, B. L. (2005). From monarchy to tyranny: *Julius Caesar* among Shakespeare's Roman works. In H. Zander (Ed.), Julius Caesar: *New critical essays* (pp. 111–126). New York, NY: Routledge.

Paster, G. (2002). 'In the spirit of men there is no blood': Blood as trope of gender in *Julius Caesar*. In R. Wilson (Ed.), *New Casebooks* Julius Caesar: *Contemporary critical essays* (pp. 149–169). New York, NY: Palgrave.

Pirie, B. (1997). *Reshaping high school English*. Urbana, IL: NCTE.

Plutarch. (n.d.). *The life of Julius Caesar*. Retrieved from http://penelope.uchicago.edu/Thayer/E/Roman/Texts/Plutarch/Lives/Caesar*.html

Plutarch. (2003). Excerpts from Plutarch. In M. Spevack (Ed.), *Julius Caesar* (pp. 178–207). Cambridge: Cambridge UP.

Plutarchus. (1898). *Plutarch's Lives, Englished by Sir Thomas North in Ten Volumes* (W. H. D. Rouse, Ed.). London, England: J. M. Dent.

Raphael, T. E. (1986). Teaching question-answer relationships. *Reading Teacher, 39*, 516–520.

Rebhorn, W. (2002). The crisis of the aristocracy in *Julius Caesar*. In R. Wilson (Ed.), *New Casebooks* Julius Caesar: *Contemporary critical essays* (pp. 29–54). New York, NY: Palgrave.

Rocklin E. L. (2005). *Performance approaches to teaching Shakespeare*. Urbana, IL: NCTE.

Rosenblatt, L. (1983). *Literature as exploration*. New York, NY: Noble & Noble.

Shakespeare, W. (1969). Sonnet 116. In A. Harbage (Ed.), *William Shakespeare: The complete works: The Pelican Text revised* (p. 1472). New York, NY: Viking. (Original work published 1593–1609)

Shakespeare, W. (1992a). *Hamlet* (B. A. Mowat & P. Werstine, Eds.). New York, NY: Washington Square Press. (Original work published 1603–1605)

Shakespeare, W. (1992b). *Julius Caesar* (B. A. Mowat & P. Werstine, Eds.). New York, NY: Washington Square Press. (Original work published 1623)

Shakespeare, W. (1992c). *Macbeth* (B. A. Mowat & P. Werstine, Eds.). New York, NY: Washington Square Press. (Original work published 1623)

Shakespeare, W. (1992d). *Romeo and Juliet* (B. A. Mowat & P. Werstine, Eds.). New York, NY: Washington Square Press. (Original work published 1597)

Shakespeare, W. (1993a). *A midsummer night's dream* (B. A. Mowat & P. Werstine, Eds.). New York, NY: Washington Square Press. (Original work published 1600)

Shakespeare, W. (1993b). *Othello* (B. A. Mowat & P. Werstine, Eds.). New York, NY: Washington Square Press. (Original work published 1623)

Shakespeare, W. (1998). *Signet Classic Shakespeare: Julius Caesar, newly revised edition* (S. Barnet, Ed.). New York, NY: Penguin Putnam.

Shapiro, J. (2005). *A year in the life of William Shakespeare: 1599.* New York, NY: HarperCollins.

Sizer, T. R., & Sizer, N. F. (1999). Grappling. *Phi Delta Kappan, 81,* 184–190.

Snell, P. (Producer), & Burge, S. (Director). (1970). *Julius Caesar* [Motion Picture]. UK: Commonwealth United Entertainment.

Spencer, T. J. B. (1968). *Shakespeare's Plutarch: The lives of Julius Caesar, Brutus, Marcus Antonius, and Coriolanus in the translation of Sir Thomas North.* Harmondsworth, England: Penguin.

Spevack, M. (2003). Introduction. In M. Spevack (Ed.), *Julius Caesar* (pp. 1–45). Cambridge, England: Cambridge University Press.

Stredder, J. (2009). *The north face of Shakespeare: Activities for teaching the plays.* Cambridge, England: Cambridge University Press.

Taylor, G. (2002). Bardicide. In R. Wilson (Ed.), *New Casebooks* Julius Caesar: *Contemporary critical essays* (pp. 188–209). New York, NY: Palgrave.

Thisted, P., & Mertens, D. (1994). Hamlet. In P. O'Brien (Ed.), *Shakespeare set free: Teaching Hamlet and Henry IV, Part 1* (pp. 69–128). New York, NY: Washington Square Press.

Thomas, V. (1992). *Twayne's new critical introductions to Shakespeare:* Julius Caesar. Boston, MA: Twayne.

Vygotsky, L. S. (1978). *Mind in society: The development of higher psychological processes.* Cambridge, MA: Harvard University Press.

Wilson, R. (2002a). Introduction. In R. Wilson (Ed.), *New Casebooks* Julius Caesar: *Contemporary critical essays* (pp. 1–28). New York, NY: Palgrave.

Wilson, R. (2002b). 'Is this a holiday?': Shakespeare's Roman carnival. In R. Wilson (Ed.), *New Casebooks* Julius Caesar: *Contemporary critical essays* (pp. 55–76). New York, NY: Palgrave.

Wilson, R. (Ed.). (2002c). *New Casebooks* Julius Caesar: *Contemporary critical essays.* New York, NY: Palgrave.

Zander, H. (2005a). *Julius Caesar* and the critical legacy. Introduction. In H. Zander (Ed.), Julius Caesar: *New critical essays.* (pp. 3–55). New York, NY: Routledge.

Zander, H. (Ed.). (2005b). Julius Caesar: *New critical essays.* New York, NY: Routledge.

About the Author

*T*imothy J. Duggan, Ed.D., coordinates the Secondary Education Program at Northeastern Illinois University, where he teaches courses in secondary English education, secondary school curriculum, and English. A former director of education for the Nebraska Shakespeare Festival, Dr. Duggan has developed Shakespeare camps, teacher in-services, and student performances in several states. He has presented on Shakespeare pedagogy at the National Council of Teachers of English annual convention and the National Association for Gifted Children national conference, and recently, he has conducted workshops for teachers through the Chicago Shakespeare Theater's extensive education program. He is also the author of *Advanced Placement Classroom: Hamlet* in Prufrock's Teaching Success Guide for the Advanced Placement Classroom series. He lives in Skokie, IL, with his wife, Heidi, and his two children, Eamon and Liesel.